Islam, Europe's Second Religion

The New Social, Cultural, and Political Landscape

Edited by
SHIREEN T. HUNTER

Foreword by
CHARLES BUCHANAN

*Published in cooperation with the
Center for Strategic and International Studies,
Washington, D.C.*

Westport, Connecticut
London

Library of Congress Cataloging-in-Publication Data

Islam, Europe's second religion : the new social, cultural, and political landscape / edited by Shireen T. Hunter ; foreword by Charles Buchanan.
    p. cm.
    Includes bibliographical references and index.
    ISBN 0–275–97608–4 (alk. paper)—ISBN 0–275–97609–2 (pbk. : alk. paper)
    1. Muslims—Europe. 2. Islam—Europe. 3. Europe—Ethnic relations. 4. Muslims—Cultural assimilation—Europe. 5. Multiculturalism—Europe. I. Hunter, Shireen.
    D1056.2.M87 I75   2002
    305.8'97104—dc21   2002070434

British Library Cataloguing in Publication Data is available.

Library of Congress Catalog Card Number: 2002070434
ISBN: 0–275–97608–4
    0–275–97609–2 (pbk.)

First published in 2002

Praeger Publishers, 88 Post Road West, Westport, CT 06881
An imprint of Greenwood Publishing Group, Inc.
www.praeger.com

Printed in the United States of America

The paper used in this book complies with the
Permanent Paper Standard issued by the National
Information Standards Organization (Z39.48–1984).

10 9 8 7 6 5 4 3 2 1

Contents

Tables

Foreword

The Luso-American Foundation took pride in associating with the Center for Strategic and International Studies (CSIS) in its research program on Islam and its contemporary global evolution. Research results presented at the conference titled "Islam in Europe," held at the foundation's headquarters in October 2000, testified to the remarkable growth of the presence of Islam in most countries of Europe. The conference underscored the heightened interest throughout Europe in the rising number of Muslims and the impact that their presence is having on the economic, social, political, cultural, and religious landscape of Europe.

Historically, Portugal has enjoyed very special relations with Islamic nations, especially those bordering the Mediterranean, and it is today reviving these historic ties in areas of culture and commerce. Therefore, research programs about the Mediterranean region, especially regarding Islam, have become of growing interest in Portuguese universities. The Luso-American Foundation hopes to be a strong supporter of this work and the international partnerships that ensue. The expansion of relations with the Islamic countries, at the levels both of governments and of civil societies, is of inestimable importance because it can lead to fuller understanding and appreciation of the rich cultural values of Islam and can facilitate the inevitable joining of cultures, which is now underway in most European cities and between the two shores of the Mediterranean.

The leadership of CSIS, in pursuing studies about Islam, under the direction of Dr. Shireen T. Hunter, is to be congratulated by all of us concerned to promote just and equitable societies. The Luso-American Foundation eagerly looks forward to further work in partnership with CSIS in this field.

Charles Buchanan
Administrator
Luso-American Foundation

Preface

The dynamics and requirements of the postwar economic reconstruction of Europe, plus those factors related to the dissolution of their colonial empires over a period of two decades (1960 to 1980), led to the migration and settlement of substantial numbers of Muslims in major industrial countries of Europe. In the 1980s and early 1990s, civil wars and revolutions in the various parts of the Islamic world became another source of Muslim migration to Europe.

Initially, when European states, for reasons of economic necessity and a sense of moral responsibility toward some citizens of their ex-colonies, allowed the migration of Muslims, they fully expected that their residence in Europe would be of a temporary nature. However, this expectation proved unjustified. Muslim immigrants and Islam were to remain in Europe and become part of its sociopolitical and cultural landscape.

The process of the implantation, adaptation, and, eventually, full incorporation of Islam and Muslims in Europe has been difficult. Nor is it likely to become easier in the foreseeable future. Many reasons account for the difficult nature of this process, most notably: (1) the move toward greater European integration and (2) the fallout of political and social turmoil in the Muslim world. Muslim immigrants, for their part, have had to adapt and adjust to their new environments, an equally difficult and at times painful process, although there are also examples of successful integration and coexistence. In the future, too, the Islamic factor will affect Europe's internal evolution and its external relations.

It was in recognition of the importance of this factor that the Center for Strategic and International Studies (CSIS) Islam and Europe Programs, in collaboration with the Luso–American Development Foundation (FLAD), organized a conference on "Islam in Europe" in Lisbon. The conference brought together distinguished scholars of Islam from Europe and the United States plus representatives of the European Union Commission.

The greatest part of this volume is based on the papers presented at the conference. The financial and logistical assistance of FLAD, which hosted the conference, was indispensable for the success of this effort. Special thanks, therefore, are due to H.E. Rui Chancellere de Machete, president of FLAD, and Charles Buchanan, its administrator and member of its executive council. The financial support of the German Marshall Fund of the United States to the CSIS Europe Program was also very important. Thus, special thanks are due to the fund and its president, Craig Kennedy.

The conference and the present book would not have been possible without the assistance of young and talented volunteers of the CSIS Islam Program, especially Sharla Dreamal, Jessica Kmiec, and Dimitris Antoniou. Also important has been the assistance of Christina Balis, research associate in the CSIS Europe Program, and Robert J. Pauly, a Ph.D. candidate in international studies at Old Dominion University. They all deserve our sincere thanks. Special thanks are also due to Paula Vicente of FLAD who made the conference participants' stay in Lisbon pleasant and the workings of the conference smooth. I would also like to thank my husband, Robert Hunter, for his support and encouragement in the completion of this work.

Introduction

Shireen T. Hunter and Simon Serfaty

In only a few decades, Islam has peacefully emerged as Europe's second largest religion after Christianity. Today, at least 15 million people in Western Europe adhere to the Muslim faith and have close cultural affinities and affiliations with the Islamic world. Furthermore, relative to a dwindling and aging European population, the percentage of Europe's Muslims, particularly the youth, is growing steadily. The presence of Muslim communities in Europe dates to the turn of the twentieth century, when Muslim immigrants began arriving from Europe's empires. The influx of Muslims reached substantial levels during the postwar years of economic reconstruction, as single male and mostly unskilled or semiskilled laborers were "invited" to work in Europe. These invitations, however, did not amount to permanent residence. The European countries fully anticipated that recovery from the Second World War would soon enable their own people to provide the labor needed for economic growth. Most immigrants, too, hoped to return home after acquiring sufficient means to provide more comfortable lives for their families. In France and Britain, the swift process of postwar decolonization accelerated Muslim immigration because the imperial powers had acquired certain moral and legal obligations toward some of their colonial subjects. Meanwhile, Germany renewed its historic ties with Turkey, when German workers from the East could no longer cross into West Germany.

From the mid-1970s, uncertain economic conditions in Europe reduced demands for labor, making Muslim workers unwelcome and a source of social tension. In response, immigration policies were tightened. Some countries tried to suspend all immigration from particular countries—like Algeria to France;[1] others, like Germany, offered financial incentives to immigrants to return home. Yet a return to the *status quo ante* proved impossible. Immigrants and Islam were to remain in Europe. During the following decades, family reunification, the natural cycle of reproduction, and the inflow of Muslim refugees fleeing revolution and civil war increased the number of Muslims and transformed their composition and character. This transformation of Muslims' migration, coupled with a growing sense that their presence in Europe would be permanent, led to a process of Muslim identity formation and assertion as well as the creation of religious and secular institutions to meet the needs of Muslim communities and to act as mediators between them and national and local authorities. By the end of the 1970s, the increase in the number of Muslims and the development of such institutions had made Islam a more visible phenomenon in many European countries—culturally, socially, and even politically.

Today, many of Europe's Muslims are second- or third-generation individuals born and raised in Europe. Some of them are fully integrated into their adopted countries. Others, because of a sense of economic deprivation, social isolation, or overall alienation from the broader society, are looking to their cultural roots, especially Islam, in order to gain a sense of identity and frame of reference. A third group is composed of those who want to be simultaneously European and Muslim. This new type of Muslim is posing the most important challenge both to other Muslims—traditionalist or assimilationist—and to European societies.

MUSLIMS IN EUROPE: PATTERNS OF CHALLENGE AND RESPONSE

As long as Europe's Muslim population consisted of single males and Islam was a largely invisible phenomenon, the impact on European societies and publics was limited. The general European public, with few exceptions, was not aware of Islam's presence. But since the late 1970s, a dynamic process of challenge and response has been operating in European–Muslim relations, eliciting different responses from both sides, at times including confrontation and violence.

When Islam became more visible, it caused discomfort and even anxiety among many Europeans. Some found many Muslims' insistence on observing religious rules related to dietary issues or the wearing of headscarves by women or beards by men distasteful and a threat to their cultural identity and values—and, in some countries such as France, a challenge to their secular traditions. It also forced largely homogeneous societies to face their new multiethnic and multicultural realities. During periods of economic decline, Muslims also became targets of animosity because they were viewed as burdens on the host societies. The effects of economic decline in the late 1970s and early 1980s hit particularly Muslim immigrants, causing large-scale unemployment among them, especially the youth. With bleak economic prospects, many of the young turned to criminal or semicriminal activities. This intensified anti-Muslim sentiment and created a vicious circle of deprivation, rejection, alienation, and antisocial behavior.

Periodic economic crises in Europe, coupled with persisting patterns of discrimination, have also meant that, despite some progress, Europe's Muslims form an economically underprivileged class. Political events in many Muslim countries, especially the emergence of Islamist movements with anti-Western undertones, resurrected old fears and negative images of Islam, which were only barely forgotten. Because some segments of Europe's Muslims found radical Islamist discourse and some even acted upon it, they damaged the image and cause of all Muslims. Political events in the Muslim world had two other effects: They led to a competition among several key Muslim states for the hearts and minds of Europe's Muslims, thus complicating the process of identity formation among Muslims and their adjustment to their new environment; and some anti-Western Muslim states tried to manipulate Europe's Muslims to their own ends or to pressure European countries to adopt certain foreign policy postures. These efforts often resulted in tensions between the Muslim communities and indigenous societies and called into question the Muslims' loyalty to their country of residence.

Despite these mutual apprehensions and grievances, over the last three decades, diverse patterns of accommodation and adjustment between European societies and their Muslim communities have been emerging. As a result of these processes, Islam is slowly but inexorably becoming part of Europe's social, cultural, and political landscape, although its full acceptance and integration in Europe's sociopolitical and cultural order are still distant prospects.

The central question now facing Europeans and Muslims is not whether Islam can be expelled from European soil, as during the Spanish *reconquista* six centuries ago, or whether the Muslims can be totally assimilated in European culture. The main questions are how best Europe can accommodate and naturalize Islam, how Muslims can become "European" without ceasing to be Muslim, how the socioeconomic conditions of Muslims—especially the youth—can be improved, how ethnic and sectarian tensions and violence and their political effects, such as the rise of racist and xenophobic political parties, can be limited, and finally how cooperative and constructive relations between Muslims and indigenous societies can be established.

FUTURE CHALLENGES

Because of several factors, the need to answer the questions raised above will grow in importance. The collapse of the Soviet empire has brought substantial indigenous (nonimmigrant) Muslim populations back into Europe. Most of the countries of southeastern Europe are unlikely to enter the European Union (EU) any time soon. But their emergence and their unstable political conditions have exacerbated fears of Islam and Muslims. The European Summit in December 1999 formally listed Turkey as a candidate country for EU membership, thus potentially opening Europe's doors to a Muslim country of 65 million people. Demographic shifts in Europe and the growing need for immigrant labor are likely to reinforce the relative and absolute presence of Muslims in Europe, as in the period 1995 to 2050 many European countries will experience a net decline in their population because of low birth rates.[2] These demographic shifts will affect the EU countries' ability to maintain high levels of economic growth and their current social security and pension systems, especially because alternative solutions are not politically viable.[3]

In the short term, part of this need for additional workers can be met by East European immigrants. But in the long term, most new immigrants for EU Europe will have to come from Asia and Africa, including from Muslim countries of the southern littoral of the Mediterranean.

In sum, the Muslim presence in Europe, along with the multifaceted challenges of accommodation and integration it is posing to indigenous Europeans and to Europe's Muslims, will become more important. This will be especially significant regarding the transformation of collective identities in Europe, at a time when Europeans are simultaneously trying to accommodate Islam and Muslims within their cultural and social frameworks and are adjusting to identity-related challenges stemming from EU enlargement to the East, the deepening of economic, monetary, and social integration, and the process of globalization. Muslims, meanwhile, are confronted with the delicate task of gaining acceptance and of becoming full European citizens while retaining their cultural and religious identity and their links to the Islamic world.

Europe's proximity to geopolitically important and demographically dynamic Muslim countries in North Africa, the Middle East, the Persian Gulf, and the former Soviet Union makes it vulnerable to developments in these regions. Meanwhile, with growing intellectual and other contacts between Europe's Muslims and the Islamic world, a dynamic process of mutual impact is being created, leading to an inescapably closer interaction between Europe and the Muslim world at several levels, although the nature and patterns of this close interaction and interpenetration remain ambiguous and their consequences unpredictable.

OBJECTIVES AND METHODOLOGY

The principal objectives of this book are to trace the history and process of Muslim immigration to and implantation in various European countries; to provide an ethnic, sectarian, and socioeconomic profile of Europe's Muslim communities—with special attention to identifying patterns of commonality and diversity; to measure the social and economic progress of Muslim communities and the level of their political participation; and to analyze the patterns of interaction within Europe's Muslim communities and between them and the broader Islamic world, especially their home countries. The book also focuses on new intellectual trends within Europe's Muslim communities and assesses their implications for the future of European Islam and Muslims' place in European societies. In particular, it addresses the twin issues of whether Europe can be transformed into a truly multicultural society capable of naturalizing Islam and whether Islam can adapt to European conditions as historically it has done in other continents. It also evaluates the impact of Muslim communities in shaping Europe's foreign policies, especially toward the Islamic world.

The book's basic methodology is comparative and empirical, with all authors' addressing similar sets of issues, in order to identify various patterns of European-Muslim interaction and accommodation as well as points of unity and diversity.

Issues raised in this book will remain important and will be the subject of further research and analysis. The hope is that this book, which in a single volume provides a statistical and analytical profile of European Islam (or Islams), will make a useful contribution to the understanding of a critical development in the history both of Europe and of Islam.

NOTES

1. James F. Hollifield, "Immigration and Modernization," in *Searching for the New France*, ed. James F. Hollifield and George Ross (New York: Routledge, 1991), 129.

2. See *Replacement Migration*, ESIA/P/WP/160 (21 March 2000), and *Demographic Statistics and Migration Statistics for 1996* (Luxembourg: European Statistics Office, 1996). See also Jonathan Steale, "Fortress Europe Confronts the Unthinkable," *The Guardian*, 13 October 2000.

3. See *Aging in OECD Countries. A Critical Policy Challenge, Social Policy Studies*, No. 20 (Paris: Organization for Economic Cooperation and Development, 1996), 99ff. See also *The Demographic Situation of the European Union, 1994 Report* (Brussels: Commission of the European Communities, 1994).

PART I

COUNTRY SURVEYS

1

Islam in France

Remy Leveau and Shireen T. Hunter

INTRODUCTION

Among European countries, France has the largest number of people of Muslim origin, estimated between 3.5 and 5 million. This Muslim presence is also of an earlier character than Muslim communities in Germany or Britain. According to Soheib Bencheikh, in 1952 the French National Office of Immigration already put the number of Muslims at 500,000. Although this number is contested, as Bencheikh points out, "the fact is that since the 1950s Muslim presence in France has become an inescapable reality."[1] This early presence of Muslims in relatively large numbers resulted from the extensive French colonial possessions in Muslim Africa; the special relations between France and Algeria, which, until independence in 1962, was considered not as a colony but as part of France; and the early recruiting of North African, and especially Algerian, labor for French industry and the army.

The dynamics of the evolution of France's Muslim community, particularly its relations with the state and broader society, also differ from those in other European countries, for three reasons: (1) The particular nature of the French concept of secularism (*laicité*), which is more strict than in other European countries and even has antireligion dimensions; (2) The close and complex relationship between France and its ex-colonies, especially Algeria. This factor makes France's Muslims more vulnerable to the effect of events in their countries of origin, thus creating negative images of Islam that shape the attitudes of large segments of the French population toward Muslims; (3) Assimilationist tendencies in France, which have traditionally been very strong. Therefore, the perceived or real inability, or unwillingness, of many Muslims completely to assimilate into French society and culture has been difficult for most French people to accept.

In the last few years, however, attitudes on both sides have begun to change in the face of two realities. First, broader society has realized that Islam in France is no longer a transitory phenomenon, in the sense that Muslims will neither return to their countries of origin nor completely assimilate into French culture. Rather, trends point toward the development of hybrid identities and the emergence of a new category of French Muslims who feel a sense of belonging and allegiance to France while remaining loyal to their religion.[2] Second, Muslims increasingly want to become engaged within the social and political life of their country of residence and citizenship while retaining their Islamic character, even if there is no consensus within the community about what exactly being Islamic means. This dual attitude has forced governmental authorities at different levels to enter into various forms of dialogue and interaction with the Muslim community, thus setting in motion a gradual process of integration, although it is ad hoc, uneven, and incremental.

Meanwhile, as in other European countries, France's Muslim community is undergoing several processes of transformation, ranging from generational to cultural. In parallel, the dynamics of interaction between the Muslim community and mainstream society and its institutions are also evolving.

MUSLIM PRESENCE IN FRANCE: A HISTORICAL BACKGROUND

The paradox of the Muslim presence in France lies in the fact that historical contacts and relations between France and the Islamic world are very old, but the presence of a Muslim community of any size is relatively recent. Moreover, this presence is the result of economic and demographic factors, namely, France's need for labor during periods of either military conflicts or economic expansion. On the Muslim side, underdevelopment and poverty, coupled in the last several decades with high birthrates and postcolonial instability, have provided the principal impetus for migrating to France.

The first wave of Muslim immigration to France came during the First World War (1914 to 1918) and was directly linked to the process of industrialization and especially the extensive exploitation of mines. Approximately 30,000 Algerians and Moroccans were recruited by various French enterprises. In addition, 175,000 Muslims were conscripted to serve in the military, either with French soldiers or as part of special native units.[3]

In 1920, labor needed for postwar reconstruction provided a new incentive to migrate; consequently, nearly 70,000 Algerians and an equal number of Moroccans arrived in France. During the Second World War, France resorted to North African labor. Instructions sent to the governors of Algiers, Oran, and Constantine demanded the dispatch of 10,000 Algerian laborers per month.[4]

Again, postwar reconstruction prompted the need for a new labor force. For example, the Monnet Plan predicted that, during a four-year period, 200,000 workers needed to be imported from the colonies.[5] Until the 1960s, however, the overwhelming majority of Muslim immigrants were Algerians, mostly from the regions around Tizi Ouzou, Setif, and Constantine. The large-scale migration of other Africans, from the north and elsewhere, began in the 1960s; Turks followed in large numbers at the beginning of the 1970s.[6]

As with other European countries, most of these immigrants were single males with few or no qualifications and who were willing to do the kinds of work that the French found repugnant. At the same time, the French managerial class found these immigrants useful in preventing upward pressure on wages in a period of boom. In fact, these migrant workers were known as the "reserve forces of capitalism." These immigrants, like their counterparts in other European countries, did not intend to settle permanently in France. There was one exception to this general rule, however: those Algerian Muslims who had fought on the French side during the War of Independence—the Harkis. They could not stay in Algeria since they were considered traitors by the new government of independent Algeria. Their reception in France also was less than warm. As noted by Alain Boyer, the Harkis were lumped together with other Algerians because the French wanted to close the book on the war. Meanwhile, French colonials returning from Algeria viewed these Muslim "fellow citizens" as former peasants (*fellah*), little better than second-class citizens.[7]

By the early 1970s, the period of economic boom had ended and with it the need for immigrants in most European countries, including France. Indeed, Europe was now faced with a problem of unemployment. Planned migration stopped, and various incentives were offered to immigrants to return home. However, these incentives had the reverse effect of pushing migrant workers to choose to remain permanently in France because of the fear that, once they left, they could not return to France.

The decision to stop new migration also changed the composition and the character of French immigration, especially after implementation of a policy to reunite families. Consequently, after the 1970s, most new

Table 1.1
Ethnic Composition

Country/Region	Numbers
Algeria	1,550,000
Morocco	1,000,000
Tunisia	350,000
Other Arab	100,000
Non-Arab, including Turks*	315,000
Asians (includes Pakistanis & Indonesians)	100,000
Asylum seekers and illegal	350,000
French converts	40,000
Others	100,000
Total	**4,155,000**

*This number may be too small, as the number of Turks in France approaches 500,000.

Source: Dossier SRI (Secretariat of Relations with Islam), *Islam in Europe* (Archdiocese of Paris, 1996).

arrivals were women and children rather than single males. This change in the composition of the immigrant population also began the process of constructing Islam in France as the symbol of asserting the identity of a particular group of people who had come to stay.

ETHNIC AND SECTARIAN PROFILE

It is difficult to provide accurate statistics about the number of Muslims in France and their ethnic and sectarian backgrounds because, following passage of the Law of 1905 establishing the separation of church and state, no official statistics regarding religious affiliation of French citizens or residents have been kept. Moreover, by what criteria should "Muslimness" be measured: the level of observance of Islamic rules or a more cultural or sociological basis? It is likewise difficult accurately to determine who is observant and who is not, since the level of observance among French Muslims varies greatly. Indeed, many French Muslims are not observant, and some of them, particularly in the second generation, declare that they have no religion at all. Thus, cultural criteria function as a better yardstick to provide some unofficial estimates.[8] According to unofficial estimates by experts, Table 1.1 demonstrates the ethnic profile of France's Muslim community. Table 1.2 depicts the increase of Muslim immigrants over the last quarter of a century.

Table 1.2
France, Stock of Foreign Population by Nationality (in thousands)

Country of origin	1975	1985	1990	Women 1990
Portugal	758.8	767.3	649.7	304.2
Algeria	710.7	805.1	614.2	253,9
Morocco	260.0	441.3	572.7	250.7
Italy	462.9	340.3	252.8	108.0
Spain	497.5	327.2	216.0	103.7
Tunisia	139.7	190.8	206.3	84.8
Turkey	50.9	122.3	197.7	87.5
Former Yugoslavia	70.3	62.5	52.5	24.5
Cambodia	4.5	37.9	47.4	22.6
Poland	93.7	64.8	47.1	28.9
Other countries	393.3	554.8	740.2	345.3
Total	**3,442.0**	**3,714.2**	**3,596.6**	**1,614.3**
Of which: EU	1,869.9	1,594.8	1,311.9	613.9
Total women	1,381.6	1,594.6	1,614.3	

Source: Systeme d'observation permanente des migrations internationales (SOPEMI) [Continuous reporting system on migration] (Paris: Organization for Economic Cooperation and Development, 1999).

An important aspect of France's Muslim community, with significant social and political implications, is its youthfulness and high birthrate, although, as the community's economic and social conditions have improved, the birthrate has stabilized.

In view of their ethnic origins, most of France's Muslims are Sunnis. The Shi'as in France consist mostly of Iranians, along with Lebanese students and refugees. These groups adhere to the Ja'afari (Twelver) School of Shi'ism. There is also an important Ismaili community. In fact, the Agha Khan, leader of the Ismailis, has his community's headquarters in Paris.

Various Sufi brotherhoods are also active among France's Muslims, particularly those from black Africa. In some instances, the Sufi Tariqas reflect the most significant aspect of organizational activity of some groups of Muslims. For example, the organizational activity of Muslims from Senegal and Mali is concentrated in Tariqas and an expression of the Muridist traditions of these countries. The Alawiyya order is popular with the Algerians, as the Naqshbendi is with the Turks. According to one expert, "France has probably the most lively and extensive Sufi activity among Muslims within all Western European countries."[9]

GEOGRAPHIC DISTRIBUTION

The distribution of the Muslim community follows a highly skewed and unequal pattern, with a heavy concentration in a few large cities and their suburbs. For example, Paris and its surroundings account for 38 percent of the total population of French Muslims. This is followed by Provence-Alpes-Côte d'Azur with 13 percent and then Rhône-Alpes (which includes Lyons) at 10 percent; the Northern Region and Pas de Calais comprise 5 percent.[10] In these regions, Muslims are concentrated in a few, generally depressed neighborhoods, which makes Islam to a great extent a "ghetto" phenomenon.[11]

Within this general pattern, there are some differences among various ethnic groups. For example, the Moroccans are more widely spread throughout the country, whereas black Africans reside mostly in Paris and its surroundings, and the Turks are concentrated in Paris and in Alsace and Lorraine.[12]

This pattern of distribution has made Islam more prominent, and seemingly threatening, in several cities. For example, in Marseilles a quarter of the city's population—roughly 200,000 individuals—is Muslim. In La Bricarde housing project north of the city center, 85 percent of the Muslim residents trace their ancestry to the Maghreb countries.[13] These concentrated pockets, with their social and economic problems, fuel tensions between Muslims and non-Muslims and are manipulated by right-wing and other xenophobic elements.

SOCIAL AND ECONOMIC CONDITIONS

France's Muslim community is not only ethnically diverse but also divided along social and economic lines. As noted by Bencheikh, within the community, one finds "big property owners, businessmen. . . . Economic, social and cultural differences exist in an extreme form."[14]

The Muslim community has made considerable progress in terms of education. Early immigrants were mostly illiterate. Today, most immigrants' children are incorporated within the French educational system. However, they still face problems at school, caused largely by their economic position and other problems such as cramped living quarters. The number of immigrant students who drop out after high school is quite high; many leave the educational system without acquiring a diploma. However, an increasing number of children of immigrants are now finishing high school and pursuing higher studies at university.[15]

Despite these gains, most Muslims have a much lower socioeconomic status than the national average. Unemployment figures indicate this inferior status. Unemployment among Muslims is more than double the national average (10.2 percent in 1999), especially among the young, even including those who completed secondary education. In January 1999, the rate of unemployment among North African Muslims stood at 33 percent.[16] The rate is even higher in the suburbs. According to Didier Bonnet, director of a social service organization in Marseilles, in fall 2000, the rate of unemployment was 20 percent in the city as a whole and 50 percent in the Muslim enclave of La Bricarde.[17]

Moreover, because of discrimination based on ethnic differences, most Muslims are still employed in unskilled and low-paying jobs. However, with advances in education, the number of immigrants working in the professional field has increased. Meanwhile, unlike in other European countries, Muslim-owned small businesses, such as restaurants and grocery stores, do not constitute a developed sector.

Here, too, some expansion and diversification are notable. Nevertheless, most is due to associations subsidized by the state or municipalities, with the goal of finding jobs for those who have a diploma, thus improving the conditions of the community. In fact, since 1998, the government has been implementing a policy of "positive discrimination," a kind of affirmative action toward the community and especially the young. The hope is that this type of intervention will integrate young Muslims in the labor market.

Meanwhile, Muslims seem to make inroads in the service sector, especially in large businesses, which seem to have a more open attitude toward them than small or medium-size businesses. Owing to this policy, those Muslims who are French citizens have more opportunities to find jobs in the public sector such as police forces, hospitals, the army, and the SNCF (French railroad).

IDEOLOGICAL DIFFERENCES

Islam in France is also characterized by its ideological diversity, in the sense that various tendencies, ranging from secular to conservative and Islamist, can be observed within its Muslim community. Most of France's Muslims practice a traditional and quietist Islam, which is principally concerned with observing basic tenets of the religion such as prayers and, to a lesser extent, the Hajj, as well as marking life's important passages, such as birth, marriage, and death, according to Islamic ritual. This Islam does not have any particular claim beyond that of being allowed to live in peace. Those who follow it have also adapted themselves to the French legal and political environment, notably the principles of separation of church and state and the supremacy of republican laws whenever they conflict with Qur'anic prescriptions.[18] Nevertheless, these Muslims expect the government to intercede on their behalf on certain issues, such as construction of mosques or provision of Muslim burial places, without realizing that such intercession is against secular logic and the principle of separation of church and state.

Secular Muslims

Some Muslims in France subscribe to a strictly secular ideology with antireligion undertones, similar to that practiced in Turkey and Tunisia. This group advocates extensive Westernization and a rather loose adherence to Islamic ritual. Nevertheless, they still take pride in the periods of Islam's cultural flourishing. Their principal goal is to create a synthesis between Islam and modernity and thus promote an intellectual and cultural revival of the Islamic world. This type of Islam is represented mostly by intellectuals, such as university professors and writers, and is linked with the leftist spectrum of politics in France, notably the Socialist Party.[19]

Conservatives

The absolute secularists form a minority within France's Muslim community. Most follow a line that can be best characterized as "moderate conservatism." This trend favors the observance of Muslim religious prescriptions while trying to live within the framework of republican laws. It also favors being open to new interpretations of Islamic principles (*ijtihad*). Furthermore, it stresses Islam's contribution to world culture. However, it opposes any radical reinterpretation of Islamic principles and laws that could threaten the unity of Sunni Islam and its four principal schools or otherwise cause a rupture with the Western world.[20]

Fundamentalists

The fundamentalist trend insists on the strict observance of all religious prescriptions, based on the Qur'an, Sunna, and Hadith, regarding Muslim rights and relations both among Muslims and with non-Muslims. Adherents of this trend consider these rules to be immutable and not subject to reinterpretation or change, despite new circumstances and historical evolution. In political matters, they are conservative and have no ambition to change existing social and political structures in the Islamic world. Although there are considerable differences within this trend, regarding both doctrine and practice, the fundamentalists' primary goal is to encourage a revival of Islam and Islamic principles. A crucial agent of this movement is *Foi et Pratique* (Faith and Practice), inspired by the *Tabligh* movement and with financial and other support from the World Islamic League, based in Saudi Arabia. The *Tabligh*'s main goal is to encourage Muslims to become more observant. Its activities have important social ramifications; because of the rigidity of its interpretations, the *Tabligh* makes the process of Muslims' integration within broader society more difficult.[21]

Islamists

In terms of their attitude toward the kind of Islam that Muslims should observe and its strictness of observance, Islamists and fundamentalists are similar. Distinguishing the Islamists from the fundamentalists is the former's political agenda, which aims at ridding the Muslim world of corrupt governments and at re-creating the ideal Islamic society and polity that existed at the time of the Prophet.

The Islamist movement is very diverse and comprises various branches, which exist in the Islamic world from Algeria to Afghanistan.[22] In terms of the number of active adherents, this movement is not very significant. However, it is important because it appeals to a segment of Muslim youth who feel frustrated and excluded. It also often puts other Muslims on the defensive, making them feel that they must establish their Islamic credentials.[23]

PRINCIPAL INSTITUTIONS

Today there exist more than 1,000 Islamic associations, formed according to the Law of Associations of July 1901, and about 10 Muslim cultural associations formed on the basis of the Law of 1905. These associations cover a wide range of activities, including charitable and educational goals. This number is not exhaustive. For example, it does not include associations based on ethnic affiliation, such as the Amicale des Algeriens or Amicales des Travailleurs et Commercants Marocains, or Turkish associations like the L'Association Cultural et Entraide des Travailleurs Turques. While not specifically religious, they are nevertheless influenced by the basic Islamic culture of their countries of origin.[24]

Muslim institutions in France can be roughly divided into three categories:

1. Those developed around major mosques.
2. Umbrella organizations trying to bring together various smaller institutions.
3. Organizations affiliated with political parties or other groups in the immigrants' countries of origin and those affiliated with worldwide Islamic movements.

Among the first category, the Paris mosque is most important. It was established in 1929, in part as a symbolic recognition of services rendered by Muslims to France's war efforts (1914 to 1918). The mosque has been traditionally identified with the Algerians, particularly the government. For this reason, many other Muslims, especially Turks, have not associated with it.[25] There have also been considerable rivalries and infighting within the mosque's leadership.[26] Nevertheless, because of its historical roots and the fact that it has generally been favored by French authorities as an interlocutor, the Paris mosque remains an influential force.

Other important mosques include that of Avicenne du petit Bard in Montpellier and various mosques in Lille, Evry, Masserille, Lyons, Strasbourg, and Rheims. In all, there are only nine mosques that have the outward characteristics of traditional or so-called purpose-built mosques that can accommodate more than 1,000 worshippers. In addition, there are around 1,300 prayer halls. Many of them cater to a particular ethnic group; the sermon is generally said in Arabic but also in Turkish and occasionally in French.

UMBRELLA ORGANIZATIONS

The diverse nature of France's Muslim community has meant that it has been difficult to create umbrella organizations that can represent all Muslims. For example, in 1981, Si Hamza Abubaker of the Paris mosque tried to create a *Conseil Superieur des Affairs Islamiques*. However, this effort was unsuccessful, owing to disagreement among various tendencies, and did not lead anywhere. In 1985, two more initiatives were undertaken that, while failing to create a single representative organization, have been more successful. The first initiative, involving the Paris bureau of the Muslim World League, led to the establishment of the Federation Nationals des Musulmans en France (FNMF). Unfortunately, West African Muslims stayed out and the Algerians boycotted it. This was natural because the federation was formed partly in reaction to Algerian domination of the Paris mosque. The federation claims 500 organizations across France as members. The ethnic and cultural composition of the FNMF is very mixed and includes a number of French converts. In December 1985, the Paris mosque established the *Rassemblement Islamique*, which brings together mostly Algerian groups.

Another important, and perhaps the most tightly structured, organization, founded in 1983, is the L'Union des Organization Islamiques de France (UOIF). It is ideologically close to the Muslim brotherhood and therefore falls into the category of the fundamentalist tendency, albeit in its more moderate version. The UOIF affirms its respect for the laws of the host country. It bases its attitude on the theory of *dar ul-ahd* (land of contract). The UOIF gathers together close to 200 associations. However, it does not control any major mosques except for the one in Lille. Moroccan and Tunisian personalities are more prominent within the UOIF. It is also supported by the active youth movement *Les Jeunes Musulmans de France* and publishes the newsletter *La Lettre de l'UOIF*.

The third category of organization consists of those linked with political groups based in immigrants' countries of origin or with worldwide Islamic movements. Among the former group, the following examples are worth noting: (1) *Groupement Islamique en France*. The main opposition group to Habib Boughiba's regime in Tunisia created this organization in 1980. Its intellectual roots are in the Muslim brotherhood; this may be one reason why it has been more willing to enter into cooperative arrangements with other organizations. (2) Various Turkish movements—Islamic and secular—have their branches in France. The chief Turkish Islamic political party, which under different names had until recently been identified with Necmettin Erbakan, is represented in France by *L'Union Islamique en France*. To these must be added various Sufi brotherhoods. Among the worldwide movements, the *Jama'at-ul-Tabligh* is very active in France through its organization *Foi et Pratique*. Its main goal is not so much to gain recognition for Islam's presence in France but rather to revive the practice of Islam among Muslims. Pakistani Muslims and preachers use this organization to spread their message.

However, Muslim associative life in France is currently in a state of flux, with new associations emerging, such as those created by women and families plus student and youth organizations. The most important student organizations include *L'Union Islamique des Etudiants de France*, which has its headquarters in Bordeaux; in 1996, it changed its name to *Etudiants Musulmans de France*. There is also the *L'Associations des Etudiants Islamiques de France*, which was established in 1963. These new and evolving associations cover a wide spectrum of ideas and orientations. Many also receive help from Christian groups. For example, the Association of Muslim Families received assistance from similar Protestant organizations. This type of organization appears at both the national and the municipal levels.

INTRA-MUSLIM RELATIONS

Disagreement and division along ethnic, linguistic, ideological, and sectarian lines, rather than agreement and cooperation, heavily characterize relations among France's Muslims. The foregoing discussion regarding ideological tendencies and the various institutions to which they have given rise has provided a sense of the community's diversity. Its result is often intense rivalry within various organizations, among individuals for leadership, and among different ideological trends regarding the tone and direction of the organization's activities. This situation in turn prevents the emergence of a unified Muslim voice that could interact effectively with the French political system and society and achieve for Islam a status equal to that of other religions.

The proliferation of Muslim organizations, which is favored by various French tendencies from right to left, is also the result of a desire on the part of the French society (1) to delay the institutionalization of Islam on an equal basis with other religions and (2) to compensate for the inadequate degree of political and economic integration of Muslims within French society. For example, at the political level, the granting of the right to citizenship—which some Muslims have seen as inoculation against expulsion—has not led to the creation of a Muslim elite at the national level. Meanwhile, the devolving of certain rights to various associations has created a limited elite concerned with the management of communitarian affairs at local levels.

At the economic level, these associations, which receive considerable funds from public sources in the form of subsidies, tend to compensate for the low level of economic integration and act as a kind of "ethnic business."

It is unlikely that these divisions within the Muslim community and their consequences for France's Muslims will disappear soon. Nevertheless, as many young Muslims attempt to develop a distinctly French Islam and to function both as fully fledged French citizens and as often-observant Muslims, a new generation transcending ethnic and ideological barriers may emerge in the not too distant future.

RELATIONS WITH COUNTRIES OF ORIGIN AND THE MUSLIM WORLD

A variety of relations link France's Muslim community with both the countries of origin and the rest of the Islamic world. In analyzing these links, it is necessary to distinguish between two categories of Muslims: those who are French citizens and those who remain citizens of other countries.

Quite naturally, direct and formal relations between noncitizen Muslim residents of France and the authorities of their countries of origin are more extensive and cover a wide range of legal and other functions that representatives of various Muslim countries perform for their citizens. However, even those Muslims who have French citizenship also retain the citizenship of their country of origin, because it is convenient, and maintain close ties with the authorities of that country. These Muslims carry two passports. This practice is not legal but is largely tolerated by the French authorities. Beyond these functions, the countries of origin exert influence, even control, over the Muslim community through two instruments: official imams (religious teachers and leaders) who are sometimes called *imams d'ambassade*; and provision of financial assistance to various mosques and institutions, including the salaries of imams. The official imams perform an important function in terms of preventing the complete assimilation of immigrants and their subscription to certain interpretations of Islam or secular ideologies, which may be considered subversive by the governments of their countries of origin.

The phenomenon of the foreign imam, educated at various religious institutions like Al-Azhar in Cairo or Zitouna in Tunis, certainly does not contribute to greater unity among France's Muslim population. Moreover, many of the foreign imams do not seem fully to understand the needs of the new generation of Muslims in France, some of whom are not even fluent in Arabic. For this reason, since the 1990s, there have been efforts to train imams in France, so far without great success. For instance, the *Faculté de Theologic Musulmane*, created by the Paris mosque in the early 1990s and inaugurated by French Minister of Interior Charles Pasqua, has had to stop its activities because it could not obtain the necessary subsidies.

Currently there are two institutions that, in one form or another, are involved in educating what could be called French imams: One affiliated with the UOIF is the Institut Europeanne des Sciences Humaines de Bouteloin in Saint-Leger de Fougeret, along with the Institut d'Etude Islamique de Paris. However, these efforts so far have not significantly increased the number of imams with French citizenship. For example, in 1990, of 500 full-time, paid imams, only 4 percent had French citizenship.[27]

French Muslims are affected not only by politics of their countries of origin but also by the general politics of the Islamic world. At times, these influences create security problems for the host country, as radical elements try to recruit alienated youth to carry out illegal and often violent acts.

For example, during 1995 to 1996, the terrorist activities linked to the Algerian civil war led to subversive acts in France. The most dramatic of these was a series of subway bombings in 1995 perpetrated by a group of disillusioned North Africans, many of whom grew up in the Lyons suburb of Vaulx-en-Velin and were recruited by the radical Algerian Armed Islamic Group. The bombings in the Paris area were carried out in part by a terrorist cell headed by Khaled Kelkal, an unemployed twenty-four-year-old Algerian living in Vaulx-en-Velin who had served time in prison; here, he had converted to extremist Islam. Shot by French riot police, he died in September 1995. Subsequently, this act caused some disturbances among North Africans in the suburbs.[28] However, these disturbances were prevented from escalating into full-scale riots by the efforts of Muslim organizations that tried to calm the Muslim population. The case of Kelkal is tragic; he had been a promising student at high school, but because of the psychological difficulties he faced in integrating into French society, the pressures of his family who wanted him to succeed, and other temptations, he drifted into antisocial behavior. In an interview with the German sociologist Dietmar Loch, which was published in *Le Monde* after his death, Kelkal said that he had the possibility of succeeding, but this meant total assimilation, something that he could not do. In the interview, he said, "Total integration is impossible; I cannot forget my culture or eat pork."[29]

Yet, whatever their grievances may be against the French state, many of the frustrated youth of depressed suburbs have not been receptive to radical ideas and acts (notwithstanding some difficult episodes, as noted above), which could endanger their integration into the French society.

More recently, rising terrorism in the Middle East, beginning in autumn 2000, resonated in the suburbs and led to some anti-Semitic protests. Yet even in this case, most Muslims expressed their loyalty to France and their desire to prevent the importation of violence from the Middle East.

Another form of interaction between France's Muslims and the rest of the Islamic world is the financial help that they receive for the construction of mosques, purchase of prayer halls, and other activities. For example, the grand mosque of Lyon, inaugurated in 1994, was built with financial assistance from Saudi Arabia.[30]

The dynamics of interaction between France's Muslims, on the one hand, and their countries of origin, on the other, have become more complex as the new generations develop their own views and interpretations of Islam within the more open political system of France. For instance, many countries whose populations form a relatively large community in France are concerned that the more democratic interpretations of Islam currently being elaborated in France will infiltrate their countries and pose a challenge to their political systems. Not all Muslim immigrants in France are active opponents of the governments of their countries of origin, along the model of Cuban immigrants in Miami, Florida, USA.[31] Nevertheless, the divergences between the interests of immigrants and their countries of origin are growing, despite efforts to hide them. Consequently, these countries do not favor significant involvement of their expatriate communities in France's social and political life, let alone their total integration within its democratic system.

In fact, some Muslim countries and organizations that they support actively discourage Muslims from such involvement. According to the Swiss-Egyptian Muslim scholar Tariq Ramadan, the attitude of the French and some other European governments is ambivalent in the sense that, at times, they prefer a traditionalist and quietist Muslim community to a more modern and activist one, which wants full participation in the system and equal treatment as fully fledged citizens of France and other

European countries. Despite these misgivings, however, the gradual loosening of ties, dilution of the practice of a pure Islam, and steady integration continue. The most important factor is the increase in the number of mixed marriages, which in the case of the Algerians account for 50 percent of all marriages.

THE LEVEL OF POLITICAL INVOLVEMENT

More than half of France's Muslim population has French citizenship, the largest group being the Algerians. This is due to the fact that, until 1962, Algeria was considered part of territorial France. Therefore, any child born of Algerian parents in France after 1962 automatically became French. Yet until recently, Muslim involvement in the political process has been limited. For instance, there are only a few hundred Muslim elected local officials and a few members of the European Parliament. This is partly due to the nature of France's electoral system for choosing both delegates to the national assembly and senators, which works against ethnic candidates.

This situation is also caused by some religious leaders who discourage Muslims linked to their countries of origin from voting, because they fear that this would lead to the development of a more democratic and progressive Islam that could eventually influence developments in the immigrants' home countries. However, during presidential and parliamentary elections, such successful North African Muslims as Zinedine Zidane, the captain of France's soccer team, will be highly courted by various candidates. Historically, French citizens of North African origin have voted for leftist parties. But recently, parties on the right of the political spectrum have tried to appeal to this section of the electorate. At the local level, even the extreme right parties at times seek the Muslim vote.

It appears justified, therefore, to predict that, gradually, the Muslim electorate will increasingly vote on the basis of economic and social considerations. In other words, it will vote for the party most likely to improve the conditions of their community and respond to their needs and grievances.

THE EVOLUTION OF MUSLIM IDENTITY IN FRANCE AND ITS CONSEQUENCES

The Muslims who arrived in France as part of the so-called reserve forces of capitalism gradually asserted their identity as Muslims through a series of atypical social conflicts. These conflicts occurred first within the industries in decline, in various living spaces such as housing developments, and in institutions with symbolic significance, such as schools. These conflicts were not organized by clandestine leaders. Rather, they resulted from the collapse or total absence of older forms of management of social relations. By their mere existence, these conflicts created new forms of integration, which tended to evolve from individual to collective patterns. However, they did not lead to the development of clear rules of the game. Instead, they resulted in a mixing of old and new forms in a somewhat confused and, at times, conflictual manner.

In France, the real cause of conflict among the specialized workforce (*ouvriers spécialises*) in the auto industry, which had witnessed the arrival of Muslims during the 1970s, was the transformation of working conditions following the change from the Ford system (assembly line) to automation. The result was that nearly all of the earlier immigrant workers who had adapted to the Ford system, as the peasants from southern Europe had done before them, became redundant. When this change occurred, no organization that had played an important role in the process of integration of previous migrant workers, such as the political parties, especially the Communist party, or trade unions, especially the CGT (*Confédération Générale du Travail*), was in a position to help Muslim immigrant workers. These organizations had other priorities and thus could not focus on taking care of a group of people who, at the time, did not appear as potential and lasting members or voters. Moreover, their demand that their interests be taken into account conflicted with the demands of earlier immigrants, who were well represented both within the party and the trade unions for access to employment and social benefits. Therefore, in the case of these Muslim workers, the social conflicts of the postwar period and Communist messianism, which had helped integrate earlier immigrants, were no longer effective. Compared with the successful examples of integration in the case of Italian and Polish workers, the North Africans appeared as atypical players in a transitory situation. Coming from countries that had barely emerged from long and violent anticolonial conflicts and had recently acquired independence, they did not ask for French citizenship, and nobody offered them the option. Yet they also refused to be abandoned to their fate because of a technological change in an industry to which they had contributed as workers. On this basis, they demanded a right to remain in France and to be treated as autonomous actors in relation both to French and to North African governments, which claimed the right to decide their future for them. By doing so, they entered into competition with the earlier immigrants defended by the political parties and the trade unions. They also entered into conflict with the North African governments, which were willing to accept their repatriation in exchange for financial assistance for their reintegration, which they would administer. Thus caught in a position of isolation, they intuitively saw Islam as the only legitimate means that could enable them to assert their collective identity and to defend their individual rights vis-à-vis employers, competitors, and their countries of origin, which were willing to abandon them in exchange for financial compensation by the industrial countries.

FORMS OF ASSERTION OF MUSLIM IDENTITY

Muslims' attempt to assert their identity was first done by demanding that prayer halls be made available for them at the workplace and that working hours be arranged in a way that would allow them to pray at required hours. These demands initially were made by small groups and in a spontaneous fashion. Gradually, Muslims working in a particular place resorted to collective forms of action and in the process became communities that were negotiating simultaneously with management and with the trade unions. As a result, self-proclaimed imams—or those accepted by the group—became interlocutors with management and trade unions, and they acted as intermediaries or mediators in disputes. They could not prevent the closure of factories or the process of robotization. But their intervention led to a more controlled evolution of the situation and, to a degree, helped protect the interests and dignity of workers.

Consequently, the more difficult periods in terms of loss of jobs became less violent than earlier ones, when badly organized and badly informed workers who had been traumatized by changes tended to adopt more uncompromising and unrealistic stands. It appeared that the assertion of a religious identity had helped to create some form of communication, solved some problems, and had made the acceptance of an inevitable evolution more palatable.

A similar process occurred in various housing projects following the strikes, which took place in the workers' home districts during the 1970s. The management of disputes over the payment of rents led to the emergence of a recognized religious presence in those housing projects where the majority of residents were Muslims. The emergence of these communitarian structures meant that rules accepted by the majority, such as prohibition of alcohol and the observance of Ramadan, could be imposed on nonobservant Muslims. In this context, too, the establishment of prayer halls—which replaced the bars—and the emergence of imams led to a more measured handling of conflicts, which in earlier times had taken a more radical turn. In the following years, the Muslim religious presence expanded—often discretely by taking advantage of the granting of the right of forming associations to foreigners by the French government in 1981. As a result, the number of cultural associations increased, as did the number of prayer halls, which were called mosques, although they lacked the architectural characteristics of traditional Muslim mosques.

There has, however, been resistance to this increasing visibility of Islam. Those who oppose a more visible Muslim presence use urban planning rules at various municipalities. Meanwhile, the French government does not intervene in favor of Muslims. On the contrary, at times the state acts in favor of the opponents of any highly visible Muslim presence. For example, when Muslims obtained permission to build a traditional mosque in the new town of Evry, the state welcomed demands to help construct a new cathedral so that the mosque would not become the most visible symbol of the town.

Nevertheless, these gains allow the legal structuring of collective action. To these would be added the granting of ten-year residence permits and the gradual acquisition of French citizenship by the Muslim elite. From this point onward, the assertion of Muslim identity would acquire a national character without losing its religious vigor.

EXTERNAL DEVELOPMENTS: IMPACT ON THE EVOLUTION OF MUSLIM IDENTITY

External developments, especially the emergence of Islamist movements in the Arab and Islamic world, have also impacted on the process of affirming Muslim identity. It seems that second-generation North Africans who were having difficulties integrating into French society used the fear that the rise of Islamic militancy had created among the public in order to ensure that Islam was treated on an equal basis with other religions. In other words, Islam appeared to be a useful means of negotiating a better deal for Muslims in French society. As a result, Islam was transformed into an instrument of social and political bargaining.

Of course, Islam was not the only means used by Muslim immigrants to get a better deal. Many Muslims joined antiracist groups or other forces working for better treatment of immigrants. Three factors contributed to Islam's acquiring a greater importance as a focus of identity and as an instrument of social and political bargaining: (1) A considerable number of the young, despite the fact that they were immersed in French culture through school, leisure activities, and everyday life, remained nostalgic about their past values that had not been transmitted to them and the land of their ancestors. These young Muslims are searching for an individual and collective identity; (2) The many problems of Arab countries, including those of North Africa, coupled with intra-Arab disputes and divisions, rendered Arabism an inadequate focus of identity; and (3) Islam's political revival and unifying dimension enable Muslims belonging to different ethnic origins to transcend their differences. As a result, Islam became an important and voluntarily chosen element of identity that enabled Muslims to raise the issue of their place in French society and to negotiate over a wide range of issues, such as Islamic values, secularism, religious freedom, and equality among religions.[32]

To these factors must be added such events as the Persian Gulf War of 1990 to 1991 and the war in Bosnia. In addition, the reaction of French society to the growing visibility of Islam in France—which it saw as a threat to French culture, especially its secular traditions—created an opportunity for Muslim activists to present Islam as the only defense against what they characterized as French racism.

THE MUSLIM COMMUNITY AND THE FRENCH REPUBLICAN SYSTEM: CHALLENGE TO THE SECULAR ACCORD

The efforts of France's Muslim community to preserve its identity through a variety of means and its demands for the granting of certain rights created a perception of Islam as a factor in a process of negotiation of a conflictual situation, which reflects a new social setting whose implications are not well understood by French society. This perception and misunderstanding generated resistance on the part of French society to the Muslim presence. It raised sharp debate about the relationship between Islam's presence and the French secular ethos as well as disagreements about what Islam and secularism exactly mean, and it also led to clashes on a number of issues.

Interestingly, the industrial and other enterprises that employed Muslim immigrants and the housing authorities where Muslims lived have reacted less strongly to this assertion of Muslim identity than have governmental authorities, at both the municipal and the national levels. For example, the presence since 1989 of what has been characterized as the Islamic veil (*voile islamique*) in France's public schools caused a major conflict that drew the attention of the media. The controversy began when, in October 1989, three female students of Moroccan origin attempted to wear the Islamic headcover at school in Creil, just north of Paris. The wearing of the Islamic headcover, which is considered insignificant in most European countries, acquired a conflictual characteristic because it was characterized as an act of proselytization in a public sphere. As such, it became part of the prohibitions that were included in the Law of 1905, codifying the principle of the separation of church and state. On this basis, the students were barred from classes.[33] Soon, laws and jurisprudence regarding the wearing of the Christian cross at school were invoked.

Initially, students who wore the Islamic headdress had no intention of challenging the established order. However, various associations for the support of these students adopted more ambiguous positions and finally challenged the government to change its attitude and practices in compliance with the rules of the European Union (EU). Consequently, this conflict generated a reverse identity dimension in the sense that the majority—the native French—reacted like a threatened minority. Moreover, the conflictual perception of Islam encouraged by the Iranian and later Algerian experience was superimposed on these concerns. Thus, the Islamic headcover came to be seen as a symbol of *jihad* (holy war). The fact that this incident occurred at the height of the controversy over Salman Rushdie's book, *The Satanic Verses*, intensified the symbolic significance of the controversy.

The high birthrate of the countries of origins was also perceived as a weapon used through immigration to force the transformation of French society according to a multicultural pattern, as seen in the United States or the United Kingdom. Other exaggerated notions were used to explain the collective fear of a changing social scene. The political groups on the right and extreme right used the issue as an instrument against the socialist government, which they accused of favoring the implantation of immigrant Muslim culture in France. By granting the right of association to foreigners, the government of Pierre Mauroy, without intending to do so, offered a legal framework for the formation of religious associations. Furthermore, the granting of a ten-year residence permit eliminated the anxiety of Muslims regarding their legitimate right to remain in France. Eventually, the government also moved toward granting French citizenship to those born in France. Thus, without going as far as an official recognition of Islam along the Belgian and Austrian models, a transitional framework gradually began to take shape.

ESTABLISHING A DIALOGUE WITH ISLAM

In the context of French tradition, which took shape in the nineteenth century after the revolutionary turmoil, the state designates as interlocutors those whom it wants to represent a given community. Once this task is accomplished, it then officially recognizes the community and provides it with the necessary resources that allow it to create a clientelist network and act as intermediaries between the community and the government.

Thus, until 1905, it was able to accord the Catholic Church a prominent place while, at the same time, integrating the Protestants and the Jews as recognized minorities and creating conditions for the free exercise of their religion and the maintenance of the cohesion of their respective communities. The state thus proposed the same arrangement for the Muslims. But the latter often did not quite appreciate all that was involved in the historic construction of a pluralist system that does not allow a place for religion in the public sphere.

The Muslims are willing to give up a large part of their behavior linked to a majority faith as practiced in their countries of origin. But they are not convinced that they should adhere to all aspects of the secular pact, which was negotiated without their participation under conditions they do not find congenial. The last people to become part of the French religious landscape, the Muslims have not inherited the places of worship designated by the state, as has been the case with Protestants and Jews after the Napoleonic concord. Nor can they rely on a prosperous community to build these places. Consequently, they have to appeal either to their countries of origin or to such rich Muslim states as Saudi Arabia. This request places them in a state of dependency, for which they are in turn blamed.

A solution can be found in the official recognition of a religious authority that could be in charge of managing dietary issues, such as *halal* meat, and who is paid by the community.

Since the early 1980s, efforts have been made to deal with this problem. But each time that a governmental authority has tried to designate such a religious authority, opposition has arisen both from within the community and from so-called "external Islam"—countries of origin— which have felt excluded.

Thus, the effort at institutionalization by designation from above, whether proposed by Pierre Joxe or Jean-Pierre Chevènement, ministers of interior of the left, or by Charles Pasqua of the right, have failed to satisfy everybody. The reason is that the community could not agree on a representative who could be acceptable to the state. In fact, various Muslim groups were not in a hurry to reach an agreement with the state unless they could be sure that any arrangement would secure them a dominant position.

The state, for its part, adjusted to this situation of disorder and fragmentation while at the same time deploring it. In fact, a solid Muslim religious authority would have caused it more anxiety. Nevertheless, some efforts were made to create mechanisms for a structured dialogue, such as the establishment of the *Conseil d'Orientation et de Réflexion sur l'Islam en France* by Pierre Joxe in April 2000 and the creation of a joint government-Muslim council by Jean-Pierre Chevènement to improve domestic Franco-Muslim relations.[34]

Despite these efforts, the French authorities, while declaring the necessity of a religious representation, adopted the strategy of encouraging the formation of civic organizations that, while ensuring for Muslims a degree of representation, would not highlight their religious character.

Associations such as *France Plus* or *SOS racisme*, directed from above, would perform this function, bringing together Muslims without any official reference to Islam and thus placing them within a framework that goes beyond Islam's confines. In this way, republican rhetoric would transcend religious particularism.

As a result of this strategy, the religious dimension finds its place within a multiplicity of local cultural associations, which, to some degree, ensure the practice of the faith. In this way, a certain level of structuring of the Islamic environment and a measure of representation for the Muslims are achieved, and intermediaries for a dialogue with various authorities are created with everyone finding the maintenance of a degree of ambiguity in relations to their benefit.

Thus, the political parties, trade unions, and municipalities use these associations when looking for members or followers. Meanwhile, those in charge of these associations play the game because they realize that this allows them some chance of upward social mobility, which they would not have been able to achieve through other venues.

This encounter of contradictory, but reconcilable, interests has so far guaranteed a degree of management of the needs of the Muslim community. It does not amount to official religious and cultural recognition of Islam, which different partners desire. But it has been able to compensate for various deficiencies of public policies and the overall system, at both an economic and a political level.

EMERGING EUROPEAN DIMENSION

The evolution of France's Muslim community must also take into account a Europe-wide phenomenon: namely, the problems of institutionalizing Islam as a symbol of the assertion of identity of immigrants coming from the south and settling in declining industrial societies.

The free movement of people legally established in the European space constitutes a factor of homogenization. It also enables Muslims to claim similar advantages obtained by Muslims in various European countries, more in the name of human rights than of religion.

Europe introduces a new dimension, a sort of court of appeals, in the context of an unequal debate between the state and the individual. It is not necessarily hostile to the idea of community and the protection of the rights of minorities. It does not present itself as a pole of identification but rather as an instrument of harmonization and arbitration. It also extends its influence to the countries of the southern Mediterranean as best exemplified by the Euro-Mediterranean partnership and the Barcelona process. (On the Barcelona process, see chapter 15.) This program should establish a base for dialogue with the immigrants' countries of origin. This should help avoid conflicts of identity and to manage the external dimensions of a process of integration, which develops also in relation to real or imagined connections with the Palestinians or Bosnian Muslims and in the shadow of tensions in the Maghreb. In short, Muslims are developing a double sense of identification: one with an emerging European Islam, with all its local variations, from Marseilles to

Hamburg, and the other with an exterior Islam, a sort of externalized painful memory of the trauma of exile.

It is through this filter that a number of important compromises—more important than is generally assumed—are achieved. First, identification with the painful memories of "elsewhere" (countries of origin) neither leads to violence nor reduces loyalty to France. This became apparent during the Gulf War and the Algerian civil war. French Muslims, by focusing their loyalty on the person of the president—Mitterrand or Chirac—affirmed their allegiance to France and under no circumstances wanted to endanger their right to peaceful residence in France.

At a deeper level, this debate about extreme poles of solidarity hides an extensive process of mixing through schools, workplace, and marriages. Nationality is no longer a problem from the moment the "other" recognizes their (Muslims') right to a different history.

The evolution toward the Europeanization of Islam's position is still done through practical and comparative measures rather than through legislation. However, in the future, some form of supranational intervention in the field of norms and values, with implications for the place and role of religion, cannot be ruled out, although presently the religious field is not within the EU's competence. Nonetheless, issues related to migration, asylum rights, and the status of minorities (which are within the EU's competence) provide venues for action that could overcome the barrier set by the exclusion of religious issues from the range of EU competencies.

The development of a compromise of a pluralist nature between religion and politics can only take place at this level and with the inclusion of Islam as one of the legitimate components of European culture and identity. Such a vision presupposes that Europe will develop a nonconflictual vision of Islam and will establish relations of good neighborliness and assistance with Muslim countries of the south and east Mediterranean, from whence most immigrants arrive. It further presupposes that Europe's Muslims will develop a theological framework appropriate to the practice of a minority religion implanted within urban societies of predominantly Christian heritage and will be capable of solving problems of coexistence with other groups.

CONCLUSIONS AND PROSPECTS

Islam's presence in France is a direct consequence of France's colonial past in the Muslim world, especially North Africa, as well as its needs for manpower over a period of fifty years. France's Muslim community, although overwhelmingly of Maghrebian origin, is divided along many lines, which makes it difficult to talk of a single community.

Economically and socially, the community lags far behind the general population. In particular, the existence of pockets of youth unemployment and poverty in major urban centers is disturbing. Nevertheless, improvements in these areas have occurred in part as a result of a kind of affirmative action by the government on behalf of those Muslims who are French citizens. As more and more Muslims acquire French citizenship by virtue of birth or naturalization, the position of the entire community should improve. Problems of so-called "ghettoized" Islam, however, may be more intractable.

Despite the fact that a minority of France's Muslims, notably the youth, are attracted to extremist ideas, and notwithstanding some turbulent periods when France was subjected to subversive acts by extremists, France's Muslims have retained their loyalty to the state and the country of their residence or citizenship.

Relations with countries of origin remain extensive and multidimensional, but they are becoming more complex, especially as the new generation of French Muslims do not accept the cultural and political tutelage of the authorities of their ancestral homelands. Rather, the trend is to develop new interpretations of Islam and new syntheses of Islamic and French values that would enable the new generation to live as French and as Muslim. The process of integration is also happening through the inevitable mixing with other groups, as well as through a variety of compromises at several levels. Similarly, France's Islamic community is affected by developments at the European level.

Barring serious economic crises in France or a new wave of radicalization in the Islamic world, France's Muslim community should develop on the path of integration without assimilation, as Islam should gain recognition as a component of the country's religious and cultural landscape. However, because of the diversity of the community, the multiplicity of influences to which it is subjected, and still strong resistance to such recognition, the process will be long and difficult.

NOTES

1. Soheib Bencheikh, *Marrianne et le prophète: l'islam dans la France laïque* [Marianne and the Prophet: Islam in lay France] (Paris: Bernard Grasset, 1998), 86–87. See also Remy Leveau (ed.), *Islam(s) en Europe* [Islam(s) in Europe], (Berlin: Centre Marc Bloch, 1998), 5.

2. Today, as Tariq Ramadan has put it, the choice for the majority of Muslims in France is not between being French or Muslim; rather, the question is how to be a French Muslim. *To Be a European Muslim* (Leicester: Islamic Foundation, 1999).

3. See Bencheikh, *Marrianne et le prophète*, 83–84.

4. Ibid.

5. Ibid.

6. See Jørgen S. Nielsen, *Muslims in Western Europe*, 2nd ed. (Edinburgh: Ed-

inburgh University Press, 1995), 8; Remy Leveau and Gilles Kepel, *Les musulmans dans la société francaise* [Muslims in French society], (Paris: F.N.S.P., 1987), 9–25; and Gilles Kepel, *Les banlieues de l'islam* [The suburbs of Islam] (Paris: Seuil, 1988), 30, 55.

7. See Alain Boyer, *L'islam en France* [Islam in France] (Paris: Presses Universitaires de France, 1998), 80.

8. According to a poll conducted by *L'Institut Français d'Opinion Publique* in 1994, only 31 percent of Muslims in France prayed daily and only 16 percent went to weekly prayers. An interesting point is that the numbers had fallen by ten percentage points since 1989. *Sondage IFOP* cited in Tariq Ramadan, *Muslims in France,* (Leicester: Islamic Foundation, 1997), 37. See also Boyer, *L'islam en France,* 22–24; and Leveau, *Islam(s) en Europe,* 12.

9. See Nielsen, *Muslims in Western Europe,* 17.

10. See Boyer, *L'islam en France,* 21.

11. Ibid., 251–258. Also, Olivier Roy, "Islam in France: Religion, Ethnic Community, or Social Ghetto?" in *Muslims in Europe,* Bernard Lewis and Dominique Schnapper (New York: Pinter Publisher, 1994).

12. Boyer, *L'islam en France,* 22.

13. Christopher Caldwell, "The Crescent and the Tricolor," *Atlantic Monthly,* 286, no. 5 (November 2000): 29–30.

14. Bencheikh, *Marianne et le prophète,* 91–92.

15. Boyer, *L'islam en France,* 264–265.

16. Suzanne Thave, "Immigrant Employment in 1999," *INSEE,* no. 717 (May 2000): 1–4.

17. Caldwell, "The Crescent and the Tricolor," 30.

18. Boyer, *L'islam en France,* 268.

19. Ibid., 269–270.

20. Ibid.

21. Ibid., 272–274.

22. On various Islamist movements in France, see Gilles Kepel, *Allah in the West: Islamic Movements in America and Europe,* trans. Susan Milner (Stanford: Stanford University Press, 1997).

23. Boyer, *L'islam en France,* 274–275.

24. Nielsen, *Muslims in Western Europe,* 16–17.

25. On the Paris Mosque and its evolution, see Boyer, *L'islam en France,* 282–285.

26. For more details, see ibid., 285–298.

27. Ibid., 243–246.

28. On the bombings, see "To Discourage the Others," *The Economist* (7 October 1995); also Alex G. Hargreaves, "The Bourgeoisie: Mediation or Mirage," *Journal of European Studies* 28, parts 1 and 2 (March/June 1998): 94–95.

29. See Dietmar Loch, "Moi, Khaled Kelkal," *Le Monde,* 7 October 1995.

30. See Milton Viorst, "The Muslims of France," *Foreign Affairs* 75 (September/October 1996): 81.

31. See, for instance, Tariq Ramadan, *To Be a European Muslim* (Leicester: Islamic Foundation, 1999).

32. See Boyer, *L'islam en France,* 116–117.

33. Government officials supported the decision of the school's headmaster,

albeit in an ambiguous fashion, which suggested that such cases should be settled on a case-by-case basis at the local level. See Maxim Silverman, *Deconstructing the Nation: Immigration, Race, and Citizenship in Modern France* (New York: Routledge, 1992).

34. Catherine Withal de Wenden, "Muslims in France," in *Muslims in the Margin: Political Responses to the Presence of Islam in Western Europe*, ed. W.A.R. Shahid and P.S. Van Koningsveld (Kampen: Kok Pharos, 1996), 64.

2

Islam in Germany

Andreas Goldberg

INTRODUCTION

In the last decade, Islam has become the second largest religion in Germany after Christianity. Today, Germany's Muslim population is conservatively estimated at 2.8 to 3 million. Two thirds of Germany's Muslims are of Turkish origin, and the rest come from countries in the Middle East, South Asia, the Balkans, and the former Soviet Union. Thus, Islam in Germany has a largely Turkish character. There are also an estimated 100,000 ethnic German Muslims.

As the number of Muslims in Germany has increased, the latent resentments against the Muslim community have also grown among largely Christian and secular Germans, because of a tendency to associate "Islam" with religious fundamentalism and political extremism. Some Islamic organizations, claiming to be official representatives of Islam in Germany, plus a few extremist groups that at times create foreign policy problems for Germany, have strengthened this view by their statements and actions. Yet only a small minority of Muslims in Germany can be described as extremists. A report by the *Verfassungsschutz* (the Federal Intelligence Organization for the Defense of the German Constitution) states that Muslim extremists constitute less than 1 percent of all Muslims in Germany.

German Muslims, especially the Turks, have established a functioning Islamic infrastructure, which is accepted by most members of the community. However, the federal government's policy regarding foreign residents has not been very concerned with the Muslims' religious or other interests; it has merely observed the formation of Islamic organizations with unease and mistrust. Meanwhile, patterns of interaction between the Muslim communities and the German society are evolving in various forms and involve elements of both coexistence and tension and even conflict.

FIRST INTENSIVE ENCOUNTERS WITH ISLAM

Muslims have been living in Germany for over 300 years, albeit in small numbers and playing a minor role in the society.[1] In the late 1940s and early 1950s, a relatively large community of Iranian businessmen was established in Hamburg. The large-scale migration of Muslims to Germany began in the mid-1950s as a result of high economic growth and shortage of labor. The first recruitment agreements were signed with Turkey in 1961, Morocco in 1963, and Tunisia in 1965. Consequently, the largest groups of Muslims, workers initially, came from these three countries. The migratory movements of foreign labor to the Federal Republic were also the result of rapid population growth and increasing unemployment in many Muslim states.

The majority of Muslim immigrants to Germany had already experienced an "internal migration," having to move from their rural homes to urban regions. Many of them had lived in large cities and had been waiting for an arrangement to immigrate. Consequently, the bulk of Muslim immigrants came from rural and traditional backgrounds, a fact that has affected the character of Islam in Germany.

The typical early labor immigrant was a single man, often employed as an unskilled worker in the manufacturing industry or in the lower services sector. Both the receiving society and the immigrants perceived their residence as temporary. Consequently, neither side made any efforts to interact socially.

Toward the end of the 1960s, it became clear that short-term labor immigrants were not economically advantageous, and thus German firms were reluctant to replace newly skilled workers with newly arriving unskilled laborers. Immigrant workers realized that they could not save enough money in a short period and decided to stay longer and bring their families to Germany. Despite these changes, the idea that immigrants should be regarded only as "guest workers" or "foreigners" who would some day leave Germany was retained. The German government's decision in 1993 to stop recruiting workers from non–European Union (EU) countries further encouraged family reunification. The existing immigrant communities believed that, with the new law, they might not be able to bring their families to Germany, a belief that accelerated the pace of family reunification. This process of family reunification marks the beginnings of Germany's evolution into an immigrant-receiving country.

Family reunification also changed the social structure of the immigrant communities in several ways: It increased the number of economically inactive and dependent immigrants; it altered the male/female ratio, gradually raising the number of women to the level of men; and the increase in the number of female immigrants made Islam more "visible" because of the practice of veiling in public. Following family reunifications, Germans had to confront those social consequences of migration that they had so far neglected because of the insistence on viewing immigrants as guest workers and thus failing to develop policies to deal with their needs. Suddenly, schools for Muslim children had to be provided. Because 80 percent of kindergartens in Germany are run by churches, most Muslim parents were unwilling to send their children there. Gradually, the public and local and federal authorities became conscious of the consequences of immigration and its multidimensional challenges to the German society.

At first, the federal government reacted to these challenges by introducing a restrictive policy on family reunification. On 2 December 1981, the age of children allowed to join their parents was reduced to sixteen. The federal government offered immigrants financial incentives to return home and on 28 November 1983 passed a law to this effect. Many immigrants were willing to return, but this was delayed for reasons such as the completion of the children's education, saving enough money, and improvement in the economic situation of home countries.

According to the 1983 law, Yugoslavs, Turks, Spaniards, Portuguese, Moroccans, Tunisians, and Koreans who returned to their countries of origin between 31 October 1983 and 30 September 1984 could receive up to DM 10,500 plus DM 1,500 per child. The pension contributions paid by the workers accumulated in pension schemes could also be given to the returning workers. About 250,000 foreigners, mostly Turks, left Germany between 1983 and 1984. Economic considerations, notably problems of unemployment, plus popular belief that Turkish immigrants could not be integrated into a Christian West European country, were the principal reasons for passing this law. The public learned about the law through the intermediary of sensationalist newspapers and in a distorted manner, which produced a negative feeling among them. Many Germans resented the offering of financial incentives to Turks. Therefore, although the immigrants got only more or less what they had contributed to pension funds, public envy and hostility toward foreigners increased.

Table 2.1
Numerical and Ethnic Composition of Muslim Communities

Country of origin	Population in 1989	Population in 1995	Population in 1999
Afghanistan	22,500	58,500	71,955
Albania	300	10,500	12,107
Algeria	5,900	17,700	17,186
Bosnia-Herzegovina	—	316,000	167,690
Iran	81,300	107,000	116,446
Iraq	4,900	16,700	51,211
Lebanon	30,100	54,800	54,063
Morocco	61,800	81,900	81,450
Pakistan	19,700	36,900	38,257
Somalia	3,000	8,200	8,350
Tunisia	24,300	26,400	24,260
Turkic Republics*	—	16,400	55,600
Turkey	1,612,600	2,014,300	2,035,564

*Azerbaijan, Kazakhstan, Kyrgyzstan, Tadjikistan, Turkmenistan, Uzbekistan.

Source: Statistisches Bundesamt, Auszählung des Ausländerzentralregisters.

SECOND-WAVE IMMIGRANTS

A second migratory wave occurred in the mid-1970s and continued into the 1980s from a wider range of Muslim-populated countries. Many of the new immigrants were victims of revolutionary upheavals or civil wars in places like Iran and Afghanistan. They represented political immigrants. These refugees benefited from Article 16 of the German Constitution, which grants right of asylum to politically persecuted persons. In the 1990s, the Soviet Union's dissolution and the civil war in Yugoslavia led to another wave of Muslim immigration, mostly from Bosnia. For a short period, Bosnians became Germany's second largest Muslim group after the Turks. But after the end of the war, many of them returned home. Since 1995, there has been a considerable inflow of refugees and immigrants from Central Asia, of which only a small portion are Muslim.

The figures in Table 2.1 do not reflect the exact number of Muslim immigrants in Germany because they do not include naturalized Muslims, although since the amendment to the citizenship law in 1999, the

Table 2.2
Distribution of Muslims in Germany Based on Country of Origin

Country of origin	Share in percentage (out of total Muslim population of 3,000,000; incl. German Muslims)
Turkey	67.9
Iran	3.9
Morocco	2.7
Afghanistan	2.4
Bosnia-Herzegovina	2.2
Iraq	1.7
Pakistan	1.3
Lebanon	1.0
Tunisia	0.8
Algeria	0.6
Albania	0.3
Somalia	0.3
From other countries	11.6
German Muslims	3.3

Source: Calculations based on Table 2.1, taking into account the religious affiliation in the respective countries (according to the *Encyclopaedia Britannica*), which is relevant for Albania, Bosnia-Herzegovina, and Lebanon.

rate of naturalization among immigrants, especially the Turks, has been steadily increasing. Over the years, 340,000 Turks have been naturalized, swelling the number of Turkish immigrants in Germany to 2.4 million. Of course, it is to be assumed that naturalized Turks remain Muslims.

Therefore, the total number of Muslims in Germany is closer to 3.3 million, with the Turks constituting 75 percent of all Muslim immigrants. They are followed by Muslims from Bosnia, Iran, Morocco, Afghanistan, Lebanon, Iraq, and Pakistan (see Tables 2.1 and 2.2). Muslims from Kosovo may well be the third or fourth largest group, but because they are counted among Yugoslav nationals, their number cannot be established with certainty. The refugee influx from Kosovo increased the number of Albanian-speaking Muslims. It is estimated that, by the end of 1999, about 140,000 Albanian-speaking Kosovars were living in Germany, but their number has been decreasing since, owing to return.[2]

In order to stem the tide of refugees, in 1993, Article 16 of the constitution was modified. According to the new law, persons who enter the Federal Republic from a "secure third country" are no longer entitled to the right of asylum in Germany. This new law has meant that politically persecuted persons from the Near East (especially from Iran, Iraq, or Afghanistan) who enter Germany via Rumania or Bulgaria—secure countries—are no longer treated according to the German asylum procedures and are sent back.

SECTARIAN DIVISIONS

The majority of Germany's Muslims are Sunnis, but there is also a Shi'a minority. Another Muslim sect is the Ahmadiyya, whose membership is estimated at around 30,000. The movement is influential with German authorities, who often praise it for its openness and its contribution to Christian-Muslim dialogue. However, because orthodox Muslims consider the sect heretical, it is doubtful that, in the absence of other more broad-based efforts, it can be effective in advancing interfaith dialogue. To the extent that the movement projects a more positive image of Islam in the long run, it can contribute to the improvement of Christian-Muslim relations.

GEOGRAPHIC DISTRIBUTION

Germany's Muslim community is concentrated in large urban centers because of the following factors: (1) proximity to a harbor or airport, (2) availability of employment opportunities, (3) more promising prospects for improved living conditions, and (4) the prior existence of relatives and friends from home countries.

Initially, most immigrants intended to return to their country of origin after a short period of residence, and thus they sought cheap accommodation and rented flats in run-down neighborhoods, where few Germans would reside. In this way, large immigrant neighborhoods grew in some of West Germany's largest cities, such as Kreuzberg in Berlin, Marxloh in Duisburg, and the Central Station area in Frankfurt. The desire of immigrants to live close to neighbors from their home country and their difficulty in finding accommodation elsewhere because of reluctance of German landlords to rent their houses to foreigners contributed to this pattern of concentration and led to the creation of large Turkish/Muslim ghettos, with populations exceeding 10,000 and with their own mosques and grocery stores in major cities. Presently, other Muslims use the infrastructure, which was created mostly by the Turks.

Prior to the fall of the Berlin Wall in 1989 and Germany's reunification, there were no Muslims in the eastern part of the country. The former German Democratic Republic did import labor, but from other socialist countries such as Vietnam. These "contract workers" made up a very small portion of the whole population, had little interaction with the rest of the society, and lived in segregated housing.

After the 1990 reunification, Muslims began to enter the new *Bundesländer* (federal states) in significant numbers. Most of them were asylum seekers from the former Yugoslavia, Turkey (Kurds), Lebanon, Afghanistan, Iraq, Iran, and Pakistan. This was due to the fact that, according to the asylum law of 1 July 1993, communes and cities of the new *Bundesländer* are obliged to accept refugees in the same manner as the old *Bundesländer*, although the number of accepted asylum seekers is principally determined by the relative size of the *Bundesländer*. Small numbers of immigrant workers from the West also moved to the industrial and populous centers of the East: Leipzig, Dresden, Halle, and Rostock. Some of these immigrants from the West have become self-employed and have established small or medium-sized enterprises. According to a 1996 study by the Centre for Studies on Turkey, 61.1 percent of those Turkish entrepreneurs who owned medium-sized firms planned to open a representation or to establish a new business in the new *Bundesländer*.[3] Others are employed in big West German construction firms, which have been active in the East as part of a policy of revitalizing the newly integrated Eastern states. Compared with the Western parts of Germany, where immigrants constitute on average 10.4 percent of the population, their percentage in the Eastern states is only between 1.3 and 2.1 percent.[4] Moreover, many of them are asylum seekers who often go west as soon as their status permits them to do so. Consequently, there is no "visible" Muslim community or Muslim infrastructure in the new *Bundesländer*, including the Eastern part of Berlin.

ECONOMIC AND SOCIAL PROFILE

Even today, problems encountered by Muslim immigrants to fully integrate into German society are attributed to the incompatibility of Muslims with Germany's Christian culture.[5] If integration is understood to mean internalizing the values of society, access to the values of the institutionalized organizing social system is crucial to this process. In this sense, access of foreign children and young people to the German educational and vocational training system plays a decisive role in determining the future of the Muslim community, in terms of their professional prospects and chances of becoming socially integrated. Thus, the ability to obtain an education or vocational training within the existing systems positively affects the process of social integration.

A weak trend of increasing participation of immigrants in high-level education can be observed from the middle of the 1980s to the 1990s. Yet, students of migrant origin are still overrepresented in extended elementary and special schools. The number of school dropouts is higher among immigrant youth. Despite a considerable increase in the number of university students of migrant origin, the prospects of finding jobs in the German employment market are less promising for them than for German graduates.

Regarding vocational education, the percentage of migrant trainees (apprentices) is still much lower than Germans of similar age. More than half of young immigrant women and nearly half of young men between the ages of twenty and thirty have no professional diplomas. Immigrant trainees are concentrated in a small number of professions. In 1996, 23.9 percent of young women preferred to train as hairdressers and 13.2 percent as medical doctors' or dentists' receptionists, whereas 13.3 percent of young men were training as mechanics and 11.3 percent as electricians.[6] Young people of foreign origin participate less in the educational system than do young Germans. Young Turks form an especially problematic group. Some of them are jobless. Others, mostly young women, have withdrawn from the labor market, and a large group of mostly young men work only sporadically.

Since the beginning of labor migration in the 1960s, the segmentation of the labor market in Germany has stabilized. This means that the Muslim immigrant workers have been employed in the mining and manufacturing industries, both of which are today in difficult economic conditions. Thus, like in the mid-1980s, a high percentage of immigrants are threatened by job losses. In the last fifteen years, unemployment has risen disproportionately among immigrants. While jobs have been lost mainly in the manufacturing and mining industries, where Muslim migrant workers are traditionally employed, new jobs have been created in the service sector. Germans have found jobs in the newly created service sectors, but immigrants have been less successful and have been employed only in low-paying jobs such as cleaning and cooking.

Immigrants are employed mostly as unskilled or semiskilled workers. The conditions of recruitment in the 1960s, poor language skills, and the original aim to return home were reasons for their low level of professional qualification. However, because of structural changes, an increasing shift in demand, that is, from low-qualified to higher-qualified staff, is taking place in the labor market. Thus, if Muslims hope to become upwardly mobile, they must improve their professional qualifications. But the German educational system does not provide them with many opportunities to acquire the needed skills. Certain religious and cultural factors also affect the Muslims' choice of occupation and their situation in the labor market. Wearing a headscarf while looking for a job reduces female Muslims' chances of finding employment.

In the last ten years, there has been a visible increase in the number of self-employed immigrants, including a considerable number of Muslim immigrants, particularly Turks, Moroccans, Tunisians, Lebanese, and, to a lesser degree, Bosnians and Albanians. Since the late 1980s, a growing number of Muslim business organizations have been formed—

Table 2.3
Contribution of the Turkish Population Living in the EU to the GDP, 1998

	Total GDP		Contribution of Turks	
	Euro (in billions)	DM (in billions)	Euro (in billions)	DM (in billions)
EU countries (total)	7,472.5	14,614.9	55.1	107.8
Belgium	223.6	437.3	1.4	2.7
Denmark	150.9	295.1	0.8	1.5
Germany	1,910.3	3,736.2	40.2	78.6
France	1,274.5	2,492.7	4.0	7.8
Netherlands	336.7	658.5	4.3	8.5
Austria	189.8	371.2	3.1	6.1
Sweden	202.6	362.3	0.4	0.8
United Kingdom	1,220.4	2,386.9	0.9	1.8

Source: Centre for Studies on Turkey (Essen, Germany).

the most important of which is the Association of Independent Industrialists and Entrepreneurs. In the framework of this organization, Muslim businessmen have formed an interest group; they exchange information and are active in cultural matters and issues connected with immigration.

According to recent statistics, there were 124,000 independent professionals with a foreign passport (including EU) in 1988 and 279,000 in 1998.[7] Over the same period, the number of Turkish independent professionals rose from 28,000 to 51,000, forming the biggest group of foreign businessmen. As of 2000, there were an estimated 55,200 Turkish businesses in Germany. Moreover, Turkish businesses, which were initially based on restaurants and grocery stores, have undergone a process of diversification. By 1999, 20 percent of Turkish independent professionals had established themselves in the areas of production, construction, handicraft, and wholesale trade. They have also been employing venture capital as part of a general trend of adaptation to the new economy.

About one third of Turks residing in Germany are economically active; that is, they are either registered employees or are self-employed. The remaining two thirds are dependent family members. Currently, the contribution of Turks to the gross domestic product (GDP) in Germany corresponds to more than 2 percent of the total GDP (see Table 2.3). Germany's Turkish population contributed DM 77.1 billion in 1997 and DM 78.6 billion in 1998 to the GDP. Despite the slight increase in 1998,

however, Turks' contribution to the country's GDP remains slightly below the ratio of their population within the total population (2.6 percent).

Two factors account for the significant increase in the number of independent professions among Germany's Turkish immigrants: (1) improvement in the level of education, with an increase in the number of
university students by over 120 percent between 1988 and 1998; and (2)
deterioration of the job market, which pushes immigrants to take the risk
of founding a business. Germany has the highest rate of independent
Turkish professionals among EU countries, amounting to 6.6 percent of
the total employed population.

Germany's other ethnic groups follow similar trends. In 1987, 73.7 percent of all foreigners were workers. In 1998, this number was reduced
to just over 60 percent. The number of professionals and self-employed
individuals is higher among young generations, which have had a
German education. The professional profile of immigrants is becoming
more like that of nationals, although most immigrants are still employed
in unskilled, low-paying jobs.

Because economic considerations play such a key role in determining
Western politics and thinking, the increasing importance and visibility
of Turkish business in Germany may have a positive effect on German
perceptions of these immigrants and change popular views regarding
their involvement in the country's political process. Because Turks are
strongly identified with Islam, their educational and economic progress
may also positively affect the public's view of Islam.

ORGANIZATIONAL DEVELOPMENT OF ISLAM AND ITS CAUSES

When the first-wave immigrant workers arrived in Germany, there
were almost no mosques in the country because no provisions were
made in the recruitment agreements for the immigrants' religious needs.[8]
Turkish Muslims first requested the establishment of places for daily
prayer in the hostels where they lived and in factory buildings. The first
imams were primarily workers who had no special religious training.
The character of this early Islam was that of popular Islam, based on the
migrant workers' daily experiences and habits, and did not contain any
orthodox theological principles. Within the immigrant community,
strictly religious persons were the exception. During this phase of Turkish immigration, especially before family reunifications, the majority of
workers were organized within political rather than religious associations. The move from workers' hostels to houses after 1974, necessitated
by family reunifications, increased interest in religion and demand for
places of worship. The first mosques were set up in former factory and
office buildings and backyards. Then, many imams from Turkey came

to Germany to administer the mosques and attend to the believers' needs. The growing significance of Islam within the immigrant community resulted from its new demographic makeup, as the presence of women and children strengthened social control among Turkish Muslims. The move from hostels to homogeneous communities, although providing a secure haven from uncertainties, led to isolation from the German society, drawing the immigrants closer to Islam as a means to maintain their cultural identity and values. This tendency was stronger among the elderly.

Economic recession in Germany and the ensuing unemployment also encouraged the creation of Islamic organizations, with their own informal system of social protection. Thus, although the predominant desire of Muslim immigrants is to practice their religion and transmit it to the next generation, new functions of Islam are changing the face of Islam in Germany.

In the last few years, racially motivated attacks against Turks, such as arson attacks in Möllen (1992) and Solingen (1993) on their houses, have spurred religious activism among the Muslim community. Islamic organizations have protested against violence toward foreigners and have acted as advocates for their community. The lack of legal and social recognition of immigrant groups including the second generation, their labeling—at least socially—as "foreigners" and the ensuing problems in terms of employment and participation in public life, plus the fact that they are legally barred from political participation, strengthen their tendency to form Islamic associations. Even the change in the law on citizenship has not altered the basic thinking of the majority of the Germans regarding what it means to be "German" or who can be called so. Rather, public opinion spoke against further liberalization of citizenship laws or the redefinition of "Germanness." Consequently, Germany's policy on foreigners has not yet evolved into an immigrant policy and thus does not include provisions against racism or for ensuring equal opportunities for immigrants. It demands that immigrants completely adapt to the German societal system as a prerequisite for enjoying equal treatment.

Because of the limited possibilities for immigrants to become politically active and to participate in the decision-making processes, the lack of a policy on immigrants' integration, and the immigrants' inadequate mastery of the German language, Muslims are little involved in German politics. These factors strengthen the tendency to create ethnic and religious organizations. Within the Turkish community, a highly diverse Turkish-speaking infrastructure, including newspapers, TV channels, and businesses, exists. This situation has two consequences: (1) It makes opting out of a German-speaking society permissible and (2) it makes Germany's Turks better informed about issues in their home country than about German politics. In short, although the majority of Germany's

Turks no longer believe in the "myth of return," political activity takes place primarily within Turkish associations. Nevertheless, these associations try to raise the community's political awareness and fight for the right to acquire dual citizenship, vote in communal elections, and gain the authorities' recognition of Muslim organizations as equal to their German counterparts.

TYPES AND CHARACTERISTICS OF MUSLIM ORGANIZATIONS

Most Muslim organizations in Germany are still based on the mosque associations. According to the estimates of the Central Institute-Islam Archive Germany, there are presently about 2,200 mosque associations in Germany, most of which follow the Turkish interpretation of Sunni Islam.[9] Most of the mosques are not recognizable from the outside and have names such as Center for Islamic Culture or Islamic Cultural Association. Throughout Germany, there are only sixty-six purpose-built mosques, and as of 2000, another twenty-six were under construction. Mosques provide a wide variety of activities and services to their members, such as Qur'an courses, German language classes, sports, and rooms for religious and other feasts, and many have book, video, or grocery stores.[10]

Most of the mosques are Sunni, but there is a major Shi'a mosque in Hamburg. The origins of this mosque go to the foundation of an Iranian community center in 1953. The mosque was finally finished in the 1990s. It is a purpose-built mosque in the Persian style. There are a few smaller Shi'a mosques in other cities, notably Berlin. The Ahmadiyya community has a few purpose-built mosques.

Education is a primary focus of Islamic organizations. Therefore, they try to establish proper educational institutions, including research centers, facilities to train preachers and imams, plus after-school support structures such as help with homework, language training, and computer courses. Many of the larger Muslim educational institutions are trying to obtain the status of recognized private schools. Muslim organizations help protect and solidify the community, maintain and transmit indigenous culture, strengthen the members' sense of identity, represent their political interests, and act as a bridge between the community and the host country.[11]

Turkish Muslims are the best-organized segment of Germany's ethnic and religious minorities. According to a study by the Centre for Studies on Turkey, focusing on the North Rhine–Westphalia region, there are 1,228 immigrants' associations with an average membership of 139.[12] Assuming that a third of the Turkish immigrants live in this *Bundesland*, one can estimate that there are a total of about 3,700 such associations throughout Germany, with over 500,000 members, of which 40 percent have a religious orientation.

Other ethnic groups have their own mosques. In Berlin, in addition to fifty-eight mosques run by Turks, two are run by Kurds, six by Arabs, two by Ahmadiyya Pakistanis, one by Bosnians, one by Albanians, and three by Germans. There is no African mosque, despite the considerable number of Somalis, Nigerians, and Senegalese immigrants. Only four of these fifty-eight mosques are purpose-built.[13] The major non-Turkish Muslim organization is the World Islamic Council based in Frankfurt, which is supported by Saudi Arabia. It accepts only Sunni associations and claims to have 700 members. In the 1990s, the King Fahd Academy was established in Bonn and serves as both an educational and a cultural center. A principal characteristic of Iranian and Arab institutions is that they are more concerned with religious and cultural matters than with broader questions of immigration and related problems. The other non-Turkish organization is the Ahmadiyya-Muslim Jama'at in Frankfurt. The Bosnians and Moroccans are weakly organized, although there is an Islamic Community of Bosnians.

PRINCIPAL TURKISH ORGANIZATIONS

Turkish Islamic organizations are incorporated within ten big umbrella associations. The largest organization, which is affiliated with the Turkish government, is the Turkish Islamic Union of the Turkish Institute for Religious Affairs (DİTİB). DİTİB comprises 740 mosque associations, which are served by their clergymen from Turkey. They are replaced every five years. The second organization is the National View with 274 mosque associations. Other organizations include the Suleymanci (Süleymanli) with 290 branches; militant Islamist groups that follow Cemaletin Kaplan, with about 50 associations; the Turkish Islamic Union in Europe with 125 associations; the nationalistic Turkish Idealists' Association (Türk Federasyonu; also known as Gray Wolves), with 180 associations; and the intellectual religious orders of the Nurculuk movement, which has 30 educational centers. Recently, the European Federation for World Order was established, with twenty associations.

Nurculuk is an internationally widespread and intellectually oriented mystical movement with roots in the Naqshbendi Sufi order. The movement sees itself as a religious reform movement trying to combine modernism with Islam. Its followers number around 5,000 to 6,000 and are organized within different mosque associations.[14] The movement does not set up mosque associations but establishes educational centers, especially for the youth. There is also a community of followers of Fethullah Gülen, a Turkish religious scholar. The community of Fethullah Gülen has about seventy local associations that organize training and recreational activities. The movement has its own TV channel in Turkey, and its broadcasts can be received via satellite in Europe and Central Asia. Various newspapers and journals published in Turkey, Germany, and elsewhere propagate the movement's philosophy. However, the movement denies having any political agenda.

Another large group of Muslims in Germany are the Alawis (Alevites). There are two umbrella associations of the Alawi communities, namely the Federation of Alawi Communities with ninety-five associations and the Republican Foundation for Education and Culture with 20 associations.[15] There are no Alawi mosques since their religious practice does not require them. Instead they have *Jam Khaneh* (place of Alawi worship). The Alawis claim that they constitute one quarter of all Turkish immigrants. However, a large portion of the Alawis are Kurds.

The foregoing has illustrated the highly diverse character of Turkish Islam in Germany, which ranges from strongly secular to nationalistic and Islamist. Some associations are oriented toward Turkey, while others see their role as supporting the believers in the German society. Despite frequent rejections, these groups are open to the German society. Most mosques still receive their imams from Turkey, but the number of those trained in Germany is increasing. There are also marginal groups, which could not have operated in Turkey, but are active in Germany. Such groups present to the German public a face of Islam that is conservative and closed and denotes a degree of conspiratorial sectarianism. Furthermore, since the 1980s, there has been growing competition among various Turkish Islamic organizations for the loyalty of Turkish Muslims. Certain groups have become less tolerant of orientations that differ from their own. This attitude, however, applies only to Turks.

Associations formed by other Muslim immigrants of a more recent history of arrival are more oriented toward their countries of origin. There is not much interethnic contact among Muslims at the level of mosque-based organizations. But informal interaction along generational lines or the immigrants' personal interests is not infrequent.[16] Many associations are formed along these lines, but there are no reliable statistics concerning their national composition, religious affiliation, or degree of political involvement.[17] Assimilationist tendencies coexist with communalist impulses, and it is difficult to measure their relative strength.

TRANSETHNIC ORGANIZATIONS

Until recently, there was no umbrella organization incorporating all Islamic organizations or even all Turkish Islamic associations. In the last few years, a trend can be observed toward the establishment of a central authority that could represent the interests of all Muslims. This trend has resulted in the creation of two important councils: the Islam Council

(*Islamrat für die Bundesrepublik Deutschland*), established in November 1986, and the Central Council of Muslims (*Zentralrat der Muslime in Deutschland*), founded in December 1994. These organizations represent different ethnic groups and religious tendencies, which cooperate with each other. Both organizations claim to speak for Germany's Muslims, including those who are not organized within the member associations of each council.[18]

The Central Council of Muslims has been successful in gaining some official recognition in the last few years through its effective public relations strategy, although this strategy does not necessarily reflect the traditional, and partly conservative, character of its member organizations. The council sees itself as an integral part of the pluralistic German society, as a partner in its social life and a participant in the religious, cultural, and political discussions, and as an authority on questions concerning Germany's Muslims. The Central Council of Muslims is also engaged in broader activities concerning women, environmental preservation, protection of animals, plus setting up of Islamic kindergartens and religious classes in schools.

The Islam Council focuses more on the care and protection of Islamic beliefs and culture and on answering questions related to religious matters. Its administrative structure is run by clerics, and the council's chairman has the title of Shaikh ul-Islam.

Despite their differences and rivalries, Islamic organizations in Germany agree on a number of demands directed at German authorities, mainly the recognition of Islam as a legal public body; special permission to slaughter according to Islamic rule, similar to the Jewish community; support from local authorities to construct purpose-built mosques; and the introduction of regular Islamic religious courses in schools.

GERMAN CITIZENSHIP AND THE MUSLIM COMMUNITY

Citizenship in Germany has traditionally been based on the principle of *jus sanguinis* (blood relationship) and not *jus solis* (place of birth). The new law on citizenship, which came into force in January 2000, has introduced the territorial principle into the German conception of citizenship. Therefore, children of foreigners born in Germany automatically obtain German citizenship, provided one parent has resided in Germany for at least eight years. Obtaining citizenship for adults has been facilitated, but dual nationality was ruled out after a long and animated debate.

Those Muslims who came to Germany as workers can obtain German citizenship after eight years of residence, provided that they do not receive unemployment benefits or other social aid. Muslim refugees and asylum seekers are denied this right because, according to the Geneva Convention for Refugees and Articles 1 and 2 of the German Constitution, the state is only obliged to protect their life and human dignity. Therefore, refugees from Bosnia-Herzegovina obtain only a temporary right to stay, and refugees from countries like Afghanistan or Algeria, where control over the country is disputed, have merely the right to stay for legal or humanitarian reasons. This means that this category of immigrants—irrespective of how long they have lived in Germany—will be deported to their country of origin if the federal government feels there is sufficient reason to deny an extension of their permits. About 50 percent of asylum seekers in Germany fall into this category.

Regulations for acquiring citizenship and the still-restrictive policy toward immigrants are not specifically directed at Muslims. Nevertheless, Muslims are most adversely affected by these laws because these laws are valid only for immigrants from Muslim countries and have no effect on immigrant workers from the EU countries, who benefit from the rights accorded to EU citizens. They can vote in local elections and enjoy freedom of movement within the EU. This situation adversely affects many aspects of the daily life of Muslims. For example, when there is a class trip to Britain, unlike German pupils and children of EU-origin immigrants, Muslim pupils must obtain a visa.

CHALLENGES POSED BY THE MUSLIM PRESENCE

A relatively large Muslim community has existed in Germany for four decades. Yet, Islam's presence still poses a number of challenges for German society and polity. Islam is the third largest religion in Germany after Catholicism and Protestantism. Yet, unlike them, it is not officially recognized as a legal public body. This is due to the fact that there is no official church in Islam that could be recognized as representing the interests of Muslims. This situation creates many administrative restrictions, which limit the Islamic community's scope of action. Consequently, very often Christian churches are asked by German authorities to deliver statements on questions related to Islam, Muslims, and Islamic traditions because they have difficulty in finding a legitimate representative who can speak for all Muslims. Thus, the official reason for the refusal to grant a recognized status to Islam is based on the argument that there is no single official Muslim institution that can represent all Muslims. While understandable, this does not explain many discriminatory policies. For instance, the requirement for Muslims to eat only *halal* meat contradicts German laws regarding the protection of animals, and thus slaughtering according to Muslim rituals is not permitted. Yet, the Jewish community has been granted special treatment on this matter. The forms of burial in German cemeteries do not comply with Islam's religious requirements. Therefore, because of conflicts over land rights, differences have emerged between local authorities and Muslims.

Some religious communities do not approve of building mosques with a minaret, especially if the minaret is taller than church towers. The call to prayer by the *muezzin* is also objected to by many residents, and there have been local initiatives against the construction of mosques. Islamic requirement to pray five times a day at fixed times also often causes friction at the workplace. Despite the large number of Muslim students, there is no efficient system of religious instruction for them, and private Qur'an courses are often the only alternative. Currently, several regions are considering requests for Islamic religious courses in schools, but this issue has not yet been resolved. The participation of female students in sports events and class outings is another source of tension between parents and teachers: The parents are concerned that mixed-gender events violate Islam's moral code. Nor have any standard regulations to allow Muslim students to abstain from attending classes during Islamic holidays been developed. The wearing of headscarves by Muslim women also produces tension because it is viewed as a barrier to women's emancipation. In 1999, a German court prevented a Muslim woman from being accepted into a teachers' faculty because she insisted on wearing a scarf. The argument was that schools should be neutral on matters of faith.

ISLAMIST ORGANIZATIONS: IMPACT ON PUBLIC PERCEPTIONS OF ISLAM

The most radical Islamist organization is the Federation of Islamic Communes and Communities (ICCB), known as the Followers of Cemalatin Kaplan—and, now that he is dead, his son, Metin. This group is believed to strive for an Islamic revolution in Turkey along the Iranian model. With the exception of the ICCB, all other Islamist organizations express their readiness for dialogue with German authorities, although their sincerity is doubtful.

The other important Islamist organization in Germany is the Islamic Community National View (*Islamische Gemeinschaft Milli Görüs*—IGMG), which was set up in 1972 under a different name. The IGMG qualifies as the largest independent Islamic community in Germany and in Western Europe and has close relations with the now-banned Virtue party (formerly the Welfare party). The German *Verfassungsschutz* accuses the IGMG of wanting to replace the secular state order in Turkey by an Islamic state based exclusively on the Qur'an and the *shar'ia* and eventually worldwide Islamization.

There are different ideological orientations among Islamist organizations. Some have no recognizable connections with a specific political party and make no open political statements, although they prefer an Islamic legal system and reject Western integration concepts. They can be defined as neo-traditionalists. Others demand the conversion of the state through political and social mechanisms into an Islamic state. This group can be divided into two categories: the pragmatists and the fundamentalists. The pragmatists are willing to compromise with the ruling system and participate in it in order to alter it from within; the fundamentalists reject any form of cooperation and support the idea of revolution. Since the fundamentalists advocate the use of violence, they can be referred to as militant Islamists. The annual reports of the *Verfassungsschutz* refer to both ICCB and IGMG as Turkish Islamists and indicate that they can potentially present a danger to the free democratic order in Germany.

CONCLUSIONS AND OUTLOOK: CAN ISLAM BE INCORPORATED INTO THE GERMAN DEMOCRACY?

After four decades of Muslim presence in their country, the majority of Germans have not yet become reconciled to Islam's presence and view it as a hindrance to the immigrants' full integration into society. This attitude of rejection by the majority causes Muslims to find solace in their traditional cultural values, especially their religion. Thus, in reaction to a world perceived as discriminatory and that demands their unconditional adaptation to the lifestyle of the majority, Islam becomes a meaningful focus of identity for Muslims. One of the latest examples of such demands is the statement of the Christian Democratic mayor of Berlin, who has been quoted as saying that Muslim families living in Germany must recognize the cultural values of Christianity and humanism. "This is not a rejection of Islamic faith," he said, but rather "a limitation of the Islamic state."[19]

There was also a discussion initiated by the Christian Democratic Union (CDU) on the issue of the leading culture (*Leitkultur*) of Germany. Even though the CDU could not define what the term "leading culture" exactly meant, it was made clear that certain circles within and outside the CDU would rather wish to see only immigrants accepting the German *Leitkultur* to remain in the country. Thus, most immigrants feel that they were expected to accept the hegemony of the German culture and were tolerated according to the degree of their acceptance and obedience. The discussion on *Leitkultur* made immigrants feel insecure in Germany, and it attempted to differentiate between those foreigners who were adapting to German culture and those who refused assimilation, between those foreigners who were deemed beneficial to Germany and those who were seen only benefiting from Germany. The public debate on the *Leitkultur* has now subsided, although it can reemerge. Indeed, the leader of CDU, Angela Merkel, seems to favor a culturally assimilationist policy.[20] In short, this debate has caused resentments among Muslim immigrants.

Such resentments are exploited by various Islamic and Islamist organizations to recruit followers. Nevertheless, it must be emphasized that there is no such phenomenon as a "typical Muslim." On the contrary, in the context of integration with Western societies and cultures, new forms of Islam are emerging. Although Muslims receive ideas and encouragement from some Islamists in their countries of origin, for pragmatic considerations, they reinterpret them in the context of Western and largely secular industrial societies.

Thus, an analysis of Muslim communities' religious orientations reveals the following groups:

- Those who already had a distant relationship with Islam prior to their immigration to Germany.
- Those who practiced their belief before immigrating but became increasingly secular and their religious convictions weakened.
- Those who practice their belief without attracting too much attention.
- Those who turn strongly to Islam after immigration.
- Those who actively organize themselves within Islamically oriented associations.

German society still harbors prejudices against Islam. The way the German media report on Islamist tendencies and conflicts in Islamic countries helps strengthen existing anti-Muslim prejudices and Germans' image of Islam as backward, extremist, and hence threatening. The popularization of this image makes it difficult for the majority of Germans to perceive the more complex and diverse nature of Islam, including its moderate and modernist aspects.

Germany's administrative and political system, too, still follows exclusivist rather than inclusive policies. This basic attitude has not changed much after the formation of a coalition government by the Social Democrat and Green parties in the fall of 1998. Therefore, reducing the number of immigrants, who are deemed to impose financial costs on the society, by means of expatriation and deportation remains an important part of the policy on foreigners. The principal goal of this policy is to meet the needs of the indigenous population rather than to integrate the immigrant population within the society and offer them equal rights. Only recently has the German government begun to encourage naturalization of immigrants. Yet, the naturalization figures in Germany are still among the lowest in Western Europe, partly because fewer immigrants have availed themselves of the new possibilities. These policies, based on the idea that "Germany is not an immigration country," have meant that the only option for immigrants is to become assimilated by fully adopting German culture. Federal president Johannes Rau's "Berlin Speech" at the House of World Cultures on 12 May 2000 has altered this concept, but there is still no policy providing equal opportunities to all residents of Germany. Rather, the easing of the naturalization process has resulted from long and sustained pressure by immigrants and the emerging awareness among Germans that their country needs immigrants to sustain its economic growth. Not all Germans and their political leaders, however, agree with this approach.

In sum, although since the 1950s, Germany has become a multiethnic society, it has yet to become multicultural. Some political parties such as the Christian Democrats reject the very concept of multiculturalism. The present German immigration policy is based on the principle of equal obligations, demanding from immigrants full observance of German laws. Thus, although immigrants are required to pay taxes and obey the laws and are affected by governmental decisions and policies, they have little or no say in the decision-making process, being unable to vote or to stand in local elections. Yet, if a substantial number of people who are permanent residents cannot vote, the legitimacy of the entire political system and its decision-making process becomes impaired. Also, it is unfair to ask refugees who may be deported at the government's will and who have no prospects of gaining citizenship or permanent residency to make economic and emotional investment in a country that hosts them temporarily. A better policy would be to integrate immigrants into society through allowing them to participate in the political process. Such a policy would encourage immigrants, who are more involved in the politics of their country of origin, to become active participants in the affairs of their adopted country.

Yet, the future need not be bleak: Economic factors, including the advances made by immigrant communities, may change German attitudes and policies. Even these advances, however, are unlikely to result in the full integration of the immigrant communities into the society in the foreseeable future. The lack of acceptance of multiple loyalties at the political and societal levels is a major problem. The process of changing attitudes and creating a truly pluralist and democratic setting in Germany will not be easy. For this to happen, the country must come to terms with its own image and identity and accept the trend toward greater mobility of people within a globalized world.

From the immigrants' perspective, multiple loyalties need not be torn loyalties. Rather, they can complement each other, allowing for various levels of assimilation within often divergent political, religious, and cultural groupings. If and when acceptance of diversity and legitimacy of multiple loyalties becomes widespread, it will also extend to Islam and Muslims.

NOTES

1. Hartmut Heller, "Muslime in deutscher Erde: Frühe Grabstätten des 14. bis 18. Jahrhunderts," in *In fremder Erde. Zur Geschichte und Gegenwart der islamischen Bestattung in Deutschland* [On foreign soil. On history and present of the Islamic burial rituals in Germany] ed. Gerhard Höpp and Gerdien Jonker (Berlin: Zentrum Moderner Orient/Geisteswissenschaftliches Zentrum Berlin e.V., Arbeitshefte No. 11, 1996), 45–62.

2. Information provided by the United Nations High Commission for Refugees on the phone.

3. *Türken als unternehmer* [Turks as undertakers] (Opladen: Centre for Studies on Turkey, 1996), 75.

4. *Bericht über die Lage der Ausländer in der Bundesrepublik Deutschland* [Report on the situation of foreigners in the Federal Republic of Germany] (Berlin: Commissary of Federal Government for Issues of Foreigners, 2000), 240.

5. See P. Antes, "Dialog mit dem Islam" [Dialogue with Islam], in *Strukturen des Dialogs mit Muslimen in Europa* [Structures of dialogue with Muslims in Europe], vol. 6, ed. Peter Graf and Peter Antes (Frankfurt/Main: Europäische Bildung Region-Sprache-Identität, 1998).

6. *Statistisches Bundesamt, Berufsbildungsbericht* [Report on vocational education] (Bonn: Bundesministerium für Bildung und Forschung, 1998).

7. *Ausgewählte Statistiken zur türkischen und ausländischen Bevölkerung in der Bundesrepublik Deutschland* [Selective statistics on Turkish and foreign population in the Federal Republic of Germany] (Essen: Centre for Studies on Turkey, 2000).

8. See Andreas Kapphan, "Zuwanderung von Muslimen und ethnische Gemeindestrukturen," in *Moscheen und islamisches Leben in Berlin* [Mosques and Islamic life in Berlin] ed. Gerdien Jonker and Andreas Kapphan (Berlin: Ausländer beauf tragle des Senats von Berlin, 1999), 9–16.

9. *Neue Daten und Fakten über die islamischen Verbände in der Bundesrepublik Deutschland (Stand: 1. März 2000)* [New data and facts on Islamic associations in the Federal Republic of Germany] in Zentralinstitut Islam-Archiv-Deutschland: Moslemische Revue No. 2/2000, 112–121.

10. *Türkische Muslime in Nordrhein-Westfalen* [Turkish Muslims in Nordrhein–Westfalen] (Duisburg: Centre for Studies on Turkey, 1997), 104–115; also, Irina Leffers and Christholde Thielcke, "Zwischen Religion und Jugendarbeit" [Between religion and youth employment], in Jonker and Kapphan, *Moscheen und islamisches Leben in Berlin*, 30–34.

11. Centre for Studies on Turkey, "Bestandsaufnahme der Potentiale und Strukturen von Selbstorganisationen von Migrantinnen und Migranten türkischer, kurdischer, bosnischer und maghrebinischer Herkunft in Nordrhein-Westphalen," in *Selbstorganisationen von Migrantinnen und Migranten in NRW. Wissenschaftliche Bestandsaufnahme* [Self-organizations for female and male migrants in NRW. Scientific analysis] (Dusseldorf: Ministry for Work, Social Affairs

and Urban Development, Culture and Sports of North Rhine–Westphalia, 1999), 84–85.

12. Ibid., 106–107.

13. See Jonker and Kapphan, *Moscheen und islamisches Leben in Berlin*, 73–74.

14. *Türkische Muslime in Nordrhein-Westfalen*, 148.

15. The numbers presented here rely on information provided by each organization.

16. See Ulrich Best, "Moscheen und ihre Kontakte nach außen," in Jonker and Kapphan, *Moscheen und islamisches Leben in Berlin*, 46–51.

17. See Centre for Studies on Turkey.

18. See *Türkische Muslime in Nordhein-Westphalen*; also, the Friedrich Ebert Foundation report, *Islamische Organisationen in Deutschland* [Islamic organizations in Germany] (Bonn: 2000).

19. Roger Cohen, "Germany's Conservatives Rediscover the 'Fatherland,' " *International Herald Tribune*, 5 December 2000.

20. See "Angela Merkel: Germany's Gritty Conservative," *The Economist* (30 November 2001).

3

Islam in the United Kingdom

John Rex

INTRODUCTION

The United Kingdom has one of the largest Muslim communities in Europe. The first large-scale Muslim immigration to the UK began in the late 1950s, mostly from the Indian subcontinent and Cyprus, following political disturbances on the island in 1957. This movement was made easy, because until 1962, entry into Britain by citizens of British colonies and member countries of the Commonwealth was unrestricted. The increased influx of immigrants in the 1950s led to the passing in 1962 of the Commonwealth Immigration Control Act. Initially, this legislation prompted a rapid increase in Asian immigration, as large numbers tried to enter Britain before the ban came into effect. These immigrants built upon community foundations that had been created by earlier immigrants largely from the Punjab and from Sylhet in East Pakistan. Migration from Mirpur accelerated in the early 1960s after the construction of the Mangla dam, which flooded 250 villages. After the Commonwealth Immigration Control Act came into effect, nearly all new immigrants to Britain came as part of family reunification schemes. Immigrants from East Pakistan (later Bangladesh) arrived later than those from West Pakistan and Mirpur.

During this period, the number of Muslim immigrants from black Africa was insignificant. In the early 1960s, the Africanization policies of countries such as Kenya and Uganda led to an influx of East African Asians. The British government offered citizenship to certain nationals of its former African colonies. In 1968, the Labor government limited this practice and refused immediate right of residence to British passport holders. This policy was revised when General Idi Amin of Uganda began his persecution of Asians, forcing the British government to admit in large numbers African Asians. These immigrants were not all Muslims. Many were Ramgaria Sikhs or Catholic Goans. But among them were some Muslims, especially Ismailis—Sevener Shi'as, whose leader is the Aga Khan.

During this period, smaller numbers of immigrants from Malaysia, Morocco, and Yemen also came to the UK. The late 1970s and early 1980s saw an influx of Iranians because of the Islamic revolution. Many members of political dissident groups from Arab countries or members of communities who were under pressure by their own governments, such as Shi'as from Iraq, also came to Britain during the 1980s. These successive waves of Muslim immigration, caused by different factors, created a highly diverse British Muslim community, comprising many ethnic and sectarian groups. Its members also differ in terms of their level of education, their social and economic conditions, their degree of integration into British society, including political life, their continued links to their home countries, and their involvement in Muslim activism.[1]

THE NUMBER OF AND ETHNIC PROFILE OF BRITISH MUSLIMS

The first difficulty in assessing the number of Muslims in the UK is underlined by the fact that the British census of 1991 included no question about religious affiliation, although the respondents were asked to indicate the ethnic group to which they believed to belong.[2] This situation has led some scholars, notably Muhammad Anwar, to suggest that in trying to assess the number of British Muslims, there is no alternative but to use available information about the country of birth plus the answers provided to the 1991 census questions regarding the respondents' ethnic origin.[3]

Using first the country of birth information, Anwar has calculated that, in 1991, there were 476,000 people from Pakistan and 160,000 from Bangladesh in Britain (Table 3.1), while a total of 204,247 viewed as Muslims were born in other countries such as Turkey, Malaysia, Egypt, Libya, Morocco, Tunisia, Algeria, and the Middle East excluding Israel (Table 3.2).

On the basis of this calculation, it could be said that in 1991, there were 840,000 Muslims in Britain. But because this method does not account for children, Anwar uses the answers to the 1991 census question regarding ethnic origin. This source shows that apart from the 636,000 born in Pakistan and Bangladesh, there were an estimated 263,397 people

Table 3.1
Population of Pakistani and Bangladeshi Origin in Great Britain, 1991 (in thousands)

Country of origin	England	Wales	Scotland	Total
Pakistan	449	6	21	476
Bangladesh	156	3	1	160
Total	605	9	22	636
Total British population	47,026	2,835	4,999	54,860

Source: Office for Population, Censuses and Surveys, 1991 Census of Population: Ethnic Groups and Countries of Birth, Topic Report (London: HMSO, 1993).

born in Britain to Pakistani and Bangladeshi parents. There are also some long-established groups of Muslims like the Yemenis, many of whose members were born in Britain. Anwar also estimates that the number of Muslims among those choosing Indian as their ethnic affiliation is 134,000. Of the Cypriot immigrants, 45,000 see themselves as Turkish Cypriots. On the basis of this calculation, he estimates the number of those identifying themselves as Muslims to be 1,406,000 (Table 3.3).

According to the Fourth National Survey of Ethnic Minorities, carried out for the Policy Studies Institute in London by Tariq Modood and his colleagues, 6 percent of Indians, 15 percent of African Asians, 96 percent of Pakistanis, and 95 percent of Bangladeshis indicated that they were Muslims.[4] When asked, "How important is religion in the way you live your life?" 74 percent of these Muslims answered that it was very important. These Muslims also attended places of worship more frequently than other ethnic groups; 62 percent attended mosque at least once a week. What this study does not distinguish, however, are differences between Pakistani, Bangladeshi, Indian, African, and Asian Muslims, on the one hand, and other groups such as Turks, Turkish Cypriots, and Yemeni Muslims, on the other. Quite possibly, some of the latter groups may regard religion as less important in their daily life and attend mosque less frequently. Most Muslims of Iranian origin are also likely to fall into this category.

Considering all the available data, the total number of British Muslims can be estimated at 1.5 to 2 million—that is, 2.7 to 3.6 percent of a total British population of 54.86 million. But because of the intensity of their religious beliefs and practices, their social and cultural impact is greater than what their numbers may suggest.

According to sources close to the Muslim community, there are approximately 10,000 converts to Islam in Britain. Less than half of these converts are white British, and there is only a small community of white

Table 3.2
Population of Great Britain: Country of Birth, 1991 (selected countries)

Born in	Numbers
Cyprus	84,000
Turkey	26,597
Malaysia	43,511
Egypt	22,849
Libya	6,604
Morocco	9,073
Tunisia	2,417
Algeria	3,672
Middle East (excluding Israel)	89,524
Total excluding Cypriots	**204,247**

Source: Office of Population, Censuses and Surveys, *1991 Census of Population: Ethnic Groups and Countries of Birth*, Topic Report (London: HMSO, 1993); adapted from Muhammad Anwar, *Race and Elections* (Coventry: University of Warwick, Centre for Research in Ethnic Relations, 1994).

Muslims in Norwich. The majority of converts are black Caribbean or black British. Some of these new Muslims have converted while in prison, and a few of the latter have formed British branches of the American "Nation of Islam" movement.

SOCIAL AND ECONOMIC PROFILE

The publication of the Office of National Statistics, entitled *Ethnic Minorities in the 1991 Census* (ONS-HMSO), which came out in 1997, does not provide adequate data on the British Muslims' economic and social conditions because this survey, too, did not include the question of religious affiliation. Therefore, the social and economic profile of British Muslims can be drawn only from data regarding the position of the Pakistanis and the Bangladeshis. Information about other Muslim communities such as Indians, Turks, Turkish Cypriots, and Malaysians is merely of anecdotal nature.

Employment and Unemployment

According to Modood et al., in terms of employment, the Pakistanis and especially the Bangladeshis continue to be severely disadvantaged.

Table 3.3
Estimated Muslim Population of Britain, 1991

Country/Region of origin	Numbers
Pakistan	476,000
Bangladesh	160,000
Indian	134,000
Other Asians	80,000
Other	29,000
Turkish Cypriots	45,000
Other Muslim countries	367,000
African Muslims (New Commonwealth)	115,000
Total	**1,406,000**

Source: Muhammad Anwar, *Race and Elections* (Coventry: University of Warwick, Centre for Research in Ethnic Relations, 1994). Other sources available at http://www.islamicweb.com/begin/population.htm put the number at 1,579,229 as of the year 2000.

Since 1982, the men in these groups have experienced some improvement in their employment levels, but this has been from a very low base. They continue to be disproportionately employed in manual work, with twice as many in manual as in nonmanual work, while white men are now evenly split between these two types of jobs. Pakistanis are twice as likely and Bangladeshis more than five times as likely as white men to be in semiskilled manual work. Self-employment reduces these ratios a little, but, even so, Pakistani and Bangladeshi men are less than two thirds as likely to be professionals, managers, and employers as compared with white men. Less than half of them are likely to supervise staff, and as employees they have only two thirds the pay packet of white men and as self-employed only three quarters of the incomes of whites.[5]

Other evidence provided by Modood and his colleagues indicates that Pakistani men have the same rate of self-employment as white men, while Bangladeshi men have only half that rate. Bangladeshis are strongly represented in "self-employment with employees"; that is, while not being employees themselves, they employ others. This is due mainly to the high proportion of self-employed restaurant owners. In 1994, unemployment among Bangladeshi and Pakistani men stood at about 40 percent—the highest rate among all ethnic groups and more than two and a half times higher than the rate for white men. Meanwhile, only a third as many Pakistani women and only a tenth as many Bangladeshi women were in paid work as compared with other women.

More than four of five Pakistani and Bangladeshi households (or four times as many as white nonpensioners) have an income equivalent to less than half the national average. At the time of the 1991 census, Pakistanis and Bangladeshis were worse off than any other ethnic group. Even disadvantaged groups, such as those of Caribbean and Indian origin, excluding African Asians, experienced less discrimination than Pakistanis or Bangladeshis, while Chinese people and African Asians had "reached a position of broad parity with whites."

Anecdotal evidence suggests that Turkish Cypriots are concentrated in the restaurant trade (as self-employed) and in textile industry (as employees). Turks, many of whom are, in fact, Kurds, are engaged mostly in low-grade occupations with low incomes similar to those of Pakistanis and Bangladeshis. Their inferior economic condition is aggravated by their often insecure immigration status. A large number of Muslims from Malaysia, Singapore, and other parts of Southeast Asia were students.

Educational Standards

According to Modood et al., 48 percent of Pakistanis and 60 percent of Bangladeshis had either no or only below O-level education. In other words, the percentage of illiterate or semiliterate among these groups was higher than among other ethnic groups. Moreover, the percentage of Pakistanis and Bangladeshis with A-level or other below-degree qualifications was the lowest among all ethnic minorities, with 20 and 10 percent, respectively. But the proportion of Pakistanis (11 percent) and Bangladeshis (10 percent) holding degree qualifications was higher than that achieved by the Caribbeans and was about equal with that of whites, although substantially lower than the percentages among Chinese, Indians, and East African Asians. Among women, the percentage with no or below O-level qualification was 60 percent for Pakistanis and 73 percent for Bangladeshis, the highest rate among ethnic minorities. The percentage of Pakistani and Bangladeshi women with A-level or other below-degree qualifications was 11 and 7 percent, respectively—by far the lowest rates among all groups (white and minorities). Only 7 percent of Pakistani and 3 percent of Bangladeshi women held a degree; the only other group with such a low percentage rate was the Caribbeans with 3 percent.

Based on these indicators, Muslims appear to be doing worse educationally than other groups. However, the lack of statistical data for Turkish Cypriots, Turks, Iranians, Arabs, and Southeast Asians—groups that certainly include Muslims—as well as for Indian Muslims makes a reliable assessment of the Muslims' educational conditions difficult. What is evident is the low educational standard of Pakistani and Bangladeshi

Muslims and the comparatively better educational qualifications of Muslims of East African Asian origin.

Geographical Distribution

Britain's Muslim community is unevenly distributed with large concentrations in a few large cities. According to Nielsen, nearly half of British Muslims live in and around London.[6] Nearly all Turkish Cypriots and half of Bangladeshis live in the inner-city areas of East London. The majority of Arabs and Iranians also live in London, although their pattern of dispersion in the city is more varied. Other major centers of Muslim concentration include Birmingham, where Muslims constitute 8 percent of the city's total population, and the city of Bradford in Yorkshire.[7]

Housing

The percentage of house owners is highest among Indians (85 percent), African Asians (85 percent), and Pakistanis (79 percent), while the percentage for Bangladeshis is only 48 percent. Bangladeshis have the highest percentage (35 percent) among council tenants (those living in government-subsidized housing) and among tenants in housing associations (10 percent). The 6 percent of Pakistanis and 8 percent of Bangladeshis living in private tenancies are not significantly different from those of other groups.

These crude figures of types of tenure may be, however, misleading in drawing an accurate picture of Muslims' housing conditions. At least until 1981, it seems that Asian owner-occupiers were to be found in the worst types of urban housing complexes. This situation is partly the result of discrimination and partly due to the desire of Muslims to remain together.[8] At the time, the relative weight of these two factors was hotly debated among academics. Today, with the benefit of hindsight, it seems reasonable to assume that there are important elements of "choice" in the concentration of Asians, and even other communities, in certain areas. Clearly, they wish to remain close to their own associations, institutions, particular shops, eating places, and religious centers. Of particular importance in the case of Muslims has been the role of mosques.

SECTARIAN DIVISIONS IN BRITAIN'S MUSLIM POPULATION

The vast majority of Muslims in Britain are Sunni (probably about 85 percent), although there is also a significant Shi'a minority. The majority of the Shi'as consist of Pakistanis, followed by Iranian, Iraqi, and other Arab and East African Shi'as. The Shi'as are divided into Twelvers and Seveners (or Ismailis). There are also small groups known as Boras. These groups are drawn largely from the business classes and do not present a challenge to the British political system.

There is no overall solidarity within the Shi'a community. Consequently, they do not represent a distinct social and political force. Some of them belong to the Pakistani immigrant working class, while others are members of the business class. They are by no means all supporters of the Ayatullah Rouhullah Khomeini's Islamic revolution; some support it, but others oppose it or ignore it. On occasions as, for example, in their response to the publication of Salman Rushdie's book *The Satanic Verses*, they easily collaborated with Sunni Muslims.

The majority of Sunni Muslims are followers of the Hanafi school of Islamic law. While recognizing the importance of the *ulema*, (religious leaders) and the *shari'a* (Islamic law), they also accept the idea of secular government and, indeed, of secular law. They are therefore inherently adaptable and politically moderate groups, well capable of fitting into a multicultural society, if left free to practice their religion. Other Sunni Muslims adhere to different traditions, one of which is the Deobandi school, whose origins are to be found in the Indian theological center in Deoband. Deobandis adhere to a stricter version of Islam and are less affected by other influences such as Hinduism. The other tendency within British Sunni Islam is that of the Barelvi school. Like the Deobandis, the Barelvis represent a traditionalist group, particularly with regard to their social teaching, but their philosophy is influenced by Sufism and some elements of Shi'ism. They emphasize a religious discipline that seeks to escape from the temptations of the flesh and the importance of *pirs* (saintly leaders), who act as models for implementing this discipline. They also believe in the ability of these *pirs* to intercede with God on their behalf—a belief influenced by Shi'a notions of the intercession of the imams. Because of these tendencies, many Barelvis belong to Sufi orders, of which the most important in England is the Naqshbendi.

The relationship between the adherents of the two schools is often tense, since the Deobandis view the Barelvi traditions as being unduly influenced by elements exogenous to Islam. Another possible cause of dispute, as Francis Robinson has put it, is the fact that "if the Deobandis wanted to conserve Islam as they found it in the Hanafi law books of the Islamic Middle Ages, the Barelvis wished to conserve it as they found it in nineteenth century India."[9] More rigid in their adherence to the ancient forms of Islam are the members of the Jamiat-Ahl-I Hadith, who rely on the Prophet's Sunna as related in the Hadith. Even stricter are members of Jamiat-Ahl-I Koran, who turn only to the Qur'an for guidance.

The Barelvis have possibly more followers than the Deobandis. They also claim to represent the only true Sunni Muslims, but the Deobandis probably control more mosques, religious schools, and madrassahs. They are supported in their work by the highly influential Tablighi Jama'at, the English headquarters of which is based in Dewsbury in West Yorkshire and Bury in Lancashire. This movement has sought to infuse a new degree of commitment in Deobandi Islam. The Tablighi Jama'at originated in India, but it also has roots in Morocco. Consequently, in their missionary work in Europe, representatives of the Indian version of Tablighi find ready allies among those originating in Morocco.

Reference must also be made to the Ahmadiyya sect, which, according to Robinson, combines Muslim teaching with a recognition of Jesus and Krishna and the Mahdi in Egypt. The founder of this movement was Mirza Ghulam Ahmad (1839 to 1908). The followers of Ahmadiyya have often been persecuted in Pakistan, and their Islamic credentials have been questioned.[10] Nonetheless, there are some towns in England where Ahmadiyya followers are the main Muslim group. Because of their religious eclecticism and modern outlook, the Ahmadiyya are viewed positively by other British citizens.

IDEOLOGICAL DIFFERENCES

In addition to theological differences, Britain's Muslim community is characterized by ideological and political divergences. These divisions appear along the following lines: (1) traditional versus militant or activist Islam, whose followers are often referred to as Islamists; and (2) traditionalist versus modernist.

Modernist movements began to appear throughout the Islamic world by the mid-nineteenth century. The Indian subcontinent was not immune from this trend. Islamic modernism in the Indian subcontinent, represented in part an adjustment of leading intellectuals and civil servants to British rule and to Western civilization. It sought to dissociate itself from any aspect of Islam that was unscientific or morally unacceptable by Western standards. A major representative of Indian Muslim modernism was Sir Sayyed Ahmad Khan and the poet-philosopher Muhammad Iqbal Lahori.

Similar tendencies are observable today among middle-class Muslim intellectuals in Britain. These intellectuals have formed their own cultural associations outside the framework of the mosques, have sought to represent Islamic culture as worthy of respect by Westerners, and are often interested in doing charitable work among poorer members of the community. An important spokesman for this trend is the Pakistani author, scholar, and one-time diplomat Akbar Ahmed. Through his work, he has tried to make Islam intellectually and politically acceptable to British elites.[11]

There is also what may be called an extremist fringe within the Muslim community. Some of its members are sympathizers of Islamist movements in their country of origin, and others have sprung up in Britain. One of these movements is the Supporters of Shari'a (SOS) movement under the leadership of Abu-Hamza al-Masri. According to some reports, the group operates from the Finsbury Park mosque in North London. The SOS's own literature suggests that it was founded in 1994 by bringing together members who had been working in many parts of the world, especially Afghanistan and Bosnia. It wants to "remove the oppression created by manmade laws so that the whole of mankind can enjoy the freedom, purity, and justice of living under Allah's shari'a."[12]

Another group that could be considered to have extremist tendencies is the Al-Muhajirun, led by Omar Bafri. According to information on the group's web site, its founders "have been active with various Islamic movements who were and still are working to establish the Islamic state (Al-Khilafat) such as Hizb ut-Tahrir, the Muslim brotherhood, young Muslims and Tabligh." In Britain, they aim to prevent the spread of corrupt thoughts among Muslims and also actively—albeit through permissible means—encourage conversion to Islam.[13]

Some of these groups intended to hold a conference in September 1999 under the title "The Relationship between Rulers and Citizens in the Islamic Khilafat State." But the Royal Albert Hall, where the conference were to be held, cancelled it in part because of the inflammatory rhetoric used by Bafri on other occasions and because of a fear that this might be damaging to interethnic and interfaith relations. Other militant Islamic groups also have sympathizers within Britain's Muslim communities, including the following: (1) *jihad*, which is reportedly linked to Osama bin Laden and was responsible for the assassination of President Anwar Sadat of Egypt in 1981; (2) Gamaa Islamiyya, an extremist offshoot of the Muslim Brothers founded and based in Egypt, which was accused of terrorist attacks in Luxor in November 1997; and (3) Armed Islamic Group, an umbrella group for the most militant elements of Algeria's Islamic movement, which has been engaged in a civil war with the government.[14]

ISLAMIC RELIGIOUS, EDUCATIONAL, AND POLITICAL ORGANIZATIONS

The Mosques

The mosques are the most important institutions around which the Muslim community's life is organized. The development of mosques has been linked to the various phases of Muslim immigration. In 1963, there were only a total of thirteen registered mosques. According to Nielsen, in 1985, there were 338 "registered mosques," and by the end of the 1980s, their number had risen to almost 500.[15] Estimates offered to this author for the year 2000 put the total number at 1,000. Birmingham alone has fifty-five mosques and Bradford fifty. A main distinction that has to be made is between purpose-built mosques, which can be recognized by their external features such as minarets, etc., and those that are converted from other buildings such as houses. The headquarters of Jamiat-Ahl-I Hadith is actually in a former swimming bath. The converted buildings have usually struggled to obtain planning permission from local councils. Presently, only about a third of all mosques are purpose built, but their number is increasing.

In addition to being a place of worship, mosques often also perform educational functions, especially by providing Qur'an courses, and other more advanced centers of Muslim education are attached to mosques.

Educational/Political Institutions

Some movements have both educational and political organizations, the most important of which is the Tablighi Jama'at, belonging to the Deobandi school. The Jama'at's center in Dewsbury is known as Dar ul'Ulum (House of Knowledge). Another Tablighi educational center is in the Lancashire town of Bury. This organization serves as a center for both Islamic learning and missionary activity. As a center of learning, it has the makings of a Muslim university. As a missionary center, the Tablighi Jama'at sends out its members—who often have quite humble secular occupational roles—to revitalize the religious practice and Islamic way of life among Muslims throughout Europe.[16] The principal aim of the Tablighi Jama'at is not to proselytize non-Muslims but to revitalize the religious life of existing Muslims. The Tablighi Jama'at is not active in the Barelvi community because of doctrinal differences.

While the Tablighi Jama'at concentrates on religious, educational, and missionary work, a much more political stance is adopted by the United Kingdom Islamic Mission. It represents the philosophy and ideas espoused by the group known as Jama'at-I-Islami and based on the ideas and teachings of Mawlana Mawdudi, who is considered to be one of the principal intellectual fathers of the Islamist movement internationally.[17] Originally he did not support the creation of the state of Pakistan, although he preached the idea of an Islamic state. Once Pakistan was created, he sought to make it into an Islamic state and to persuade its leaders to apply the shari'a.[18] Theologically speaking, Mawdudi's doctrine is in no sense literally scripturalist. Rather, he places the emphasis upon *ijtihad* (interpretation of scriptures). Mawdudi, however, concerns himself with the problem of organization. Like many third-world political parties, Jama'at-I-Islami is organized along quasi-Leninist lines. Lenin once said that he wanted to include in his party not only those who would give up their spare evenings, but especially members who would be willing to sacrifice their whole lives for the organization's goals. Jama'at-I-Islami makes similar demands upon its members. At its margins are supporters under instruction, but they are ultimately controlled by an inner core, which directs the organization. The number of core members in any city is small, but they are surrounded by a much larger group, which they educate and direct politically.

This organizational capacity makes the UK Islamic Mission, linked to the Jama'at-I-Islami, a formidable rival to other groups' competing bids for influence within the Muslim community. The UK Islamic Mission is also engaged in education with its own college and research center, the Islamic Foundation, located in Leicestershire. The center has been active in research and publishing, especially in translating Mawdudi's works. Other subjects studied at this center include Islamic economics, such as Muslim attitudes toward money lending and banking, and political questions, such as the setting up of an Islamic state. Regarding the problem of paying interest on loans, the center has suggested ways that would allow banks to operate while conforming to Islamic rules. Talk of creating an Islamic state, however, is clearly an unrealistic prospect within a society where Muslims constitute only 2 or 3 percent of the total population. Perhaps for this reason, the UK Islamic Mission has not yet developed a definite view on this subject.

At the level of political thinking, the UK Islamic Mission is not focused on the critical question of the nature of the Muslims' relations with the British society at large. Rather, it seems to be more concerned either with Pakistan's problems or with the internal organization of Britain's migrant community.

Another important institution is the Muslim Education Trust. Its activities are focused on making arrangements with schools in order to provide religious instruction for Muslim students. Mention should also be made of an institution called Dawat-ul-Islam (call to Islam), which caters primarily to the Bangladeshi population and, indeed, was established in 1976 in response to Pakistan's breakup and the ensuing tensions between Pakistanis and Bangladeshis.

The Muslim Institute

The Muslim Institute was founded in London in 1980 by Kalim Siddiqi, a former journalist with *The Guardian*. In his Muslim Manifesto (1990), he said that Muslims should be ashamed to have brought their families to a country like Britain and called for the establishment of a

Muslim Parliament. While not identifying with Shi'ism or, indeed, with any of the various Muslim sects, he did suggest that all Muslims should look to Iran for leadership. Consequently, the institute got more public and media attention than was justified by the extent of its support among the Muslim community.

Siddiqi's challenge was far more radical than the one posed by Jama'at-I-Islami and its British affiliates. The latter had been careful to avoid any action or statement that could be represented as treason, and despite their theoretical commitment to an Islamic state, they certainly did not advocate loyalty to another state. By contrast, Siddiqi was less prudent.

It is still not possible to foresee the future appeal of Siddiqi and his Muslim Manifesto. It has, however, survived his death and has provided, in the shape of an entirely nominated or self-selected Muslim Parliament, a forum for the expression of more radical forms of Islam and for ideas that suggest secession, or at least isolation, from British society. However, it seems that sharp divisions and serious infighting have appeared in the institute's leadership, which bode ill for its prospects as a serious organization capable of developing a broad base of support.[19]

The Al-Khoei Foundation

The Al-Khoei Foundation is an Iraqi Shi'a organization named after the late Ayatullah Khoei, who lived in the holy city of Najaf in Iraq. It plays an important intellectual role and publishes a journal called *Dialogue*.

Institute of Islamic Studies (IIS)

This institute has close links with Iran and is located in London. It aims to be a serious research institution:

- The IIS aims to examine, facilitate, and coordinate research in the fields of Islamic history, literature, arts, culture, and civilization in close cooperation with the scholars who are actively engaged in quality researches in these fields.
- It intends to facilitate academic debates and discussions on issues that are thought to be highly important to Iran, the Middle East, Northern Africa, other Muslim countries, and the Muslim communities living in Europe and North America. These issues must be analyzed in their political, social, economic, historical, and cultural contexts.
- It helps to set up and/or support professional artistic performances (e.g., drama and music).

- It collaborates with respected universities to run purely academic conferences on useful subjects.

- It actively encourages dialogue between various world civilizations and religions.

- It endeavors to establish communicative links with the scholars of various social disciplines in Europe and America and corresponds with academic centers to encourage fruitful and healthy debate between researchers and academicians of these centers and those living in Iran.

In addition to research and publications, the Institute of Islamic Studies has organized different conferences in collaboration with Iranian and Western universities.[20]

Islamic Centre England

This institution was founded in 1995 and has close links to Iran. Its director is Ayatullah Mohsen Araki. The center offers religious advice and instruction, language courses (English, Arabic, Persian), and other training, as well as sports and educational facilities. In addition, there is a large number of Muslim associations dealing with different aspects of Muslim life in Britain.

INTERACTION AMONG MUSLIMS AND EFFORTS TO CREATE UMBRELLA ORGANIZATIONS

British Islam is dominated by Pakistanis, Bangladeshis, and Indians, and therefore their mosques are visible in most cities. There are, however, mosques that cater to a larger and ethnically more mixed constituency. In this category, the most important are the mosques in Regents Park in London and in Woking. These were established before the large-scale South Asian working-class migration of the 1950s. They also meet the needs of many of the smaller Muslim groups from other countries, though many of the Malaysians pray in university institutions, while some middle-class East African Asians may have their own separate religious meeting places. As a rule, however, mosques and madrasahs are organized along ethnic lines and are dominated by South Asians.

There have been efforts to develop greater cooperation and unity among various Muslim institutions. The first umbrella organization was the Union of Muslim Organisations of the UK and Eire, set up in the 1970s. In the mid-1980s, the Council of Mosques in the UK and Eire was established mainly through the encouragement of the Muslim World League, which is closely linked to Saudi Arabia. Almost at the same time, a Council of Imams was set up in collaboration with the Islamic Call Society linked to Libya.

Despite these efforts, the following factors have hampered the development of a single Muslim umbrella institution which could rightly claim to represent the British Muslim community: ethnic and sectarian diversity of the community; ideological differences and conflicting, or at least competing, foreign links; and the essentially local character of issues facing the Muslim community.

ASSIMILATION VERSUS COMMUNALISM

There is very little in the way of assimilation of the Muslim community, if assimilation is interpreted to imply movement toward acceptance of British beliefs, practices, and forms of worship. Insofar as there is such a tendency, it is represented by such figures as Akbar Ahmed, a former professor of Pakistani studies at the University of Cambridge, who, for a period following the military overthrow of the government in 1998, became Pakistan's high commissioner in London. Ahmed emphasizes the compatibility of Islam with British traditional and, perhaps, upper-class values. By doing so, he has played a role in Britain somewhat similar to that of Mohammad Arkoun in France. He distances himself from "fundamentalism" and argues that whereas there had been some balance in Pakistan between the influence of the administration, traditional political leaders, and the religious leaders (mullahs), the latter's influence has become dominant among Pakistanis in Britain.[21]

This assimilationist stance is not, however, shared by poorer working-class communities. While they may well negotiate with the local authorities and may share some of their values, they see their own often mosque-based communities as primary foci of belonging. Muslims in Bradford, Birmingham, Rochdale, or the East End of London live their lives largely within such communities.

MUSLIM INVOLVEMENT IN THE BRITISH POLITICAL PROCESS

In assessing the level of British Muslims' participation in the political process, the following point needs to be emphasized: Britain is unique among all European countries in that UK residents with Irish and Commonwealth nationalities have the right to vote. Until the introduction of the new Nationality Act in 1983, Commonwealth residents could acquire full UK citizenship by a simple process of registration; indeed, by the mid-1970s, most immigrants had done so. Because the overwhelming majority of UK Muslims come from Commonwealth countries, most of them are full-fledged UK citizens. This is not the case, however, with non-Commonwealth immigrants.

Therefore, in evaluating the level of Muslim political participation, the focus will be on Asian immigrants. The level of political participation could also be a good indicator for measuring the Asians' commitment to British society. This can be ascertained from their registration and voting record, the extent of their participation in the selection of candidates for local councils and the national Parliament, and their ability to field their own candidates.

Asians are more likely to register than whites, although this gap is narrowing. Of those who register, Asians are also more likely to vote than whites, especially in areas of high Asian concentration. Figures provided by Anwar are only for Pakistanis, Indians, and Bangladeshis, in general. There are no data drawn from research specifically on Muslims within this larger category.

Asians participate actively in the life of local political parties, and where there are large concentrations of registered Asian voters, they have a decisive influence in the selection of candidates and often run their own candidates. Muslims are among the most active of these Asians. Most Asians have supported Labour, while only a small minority favor the Conservative party. By the mid-1980s, however, divisions within the Labour party, plus the Conservatives' emphasis on the so-called family values, had somewhat shifted the balance. Meanwhile, independent Asian and Muslim candidates who run in elections are rarely successful.

In London and in major provincial cities such as Birmingham, Leicester, Bradford, Rochdale, and Bolton, Muslim candidates exercise considerable influence in local Labour-controlled councils, taking over the chair of major committees. They generally support the party's moderate or right-wing sections. From this position, they are able to contribute to the reduction of racial, ethnic, and religious discrimination, but they do not constitute a distinct Asian or Muslim caucus. Muslim councillors, however, are actively concerned with some specific Muslim religious matters, such as licensing *halal* butchers, providing *halal* food on civic occasions, giving planning permission for mosques, and allowing for call to prayer.

According to Anwar, in 1996, there were 136 Pakistani councillors in Britain, although there were no Pakistani members of Parliament. Solomos and Back provide evidence that white trade unions used their influence to prevent Asian representation.[22] Nearly all the councillors belonged to the Labour party, although the few Asians favoring the Conservative party were very active. Especially Asian employers were very responsive to the policies of the Thatcher government. Apart from these Thatcherite tendencies, several cities elected Asian mayors, most notably Bradford, where Muhammad Ajeeb, an active member of the Labour party, became mayor in 1985. Ajeeb had been active in the Bradford Council of Mosques that sought to promote the welfare of Muslim groups and, on becoming mayor, arranged for the city's civic religious service to be held in a mosque.

The 1997 election, which led to an overwhelming Labour victory, does not appear to have significantly affected Asian or Muslim voting patterns. Asian registration and turnout were as high as for whites. Most Asians still voted Labour, although a significant minority voted for Conservative and other candidates.[23] Yet, the representation of Asian Muslims in the British Parliament is very low. In fact, there is no Muslim representation in the House of Commons, and Nadir Ahmad is the only Muslim member in the House of Lords.

Very little research is done on the political behavior of the two main non-Asian Muslim groups, namely, the Turkish Cypriots and the Turks. As far as the former are concerned, the divisions within Cyprus resulting from the Turkish occupation are reflected in the British Cypriot community, but these differences are not based on religious distinctions. As far as the Turks are concerned, there are not enough data to show whether conflicts among different Turkish religious and political factions, which are observable within the Turkish community in Germany, are also present among Turkish residents in Britain. In the latter case, some of these Turks are, in fact, Kurds who failed to gain refugee status but were nonetheless granted exceptional permission to remain in the country. Among these Kurds, political factionalism with regard to the Partiya Karkeran Kurdistan's (Kurdish Workers Party) role was more important than any difference in religious orientation. In these circumstances, it is difficult to reach any firm conclusions about the level of Turkish Muslims' participation in Britain's political system.[24]

The conclusion to be drawn from Pakistani and other Muslim participation in the British political system is that those with citizenship rights seek to exercise them through registering to vote, voting, and involvement within Britain's main political parties.

FOREIGN LINKS AND CONFLICTING LOYALTIES

An important, and frequently posed, question is to what extent Britain's Muslims have political commitments to other states. A particularly delicate issue is the degree to which such loyalties are generated and sustained by financial and other assistance, especially from wealthy Middle Eastern countries. A related question is to what extent activities of certain Muslim dissidents and/or extremists pose security threats to the British society or create difficulties in its diplomatic relations with some countries.

Financial support received by British Muslims from abroad can be divided into two categories: (1) support for maintaining Muslim institutions such as mosques and so on; and (2) support used to exercise a degree of political control over various sects and groups that are recipients of such assistance. The first type of funding is sought and obtained by all groups, complementing contributions made by individuals from within the immigrant community and from those residing in the country of origin. All the main Middle Eastern countries provide support of the second type. The most important country involved in giving this kind of support is Saudi Arabia, but Iraq, Syria, Egypt, and Libya may also be involved. For example, a recently founded Deobandi mosque in Birmingham is called the Saddam Hussein mosque, which could indicate some form of Iraqi financial support. There are conflicts of interest and competition among these countries, some of which were evident during the Persian Gulf War of 1990 to 1991. Significant competition also exists between these countries and Iran—a situation that was brought into sharp focus by the Rushdie affair.

The principal recipients of Saudi aid are major mosques, especially the Deobandi mosques and institutions. It is less clear what the sources of financial aid are for the Barelvi institutions. Given their Sufi links, most probably they depend either on financial support from individuals or followers of particular *pirs* or on aid of a more political kind from countries with Sufi orders to which they belong. Jamiat-Ahl-I Hadith, which has its headquarters in Birmingham, is strongly committed to the cause of a liberated Azad Kashmir and to the liberation of Kashmir as a whole. Jama'at-I-Islami has complex political involvement in Pakistan, Bangladesh, Afghanistan, and Kashmir, which has enabled it to gain the support of several different countries. It is possible that a small part of this money is channeled to bodies like the UK Islamic Mission. Influence is also exercised through religious education.

Jamiat-Ahl-I Hadith represents a different type of situation. Its leader, until his death in the early 1990s, was educated in Saudi Arabia and was well schooled in Muslim theology. But the political situation in Saudi Arabia and the theological developments related to them are complex. The country's present rulers are considered to be Wahabis, but there are radical Wahabi groups that are highly critical of the ruling elite, whom they accuse of corruption. In general, it should be said that the impact of Saudi education is not uniform and does not necessarily translate into blind support for the Saudi government. Other groups obtaining Saudi funding are also connected with theological and educational centers in the Indian subcontinent, and their imams are mostly recruited from there.

Regarding the question of whether Muslim minorities in the United Kingdom constitute some sort of bridgehead across which foreign countries can influence British society, research shows the actual pattern of influences is complex, although the Saudi influence is probably predominant. Because of the role of Saudi Arabia in the cold war and later in the Gulf War, this situation means that the political influence exercised through Saudi funding may advance Western interests. The Middle Eastern states use the Muslim community in Britain to serve their interests. Meanwhile, these communities sometimes offer a base to their radical opponents.

The activities of some of these groups create problems for the British government. To illustrate, in early 1999, the Yemeni government demanded that the British government hand over Hamza Al Masri, the leader of the aforementioned SOS group, because of his links to the Islamic Army of Aden, which has been involved in terrorist activities, including kidnapping of foreign nationals.[25] However, the UK government could not comply with this request because Al Masri was a British citizen. Another case was that of the Saudi dissident Muhammad al-Masari. The Saudi government objected to his activities and requested that British authorities prosecute him. British authorities tried to solve this problem by sending him to the Caribbean. As a result of Amnesty International's intervention, however, he was allowed to remain in England but had to refrain from anti-Saudi activities.[26]

THE RESPONSE OF BRITISH MUSLIMS TO INTERNATIONAL CHALLENGES

The publication of Salman Rushdie's novel *The Satanic Verses* in 1988 shocked Muslims throughout the world. Yet, nowhere was the effect stronger than in Britain, because Rushdie, although of Indian descent, was a highly regarded English novelist and the product of an English public school. Irrespective of the book's literary merit, Muslims viewed its handling of Islam, especially of the Prophet and his family, as an insult to their religion and thus placed it within a long tradition of anti-Islamic writings in the West.

The publication of the book led to protests and riots in many Muslim countries, especially in Pakistan. Even the Indian government banned the sale of Rushdie's book. But the most dramatic reaction with broadest implications was the *fatwa* issued by the Ayatullah Rouhullah Khomeini pronouncing Rushdie an apostate and hence making it permissible for Muslims to kill him. This *fatwa* was not seen as binding by Muslims outside a hard core of supporters of the Iranian revolution. Nevertheless, the feeling of having been insulted was shared by nearly all committed Muslims and led to large-scale demonstrations against the book. The demonstrations in Bradford took the form of ritual burning of Rushdie's book, and there was a widespread call for its withdrawal by its publishers. Appeal was made to an ancient British law against blasphemy, and it was argued that refusing to apply this law to defend Islam, while it is applicable in cases of blasphemy against Christianity, was discriminatory.

Significantly, however, there was little support for the *fatwa* among Muslim leaders in Britain. It is quite possible that this was due to these leaders' Saudi orientation; of course, Saudi Arabia had no interest in supporting policies espoused by Iran's revolutionary leadership.

The hostility of Muslims to Rushdie and his book produced a strong negative reaction from believers in free speech in Britain, particularly from writers like Melvin Bragg and Fay Weldon. The reaction posed a challenge to Muslim modernists like Akbar Ahmad, who—while strongly opposing the theme of the book—supported Rushdie's right to have written it.

A second challenge to British Muslims came with Saddam Hussein's attack on Kuwait in August 1990. Hussein called for a *jihad* in support of his attack, and British Muslims were called upon, if not actually to support the attack, at least not to support the alliance that opposed and eventually defeated his forces. But because Saudi Arabia was part of the anti-Saddam alliance, British Muslim leaders, who are influenced by Saudi policy, gave little support to Saddam. Indeed, some of them emphasized the duties of British Muslims to the British state.

The Salman Rushdie affair, however, was a watershed in the evolution of Britain's Muslim community in that it made Muslims realize the importance of becoming politically better organized.

SECOND- AND THIRD-GENERATION BRITISH MUSLIMS

According to Anwar, by 1991, 51 percent of those claiming to belong to the Pakistani ethnic group were born in Britain. This percentage was lower (though rising) in the case of Bangladeshis because of their later arrival in Britain. Moreover, available data indicate that the percentage of those having one parent born in Britain was increasing among both Pakistanis and Bangladeshis, thus giving rise to a third generation of British Muslims.[27]

Given that the future character of British Islam will be determined largely by the younger Muslims, certain important questions arise: To what extent do these British-born Pakistanis and Bangladeshis still think of themselves as Muslims? Is the nature of Islam in which they believe significantly different from that of their parents? There are no single and generally accepted answers to these questions. It is noteworthy, however, that when questioned about their identity, young Pakistanis, Kashmiris, and Bangladeshis identified themselves first as Muslims and only second according to their ethnic group or color. This does not necessarily imply their acceptance of traditional Muslim family values. Rather, it seems that emphasis on Muslimness is a political act and evidence of an emerging political identity. After minor rioting and conflict with the police, which took place in Bradford in July 1996, some commentators suggested that the young people were essentially revolting against their parents' value system. Yet, some young Pakistanis that were subsequently interviewed said that their main disagreement with their parents was caused by their belief that the latter had failed to resist discrimination against Muslims and their oppression with sufficient vigor.[28]

The above seem to indicate that the second and third generations of British Muslims are emphasizing different issues and different aspects of their fate. They seem less concerned with attendance at mosques or regular prayers than with the public assertion of Muslim political values. Thus, in their own special way, militant young Muslims represent another modernizing tendency in contemporary Britain. It is of some interest that these young people regarded their Muslimness, rather than their color, nationality, or country of origin, as the basis for their identity and as giving scope for their collective political activity.

MUSLIMS IN A MULTICULTURAL SOCIETY

Despite the growing involvement of Muslims in British public life, one major question still needs to be answered: How can Muslims be expected to fit into existing British society and to what extent can they contribute to the development of an ideal multicultural society? The question has to be put in this way because the ideal type of a multicultural society is not acceptable to many native Britons. In fact, there is still a substantial amount of racism directed against all people with dark skin. In addition, certain studies tend to indicate that Muslims suffer from religious, as well as racial, prejudice. This is, for example, the conclusion reached by a study conducted by the Runnymede Trust, published in 1997 and entitled "Islamophobia: A Challenge for Us All."[29] The report refers to "a particularly dramatic aspect of social exclusion, the vulnerability of Muslims to physical violence and harassment." What is more disturbing is that strong Islamophobic tendencies exist among intellectuals, religious circles, and the press.

Yet, even those who accept British society's multicultural character do not necessarily believe in the equal treatment of all groups. To many Britons, multiculturalism merely means the recognition of the fact that more people of diverse physical and cultural characteristics are now present in British streets. This attitude says nothing about how these diverse groups are to be treated or how their culture ought to be regarded. A good example of this attitude is the behavior of Ray Honeyford, a school headmaster of working class background in Bradford and a subscriber to Conservative politics, who, in the 1980s, refused to carry out the city's multicultural educational policy. While he recognized cultural diversity as a fact, he insisted that the culture of Pakistanis was inferior to that of white Britons and that it should not be perpetuated in the schools. Prime Minister Margaret Thatcher recognized Honeyford as an important thinker and invited him to Downing Street for consultations.[30]

In contradistinction to this interpretation of multiculturalism, an attempt has been made to promote an alternative egalitarian version. Such an alternative multiculturalism would involve, in Daniele Joly's words, "making a place for Muslims in British society."[31] This progressive idea was taken up by Home Secretary Roy Jenkins, who in 1966 defined it not as "a flattening process of uniformity, but [as] cultural diversity coupled with equal opportunity in an atmosphere of mutual tolerance."[32]

This author has suggested in his writings that the success of the progressive interpretation rests upon making a distinction between public and private domains. In practice, however, this distinction is difficult to maintain, not least because the educational system straddles both domains. The task of primary socialization is one in which the primary school and the community are in competition, and this may involve some difficulties. More severe problems arise in the secondary schools, where students have to confront the modern world of the economy, which may well appear threatening to the values of some traditional young Muslims. Usually, however, Muslims seem more concerned about ensuring that schools allow time for prayer, respect Muslim dress, provide *halal* meat in school meals, and do not require girls to take part in swimming lessons.

There is also strong support within Muslim communities for separate education for girls. Some local authorities have preempted Muslim protests regarding these issues by agreeing to introduce guidelines in schools with large Muslim representation. The operation of these guidelines has weakened the demand for separate schools. A few such separate schools have now been selected as eligible for funding by the state on the same basis as Jewish, Catholic, and other Christian schools, on the condition that they be subject to inspection by governmental authorities. Yet, private Muslim schools may be less influenced by such inspections, and in a few cases, they appear to be preparing their students for living in a Muslim society that does not exist in Britain. Alternatively, some parents send their children to their country of origin for educational purposes. This practice also creates problems for schools.

There are, however, efforts to make multiculturalism an acceptable reality in Britain. Samad and I have shown in our writings how multicultural policies have begun to be implemented in Birmingham and Bradford.[33] In Birmingham, the council's Equal Opportunity Department has set up a complicated system for ethnic minorities. This involves the setting up of a standing consultative body, an umbrella organization under which a small amount of funding and access to local authorities is granted to a number of differently defined communities. These include secular as well as separate religious communities.[34] In Bradford, the Council of Mosques, set up jointly by the local authority and representatives of the Muslim community, is in a position to advise the council on religious and cultural matters while at the same time promoting equality in such spheres as employment, housing, and education. The most active figure in this council, Mohammed Ajeeb, became in due course the city's lord mayor. In Samad's own research, this entire equal opportunity and multicultural framework was found to be threatened during the period of Conservative government by a reduction in funding. In fact, Samad and many researchers in other cities found that commitment to a policy of multiculturalism was seen as part of an overall policy of equalizing opportunities and promoting welfare. When, during the Thatcher era, the latter policy had to be abandoned owing to lack of funding, the promotion of multiculturalism was more difficult to pursue.

However, as the report of the Runnymede Trust illustrates, the creation of a truly multicultural society would require more than governmental action and would succeed only by changing popular attitudes and developing mechanisms of cooperation and accommodation between Muslims and the rest of the society.

The riots that broke out in Northern England (Oldham, Bradford, and Burnley) involving Muslims in spring and summer 2001, plus the anti-foreign and anti-Muslim statements made by leaders of the British Nationalist Party, which had some modest success in the last parliamentary elections, illustrate that the task of changing attitudes on both sides will be arduous.[35]

CONCLUSIONS

Islam in the United Kingdom is a diverse and multifaceted phenomenon. The British Muslim community is divided along ethnic, sectarian, and ideological lines. Some Muslims are more inclined toward integration, whereas others exhibit ideological and communal tendencies. There is an extremist fringe within the community, but it is dangerous to use the term "fundamentalist" in reference to Muslims in general. In fact, there is a range of modernizing tendencies among all Muslim groups and sects, along with more traditional attitudes. One peculiarity of Britain's Muslim—or, more exactly, Pakistani—community is the activities of many of their members that make them influential in Muslim circles throughout Europe. While efforts have been made in developing institutions and methods to deal with an increasingly multiethnic and multicultural society, much still needs to be done by both sides. Nevertheless, there does appear to be some scope for "making a place for Islam" in Britain that would include both modernist and traditionalist tendencies in the context of a social and cultural framework that accepts diversity and fosters mutual tolerance and respect. However, the consolidation of such a framework and the development of attitudes needed for its successful functioning will be a long process.

NOTES

I wish to express my gratitude to the following people who helped me understand the sectarian divisions in Birmingham: Cornelius North in his unpublished thesis for the University of Birmingham, "Muslims in Birmingham: Religious Activity in Mosques and Paramosques" (1996); Philip Lewis in his *Islamic Britain* (Taurus Books, 1994); and Prof. Jørgen Nielsen and his Center for the Study of Islam and Christian Muslim Relations in the Selly Oak Colleges of the University of Birmingham. I also owe much to my collaboration with Yunas Samad, and I am very grateful to Professor Anwar for commenting on earlier drafts of this chapter.

1. For a history of Muslim immigration to the UK, see Jørgen S. Nielsen, *Muslims in Western Europe*, 2nd ed. (Edinburgh: Edinburgh University Press, 1995), 39–41.

2. The options offered were White, Black Afro–Caribbean, Black African, Black Other, Indian Pakistani Bangladesh, Chinese, Other Ethnic Group.

3. Muhammad Anwar, *Race and Elections* (Coventry: University of Warwick, Centre for Research in Ethnic Relations, 1994).

4. Tariq Modood et al., *Fourth National Survey of Ethnic Minorities* (London: Policy Studies Institute, 1997).

5. See Tariq Modood, Richard Berthoug, Jane Lakey, James Nazroo, Patten Smith, Satnam Veidee, and Sharon Beiskon, *Ethnic Minorities in Britain* (London: Policy Studies Institute, 1997), 337–359.

6. Nielsen, *Muslims in Western Europe*, 42.

7. Ibid., 43.

8. I had emphasized discrimination as the reason for all kinds of concentration in my own work and was criticized for this by Badra Dhaya. Vaughan Robinson saw this as involving a debate about the relative causal importance of constraint and choice. See John Rex and Robert Moore, *Race, Community and Conflict* (Oxford: Oxford University Press, 1967); also, John Rex and Sally Tomlinson, *Colonial Immigrants in a British City—A Class Analysis* (London: Routledge & Kegan Paul, 1979); Badra Dhaya, "Pakistanis in Britain: Transients or Settlers," *Race* 14 (1973); and Vaughan Robinson, *Transients, Settlers or Refugees: Asians in Britain* (Oxford: Clarendon Press, 1986).

9. Francis Robinson, "Varieties of South Asian Islam," in *Research Papers in Ethnic Relations, No. 8* (Coventry: University of Warwick, Centre for Research in Ethnic Relations, 1988), 8.

10. Ibid., 9.

11. See Akbar Ahmed, *Post-Modernism and Islam: Predicament and Promise* (London: Routledge & Kegan Paul, 1992).

12. See Muhammed al-Shafi', "Three Members of Abu Hamza al-Masri's Group Arrested in London," *Al-Shaq-al-Awsat*, 21 June 1999, 4: "The British Police have arrested three members of Abu Hamza al Masri's group, Supporters of Shari'a (SOS)."

13. See Al Muhajiroun, "The Voice, the Eyes and the Ears of the Muslims," www.mupae-rajirun.com.

14. See Muhammed al-Shafi'i, "Islamist Movement's Conference at London's Albert Hall Cancelled," *Al-Shaq-al-Awsat*, 16 September 1999, 2, on various extremist groups. Also, see "U.K.: Islamic Groups Based in Britain," *BBC News*, http://news.bbc.co.uk/fi/english/uk/newsid.25August1998.

15. See Nielsen, *Muslims in Western Europe*, 45.

16. John King, "Three Asian Associations in Britain," in *Monographs in Ethnic Relations No. 8*, (Coventry: University of Warwick, Centre for Research in Ethnic Relations, 1994); see also Philip Lewis, *Islamic Britain: Religion, Politics and Identity among British Muslims* (London: I.B. Tauris, 1994).

17. Sayyid Abul Ala Mawdudi, *Towards Understanding Islam* (Leicester: Islamic Foundation, 1981).

18. For a critical discussion of Mawdudi's position, see Ishtiaq Ahmed, *The Concept of an Islamic State* (London: Pinter, 1987).

19. See Muhammed al-Shafi'i, "Split within Islamic Shura Council of Britain's with Chairman and Deputy Chairman," *Al-Shaq-al-Awsat*, 14 January 1999, 5. Apparently, the new leader—who is the founder's son—is accused of authoritarian tendencies and wrongdoings.

20. See the institute's website at http://www.islamicstudies.org.

21. See Nielsen, *Muslims in Western Europe*, 46–48.

22. John Solomos and Les Back, *Race, Politics and Social Change* (London: Routledge, 1995).

23. Muhammad Anwar, *Ethnic Minorities and the British Political System* (Coventry: University of Warwick, Centre for Research in Ethnic Relations, 1998).

24. See Osten Wahlbeck, *Kurdish Diasporas: A Comparative Study of Kurdish Refugee Communities* (Basingstoke/New York: Macmillan/St. Martin's Press, 1999).

25. On this and other items related to Yemen's requests, see Eric Watkins, "World: Middle East Analysis: Yemen, Extremists and Britain," *BBC News*, 25 January 1999, http://news.bbc.co.uk/hi/english/world/middle_east/newsid_262000/262606.stm.

26. See Sayyid Ghaib, "London: Jungle of Islamic Organizations; Their Recent Statements Cause Change in Official and Popular Stands in Britain," *Al-Majallah*, 6–12 September 1998, 12–14.

27. See Modood et al., *Ethnic Minorities in Britain*, 60–289.

28. Based on informal interviews with young Muslims in Bradford after the disturbances.

29. http://www.runnymedetrust.org/projects/islam/summary.pdf.

30. In his earlier writings (1986), Ray Honeyford wrote with contempt of Pakistani culture. In his recent work (1998), he has accepted the idea of multiculturalism and is now against its fostering by government action. Ray Honeyford, "Education and Race—An Alternative View," in *Salisbury Review, No. 6*, (London: Claridge Press, 1986), and *The Commission for Racial Equality: British Bureaucracy and the Multi-Ethnic Society* (New Brunswick: Transaction, 1998).

31. See Daniele Joly, *Britain's Crescent: Making a Place for Islam in British Society* (Aldenshat: Avebury, 1995).

32. See Rex and Tomlinson, *Colonial Immigrants*, 8.

33. John Rex and Yunas Samad, "Multiculturalism and Political Integration in European Cities—The British Case, Birmingham and Bradford," *Innovation in Social Science* 9 (1996).

34. This structure of standing consultative bodies was further modified in 1998.

35. For a description and chronology of these events, see *BBC News*, http://news.bbc.co.uk/hi/english/uk/newsaid, for May, June, and July 2001.

4

Islam in Italy

Stefano Allievi

INTRODUCTION: THE EUROPEAN FRAMEWORK

In Europe, including Italy, Islam has become the second largest religion in terms of followers, making Europe, in the words of Felice Dassetto and Albert Bastenier, the new frontier of Islam.[1] The term "frontier" describes better the ongoing processes of Islam's growing presence in Europe than the term "periphery," popularized in the 1980s by Gilles Kepel.[2] It does more to explain the current dynamics and puts less emphasis on the feeling of marginalization and gravitation toward a "center" situated elsewhere, which was perhaps true in the case of the first generation of Muslim immigrants.[3]

The Muslim presence in Europe constitutes a dramatic cultural change that could not have been envisaged only a generation ago. Considering the tumultuous history of relations between the Islamic world and Europe, Islam's presence in Europe represents a historic watershed. In the past, one talked of Islam *and* the West; now, one increasingly speaks of Islam *in* the West and, eventually through the role of second- and third-generation immigrants and converts, of an Islam *of* Europe, if not yet of a European Islam.[4] Islam is no longer a transitory phenomenon that can eventually be sent back "home." More like the stranger described by Georg Simmel, the Muslim is not a person that "today comes and tomorrow goes, but he who today comes and tomorrow stays."[5] Italy is no exception to this general rule, although until three decades ago, it was itself a labor-exporting country.[6]

THE RETURN OF ISLAM: A HISTORICAL BACKGROUND

Historically, Islam's presence in Italy is not a novel phenomenon; it is rather a "return." Indeed, an Arab/Muslim presence existed in Sicily since the seventh century, the early days of Islam, and Muslims dominated the island from the ninth to the eleventh century. This was a period of splendor for Sicily, a fact often forgotten or underrepresented in Italian history. The Islamic heritage has also been important elsewhere in Italy; other areas of the south, as represented by the Emirate of Bari and the Muslim colony of Lucera, and to some degree in certain central and northern regions as late as the nineteenth century.

There were brief contacts and short histories, but not enough for a living memory, except in popular traditions and the folklore, which often refer to some kind of conflict or expressions of fear like "Mamma, li turchi!" (Mother, the Turks!). Traditional popular games, such as the *giostre del Sarracino*, in which the Sarrasin in question constitutes the target of attack of the participants, as well as many *torri saracene* (Sarrasin towers) built all along the Italian coast to defend it from pirates, reflect a historic memory of Islam imbued with fear and mistrust.

More recently, as during the colonial period, Islam's importance in Italy was sharply reduced, largely because Italy had no colonies in the Islamic world and hence felt no need to develop specific policies toward it. The exception was the period of Fascist rule, 1928 to 1943, when Mussolini tried to play the role of "protector" of Islam. He liked to be represented with the "sword of Islam" in his hand. In 1928, in a speech on foreign policy to the National Assembly, he defined Italy not only as a "friend of the Islamic world," but as a "great Muslim Power." But such aspirations were more dream than reality.[7] These declarations remain the only "Muslim heritage" of that period. The other remnant is the Instituto per l'Oriente, which still publishes the review *Oriente Moderno*.

The policies of the Fascist regime did not significantly affect Italian culture, which is still either unfamiliar with Islam or views it as an old enemy. This lingering image is due more to frequent incursions of the Saracen pirates on the Italian coast than to the Crusades. In fact, despite the role played by various popes who launched these battles, the French were more deeply involved in the Crusades and have been so in Arab countries. Indeed, the crusaders were often referred to as *frang*—a corruption of Frank.[8]

Because of this historical memory, coupled with geopolitical factors, notably Italy's proximity to the Muslim world, the impact of Islam's return to Italy has been strong—reflecting both past fears and preoccupation with new challenges posed to Italian society.

A NEW SOCIO-RELIGIOUS PRESENCE

Sociologically, the Muslim presence in Italy is a new phenomenon and the consequence of the growing presence of immigrants. The first significant wave of immigration began in the 1970s and consisted mainly of people from the Philippines and Catholic countries of Latin America. These immigrants were employed mostly as domestic workers. Immigrants in the 1980s and 1990s came to Italy from the Maghreb and Subsaharan African countries, plus Albania, Latin America, other Middle Eastern countries, and more recently Eastern Europe.

Some of these immigrants, especially from the Maghreb, Africa, and the Middle East, were Muslims, and they reintroduced Islam to Italy. Soon, Muslim immigration became organized, first through the setting up of mosques in several university towns by the Union of Muslim Students in Italy in the early 1970s. Before their activities, there was only a single mosque in Rome. Regarding the emergence of Muslim organizations, Italy is unique because, unlike in many other European countries, the first mosques were created not by and for immigrant workers, but by and for an intellectual elite of students from the Middle East, notably Syria and Jordan, many of whom were Palestinians. Only later did the number of workers exceed that of students, thus changing the mosques' role, character, and often their legal status. But these changes have so far not affected the character of their leadership.

During the last two decades, Islam has been establishing itself steadily in Italy, institutionally and otherwise, as reflected in the growing number of Muslim religious and cultural associations, mosques, Sufi orders (Tariqas), political movements, intellectual output such as books and tracts, transnational organizations (centered mainly in Rome), links with home countries and activities of these states, plus the presence of converts. In sum, all forms of Islamic expression exist in Italy, but they are still at a relatively fragile and evolving stage of development. This applies particularly to the community's leadership structure, especially at the national level.

ANATOMY OF ISLAM

The development of an immigrant community in Italy has certain characteristics that distinguish it from other European countries. In addition to the recent arrival of immigrants, other distinguishing characteristics include (1) diversity of countries of origin, (2) rapid pace of entry and settlement, (3) higher number of irregular immigrants, and (4) higher level of geographic dispersion. This means that, in Italy, there are no major centers of concentration of immigrant communities, for example, in industrial districts. Nor are there visible Muslim "ghettos," although there is a significant and visible presence of Muslim residents in cities such as Milan, Rome, Turin, Brescia, and Vicenza in the north and in Naples, Caserta, Catania, and Palermo in the south.

Other characteristics also set Italy's Muslim community apart from those in other European countries. The Islamic presence in Italy became visible with the entry of the first immigrants, whereas in other countries, Islam became visible only after the emergence of a second immigrant generation. Elsewhere, immigrants arrived in the 1950s and 1960s and at first were perceived as a temporary phenomenon. In those days, laws regarding immigration were more relaxed, the legislative climate was very different from today's, and entry into Europe was easy and un-problematic. This gave rise to a "myth of return" among first-generation immigrants or a feeling that they could easily move in and out of Europe. This myth was destroyed in the 1970s for two reasons: Immigrants dis-covered that once they left the host country, they might not be able to return because of changes in the labor market; and second-generation immigrants began to feel more at ease in the country in which they were born or had grown up. Unlike countries like Germany, France, and the United Kingdom where one or two ethnic groups form the bulk of Mus-lims, Italian Muslims come from a wide range of countries. Therefore, in Italy, no single ethnic group numerically dominates the Muslim com-munity, although there are more Moroccans than others. Ethnic diversity means that Islam in Italy is not identified with one ethnic group or a single country or region, either by public opinion or by the government. Therefore, the Muslim presence in Italy cannot be treated in terms of *foreign* policy, as in some other European countries. Few Muslims come from a former colony; therefore, they have little linguistic and cultural affinity with Italy. Most come from countries where Islam is a dominant cultural and social force; this was not always the case for earlier immi-grants, even those who came from the same countries. For example, only two or three decades ago, various secular ideologies such as Arab na-tionalism or socialism in its different forms (Nasserism, Ba'athism) were more widespread in the Arab Middle East than Islam, and popular lead-ers were not openly religious.

These characteristics have a number of consequences that can be ex-pressed in the following "social equation":

Greater residential and labor dispersion + smaller weight of ethnic and secular associations + immigration from countries with a higher Islamic consciousness = greater weight of cultural-religious socialization.

NUMBERS AND ETHNIC COMPOSITION OF THE
MUSLIM COMMUNITY

It is difficult to calculate the number of Muslims in Italy, in part because of the lack of official statistics on religion and the ambiguity of
available data on legal immigrants. In Italy, the problem is magnified by
the large number of illegal immigrants, a third or perhaps more of whom
are Muslim. Researchers estimate that there is a core of about 1.5 million
legal and illegal immigrants in Italy, to which a few hundred thousand
may be added, based on different estimates. The press and some politicians put the number much higher, at 2 million or more.

Moreover, who is a "Muslim"? Does that mean only practicing Muslims? Or anyone who comes from a Muslim country? The first estimate
of the number of Muslims, based on research done in 1992, put the total
at 280,000. This included those coming from Muslim countries as well
as Muslim minorities coming from non-Islamic states. Thus, Muslims
were 31 percent of the Italian immigrant population.[9] By the end of 1999,
this number had increased to 650,000 to 700,000, based on official data
of the Ministry of Interior. Of this, 436,000, or 36.5 percent, have legal
documents and permits. In addition, people under eighteen years of age
are not counted among the previous group, because they do not have
personal residence permits, but are included in their parents' permits;
and a number of people are waiting for resident permit requests to be
considered.[10] When these groups are included, the total is 544,000, without counting Italian citizens who have converted to Islam (maximum
10,000),[11] those Muslims who have acquired Italian citizenship (20,000 to
25,000), plus a number of illegal immigrants. These calculations show
that 650,000 to 700,000 is a more realistic estimate than the 2 million cited
by some Italian politicians and Muslim leaders. Nevertheless, even the
smaller estimate is large enough to make Islam Italy's second religion.
Moreover, it is a "resident" religion, because it has not yet been granted
the full rights of citizenship. But this is a transitory stage; eventually
Islam will be naturalized through the elaboration of new rules on citizenship, mixed marriages, and conversions. It will also remain an "immigrant" phenomenon since it is unlikely that the process of immigration
from Muslim countries will end.

Moroccans, the largest group, are followed by Albanians (see Table
4.1). The list of the more significant countries of origin indicates the ethnic variety and cultural plurality of Italian Islam.

The breakdown shows interesting differences from other European
countries: a modest presence of Turks (different from Germany and the
central part of Europe, from Switzerland to Sweden) and South Asians
(different from Britain), as well as a small number of Muslims coming

Table 4.1
Ethnic Breakdown of the Muslim Community in Italy

Country of origin	Total in thousands	Percentage of Muslims	Percentage of immigrants
Albania	115,755	26.5	9.2
Algeria	12,381	2.8	1.0
Bangladesh	14,767	3.4	1.2
Bosnia	10,399	2.4	0.8
Egypt	28,264	6.5	2.2
Iran	6,042	1.4	0.5
Italian converts	10,000 (est.)	2.3	—
Morocco	146,491	33.6	11.7
Other Yugoslav	10,000 (est.)	2.3	0.8
Pakistan	13,434	3.1	1.1
Senegal	37,413	8.6	3.0
Somalia	7,000	1.6	0.6
Tunisia	44,044	10.1	3.5
Turkey	6,348	1.5	0.5
Total	**4322,8**		

Source: National Statistical Bureau. Legal residents. Unofficial data by Caritas di Roma put the numbers higher, as shown in Table 4.2.

from former colonies (different from many European countries such as France, Britain, Holland, and Portugal).

SECTARIAN DIFFERENCES

The absolute majority of Italy's Muslim population (about 98 percent) is Sunni. There is also a Shi'a community, which includes 6,000 Iranians (although many of them came to Italy as students and decided to remain because of the Iranian revolution), some Lebanese, more recently some Pakistanis, and some Italians. The community has its own halls of prayers and is particularly well organized in Rome. It has close links with the Iranian embassy in Rome and in the Vatican. There is also a significant Shi'a community in Naples, with an active group of converts, who publish a Muslim review in Italian, *Il Puro Islam*. There are also Shi'a groups in Milan and elsewhere.

Table 4.2
Unofficial Estimates

Country of origin	Total in thousands
Albania	137,748
Algeria	14,733
Bangladesh	17,573
Bosnia	12,375
Egypt	33,637
Iran	7,190
Italy	—
Morocco	174,324
Other Yugoslav	12,375
Pakistan	15,986
Senegal	44,521
Somalia	8,330
Turkey	7,554
Total	**484,346**

Source: Unofficial data by Caritas di Roma.

An Ismaili group is also present in Italy, as are faiths that initially derived from Islam but are not considered Islamic by orthodox Muslims, such as the Baha'i and the Ahmadiyya. The Baha'is now consider themselves as totally separate from Islam, with their own holy book, and as one of the divinely revealed religions, similar to Abrahamic faiths.

SOCIOECONOMIC PROFILE

There has been no systematic study of the socioeconomic profile of Muslims in Italy. Generally, the educational and income levels of earlier immigrants, such as Egyptians in Milan and Reggio Emilia and Iranians in different cities, are quite high, and some are economically well off. Those who arrived with this first wave of Muslim migration in Italy are well integrated in society, with a high percentage of self-employment and liberal professions. In particular, a Syrian and Jordanian-Palestinian lobby has a significant presence within the Muslim community and leadership. Many members of this group are doctors since, for some time in the 1970s and early 1980s, the Italian government had bilateral agreements granting them the right to stay in Italy as professionals after finishing their studies. They also include families and a second generation.

More recent immigrants are still characterized by a lower level of integration in the labor market, greater mobility, and a smaller number of families. A particular problem of the Italian labor market is the high percentage of irregular jobs, which is hard to calculate, but some estimate this number as embracing as much as one third of the economy in some areas, particularly in the south. *Lavoro nero* (black work: moonlighting) is found more frequently among immigrants. This group of immigrant workers often lacks legal work and resident permits. Many black jobs are seasonal and are found in areas like agriculture, textiles, and tourism. Some of the irregular immigrants are involved in the criminal economy. In the absence of statistical data, it seems that many irregular and clandestine workers come from Muslim countries close to Italy, especially Morocco, but also Albania, Tunisia, and Turkey.

Regional differences for immigrants are increasing owing to the good economic performance of the north. In 1999, 75 percent of new employment for foreign workers was in the northeast, Lombardia, and the center. In the Veneto region alone in 1999, one tenth of new hires were immigrants; in unskilled jobs, the rate was as high as one fifth nationwide. In fact, 29.2 percent of immigrants were employed in commerce, restaurants, and bars and 23.8 percent in the metal and mechanical industry. These two sectors employ more than half of the immigrant workers, followed by the construction industry (12.6 percent), chemical and leather industry (8.7 percent), and textile and transports (both 5.5 percent). Many female workers have domestic jobs. According to unofficial estimates, of a total of 1,250,214 legal foreign residents, only 385,091 are female. The percentage of females is quite low among Muslims, with the exception of Somalis, although ratios have recently been changing somewhat.

MUSLIM ORGANIZATIONS

As in other European countries, Muslim organizations in Italy cover a wide spectrum, from essentially religious to cultural, social, and political. But these distinctions are only relative, and most organizations perform functions that cut across these lines. For example, mosques are religious organizations, but they also perform social and even political functions. Nevertheless, for the sake of clarity, the following distinctions will be made.

Religious Organizations: Mosques

The mosque is the central place for practicing Islam, the most important physical manifestation of Islam's progressive emergence in the Italian public sphere, and the focal point for the symbolic battles between Islam's followers and its opponents—where cultural tensions *about* Islam are manifested. The organization and development of Islam in Italy have been along the same lines as in other European countries, but the pace has been more rapid. Thus, in 1970, Italy had only one mosque, a small prayer hall in Rome. Today, there are 130 to 150 places of worship, 15 of which can be considered major Islamic centers. The number is even higher if the less structured, rather "makeshift," places of prayer are also included. In fact, there are only three purpose-built mosques, recognizable by their structures such as the dome and minarets. The first is the great mosque of Monte Antenne in Rome, which was officially inaugurated in June 1995, although it had been in operation for some time before that. The mosque of al-Rahman (the Merciful) in Milan has been active since 1988 and is the symbolic nucleus around which the activities of the Islamic Center of Milan—one of the most important and influential Muslim institutions in Italy—are organized. The oldest is the mosque of Omar in Catania, which was inaugurated in 1980. This mosque has a rather peculiar history, since it resulted from the enterprising spirit of a non-Muslim lawyer (whose family name, ironically, is Papa, that is, "Pope") and Libyan financing.

The mosques often cater to one particular ethnic group. Because they are so numerous, Moroccans have more mosques. Other mosques are built by large groups such as Muslim associations or transnational organizations, including the Rabita al-Alam al-Islami, which built the mosque in Rome. At times, mosques serve a diverse community, as when there is only one mosque in a town. However, once the size of a particular ethnic group increases, it tends to build its own mosque.

Sufi Brotherhoods

Next to the mosques, various Sufi brotherhoods are significant religious organizations. Nevertheless, the term "brotherhood" (*tariqa*) should not necessarily be applied together with the term "Sufism," in the sense of the mystic tendency of Islam. Several self-defined Sufis, particularly among converts, are not members of any brotherhood, at least not in a "spiritual" way. By contrast, some brotherhoods are more popular with immigrant mystic circles.

In the case of some communities, such as the Senegalese, the brotherhoods are more important than the mosque. But in general, all the brotherhoods, even when their members attend prayers at the mosques, tend to have separate organizations and places of worship. The Senegalese brotherhood of the Murides is the largest in Italy, and most Senegalese belong to it. However, this brotherhood is more a solidarity network than a Sufi group in the proper spiritual sense of the term.[12] In all other cases, brotherhoods are composed mainly of converts, for whom mysticism is one of the main attractions of Islam.[13]

Among the brotherhoods, there are the following: the Burhaniyya, an Egyptian *tariqa* that has its European center in Germany, and the Italian *zawiya* in Rome; three different branches of the Naqshbandiyya, among which is the well organized group of *shaykh* Nazim; the Darqawiyya, which has a small militant (and radical) group called the Murabitun, which has members in different countries of Europe, from Britain to Spain; the Ahmadiyya Idrissiyya, which has an active network that is also the origin of the organization *Comunitá Religiosa Islamica*/Islamic Religious Community (COREIS); and there are members of the Alawiyya school. The followers of the Alawiyya school are divided into two groups: one that follows the teachings of the main branch based in Algeria, and the other formed in Italy, which follows the teachings of Fritjof Schuon. The Turkish group of Jerrahi-Halveti is also active in Italy, and there are some members of the Tidjaniyya, which is divided into two branches: one of Arab origin and the other from Senegal, whose members, like those of the Murides, are mainly immigrant.

Political and Religious Movements

Islamic movements get more media attention but are not necessarily better organized. Principal religious movements active in other European countries are also present in Italy, including the Tablighi Jama'at. It has expanded considerably throughout Europe and is also present in Italy, although to a lesser degree compared with some other countries. It leads some mosques, particularly in the north.

Among the transnational movements, the Muslim Brotherhood (Ikhwan al-Muslimun) is very important, but more as an ideological force than a tightly organized structure. Several leaders of the (Union of Muslim Students in Italy (USMI) and the Union of Islamic Communities and Organizations in Italy (UCOII) are linked to it, mainly because of a "generational conjuncture": They belong to the first generation of organizers of Italian Islam, who arrived in the 1970s as students in different universities, where they formed the first Islamic groups. A small group of Milli Görüs is also active among the Turks.

With some exceptions, what seems to bind Muslims together are common "cultural tendencies," such as the *salafiyya*, rather than the structured movements. For example, those Muslims who are attracted to the *salafiyya* interpretation of Islam come together because of shared ideological and cultural affinity in a rather informal fashion rather than through the activities of organized networks. Nevertheless, a variety of organized groups, with both internal and international links, are active in mosques and other institutions.

In Italy, as in other countries, movements such as the *Jama'at-I-Islami* and other Islamist movements active in the immigrants' countries of origin are present within the Muslim community. However, their presence takes the form more of ideological support than of extensive and organized networks as sometimes is portrayed in the press and even in intellectual discourses on the phenomenon of Islamism.[14]

Islamic Organizations and Institutions

From the institutional point of view, the most important social actors are those trying to act as representatives of Islam at the national level, in dealing with Italian institutions. The main organizations are the following:

1. The Italian Islamic Cultural Center (*Centro Islamico Culturale d'Italia*). This is the institution behind the monumental mosque of Monte Antenne in Rome. The center existed since 1966, but the project to build the great mosque took shape only in 1974, during King Faisal's state visit to Italy. The Rome municipality donated 30,000 square meters of land in an area near the fashionable neighborhood of Parioli. At this time, Muslim immigration to Italy was just beginning; thus, the principal reasons for building the mosque were political, strategic, and symbolic. From Italy's perspective, this was especially due to the oil price revolution of 1973 and its strategic, political, and financial consequences. But from the Muslims' perspective, the symbolic dimension was crucial: The official inauguration of the center, in June 1995, which had been widely announced in Muslim (particularly Arab) media, was portrayed to be, symbolically, an important historical event—the establishment of a mosque in the very center of Christianity.

The center's political dimension is predominant. Indeed, given its size compared with other mosques, its social and cultural activities are fairly limited. It could be defined as representing diplomatic or state Islam, especially since it is managed by a council formed of ambassadors of Islamic states. Saudi Arabia exerts the greatest influence over it through financing its operations. Indeed, presently Saudi Arabia directly leads it. This financing is channeled through the intermediary of the *Rabita al-Alam al-Islami* (League of the Islamic World). The center has little to do with the world of Muslim immigrants, although it serves as the main place of worship in the Italian capital. It is not really on the same wavelength with Muslim immigrants, who go there for Friday prayers but perform daily prayers in other mosques, located in suburbs where they live and with which they have greater spiritual or cultural affinity. Nevertheless, the Islamic Cultural Center does not hide its ambition to represent Italian Islam, on both political and organizational levels.

2. The Union of the Islamic Communities and Organizations in Italy

(*Unione delle Comunitá e delle Organizazioni Islamiche in Italia*; UCOII).
Founded in 1990, this is an umbrella organization that tries to consolidate
a number of social religious institutions. The UCOII is also the organization that interacts most actively with the mass media. It promoted the
first agreement project *(intesa)* between the Muslim community and the
Italian state for the purpose of legally regulating the presence of Islam
in Italy.

Among the founders of the UCOII, there are two organizations that,
while part of it, continue their own activities: First is the Islamic Center
of Milan, founded in 1977, which is one of the oldest and most influential
in the country. It is often in opposition to the Rome center, which is
considered to represent official Islam. The Milan center, by contrast,
claims to represent popular and "real" Islam and sometimes presents an
oppositional and radical profile. Second is the *Union of Muslim Students
in Italy (Unione degli Studenti Musulmani in Italia)*. Founded in 1971, this
is the oldest of the Italian Muslim networks. But its importance has been
eroding as the number of students compared with immigrant workers
has been declining. Nevertheless, so far, most Muslim community leaders have emerged from the ranks of its membership. Of course, this may
change as the second generation of immigrants comes of age.

3. There are other Muslim organizations, including some developed
exclusively by converts. One is COREIS, which has begun to play a more
important role, especially regarding efforts to negotiate an agreement
with the state. This enhanced profile has been due partly to recent substantial Saudi financial aid and acceptance of one of the organization's
representatives on the board of the Islamic Cultural Center of Rome in
2000. It is particularly active in the cultural field; it has no link with the
Muslim immigrant community and seeks none.

4. A new umbrella body, which is supposed to federate all the others,
is the Islamic Council of Italy (*Consiglio Islamico d'Italia*). Formed in 1999,
after some initial setbacks, it was re-created in 2000. It is composed
mainly of the members of the Islamic Cultural Center of Italy and the
UCOII, in order to become the official representative of the Muslim community in dealing with the Italian state. COREIS has refused to join this
new umbrella organization, and polemics among the two bodies are
harsh, with each claiming to be *the* representative of Islam in Italy. In
light of these divergences, it is difficult to foresee the future role of this
institution.

In addition to various centers and groups that constitute the panorama
of organized Islam, also important is what could be called the 'silent
majority' of Islam. It is little or not at all organized and can best be
described as "sociological Islam." It cannot be found in the above-
mentioned networks. Rather, it is organized at local levels within associations with limited interests and often more along ethnic than religious

lines. This Islam is less politicized and less visible. However, it is equally, and perhaps even more, important for the future evaluation of Italian Islam.

THE AGREEMENT PROJECT OR *INTESA*

The legal recognition of religions in Italy by the state implies a system of agreements between it and legally recognized bodies representing different religious communities. For historical reasons, the Catholic church enjoys a special and privileged treatment on the basis of the *Concordato*, signed for the first time in 1929 during the Fascist period, later incorporated in Article 7 of the Constitution of 1948 and revised in 1984. All other religions, if they want to be included in the system of recognition that offers various juridical and economic advantages, have to sign an agreement (*intesa*) with the state. The system of agreements began to be effective in 1984. So far, several minorities have signed an *intesa*: the Waldensian-Methodist church (in Italy united in the same organizational body), the Adventist church, the Assemblies of God, the Union of Jewish Communities, the Baptist church, and the Lutheran church. The Union of Buddhists and the Jehova's Witnesses also signed an *intesa* with the Italian government in March 2000, but they have not yet received the needed ratification by Parliament.

Since the beginning of the 1990s, the Italian Muslim community has been trying to negotiate an agreement with the state in order to gain legal recognition.[15] In many respects, this Muslim demand, in principle, is legitimate. Their numbers certainly justify reaching such an agreement, since much smaller communities have successfully negotiated similar agreements. But concluding an *intesa* is not, juridically, a *duty* of the state but always a bilateral agreement with a particular religious community. The state has no obligation and can discuss—in many ways, impose— the timing and contents of an agreement. In other words, signing an agreement is a political decision. In this sense, the Muslims' request is also politically legitimate since *realpolitik* counts, and it is neither possible nor sensible to leave it out of consideration in deciding on this matter. This is true, in a certain sense, also in terms of "foreign policy." As with the donation of land for the construction of a mosque in Rome, it is probable that the legal recognition of Islam by the Italian government would be very much appreciated by Muslim (particularly Arab) countries and could be useful in terms of achieving Italy's foreign policy objectives. However, there are some aspects of Italian Islam that make reaching such an agreement more problematic than in the case of other religions:

- The most significant stumbling block is the fact that most Muslims are not Italian citizens. They are immigrants who, at some point, hope to return to their countries of origin, although they may never do so. This lack of citizenship should not be an insurmountable barrier to negotiate an agreement with the Muslim community in Italy, since other religious groups, such as the Lutherans, already have reached such agreements with the state, although most members are not Italian but foreign legal residents. The fact remains, however, that most of the agreements are with long-established communities, like the Jews, who have lived in Italy since pre-Christian times. Some more recent agreements, by contrast, have been signed with religious communities whose members arrived in Italy much more recently but who have nevertheless been in the country for a longer period than the Muslims.

- The number of Italian converts to Islam and other Muslim citizens is still relatively small. The fact that Muslims do not yet represent a powerful political group reduces the urgency of reaching an agreement with them.

- Cultural differences, notably the use of Arabic as the principal medium of religious expression and intra-Muslim communication, enhance the alien image of Islam. The identification of Islam with problems linked to immigration is also a peculiarity that plays a role in making Islam appear more "alien" than other religions.

- The fact that some of the financing for Muslim institutions, including mosques, comes from other Muslim countries contributes to this "outsider" image of Muslims, even for those who have acquired Italian citizenship.

- Other contributing factors are the recent character of Italian Islam and its weak level of organization, its lack of cohesion, the lack of adequate public awareness of Islam and the negative nature of such awareness where it exists, and the persistence of Islam's image as an enemy.

Regarding the last point, both popular sentiment and institutional attitudes in some cases tend to treat Islam as an enemy against which defenses should be built. The implication of this attitude, on the part of some parliamentarians—even if not openly expressed—is that few legal privileges should be given to the Muslims, so as not to deprive the authorities of weapons that they might need to protect the country against the disruptive potential of the Islamic presence. Considering that the Ministry of Interior, which deals with security matters, is also in charge of issues related to religion, the unwillingness to lower the guard is even stronger. No doubt, because of the presence of some radical elements within Italy's Muslim community, a degree of prudence is necessary and justified. However, if some groups of Algerians, Palestinians, or others need to be kept under observation, this should not hinder legal recognition of the religious life of all Muslims in Italy.

Indeed, Muslims are not "in essence" different from others, although their presence poses a problem quantitatively greater than that of other religious minorities. To overcome these barriers, it is necessary that the question of the juridical (and political) treatment of the presence of Muslim minorities be *de-Islamized*. It is also time to stop viewing Muslims as a special case, besides specific issues discussed earlier. Doing so would have positive effects. In particular, it would reduce public suspicion of Muslims, which at present feeds the arguments of radicals on both sides.

COMMUNALISM VERSUS INTEGRATION

The level of communalist tendencies within Italy's Muslim population is relatively low, for two reasons: (1) the lack of major centers of Muslim concentration and (2) the lack of any special policies to promote multiculturalism, which, at times, has the contrary effect of promoting a sense of being different and thus encouraging communalism. Yet, the level of acceptance of Islam by Italian society, that is, Muslims' level of integration in Italy's social and political fabric, is also not particularly high. This is due partly to the fact that, although issues of immigration are still viewed more in terms of security, illegal work, and the like, rather than in cultural and religious terms, recently anti-Muslim statements and writings have been increasing, including by some church leaders, such as Cardinal Giacomo Biffi in Bologna in September 2000.

This does not mean that there is an "official" anti-Muslim position in the Catholic Church. On the contrary, many different positions can be found. The unofficial position, particularly at the Vatican level (Pontifical Council for the Inter-Religious Dialogue), is quite open. For instance, on the question of the mosque in Rome, the Vatican has been unofficially consulted, and the response has been positive. Generally, different attitudes toward Islam can be found both in the Catholic hierarchy (the positions expressed and the texts written by Cardinal Carlo Marja Martini of Milan or Cardinal Marco Cè of Venice are very different from the one by Cardinal Biffi) and in the Catholic associations. The Caritas network, for instance, plays an important social role in policies concerning immigrants, and its positions are much more along the line drawn by the influential statements of Cardinal Martini.

It is possible to find harsh opinions about Islam inside lay circles. For example, the mosque of Monte Antenne in Rome has been perceived by some as a sort of cultural nemesis, a claiming of territory and an Islamic imprinting in the center of Christianity. A further example is the book

Pluralismo, multiculturalismo e estranei by Giovanni Sartori, a political scientist at Columbia University in New York, USA, which was published in 2000 and has been widely discussed in Italy: Ostensibly a critical essay on multiculturalism, it tends to popularize superficial and uninformed anecdotal "knowledge" on Islam. The violent anti-Muslim "crusade" of the northern secessionist party, the Lega Nord, and of its leader, Umberto Bossi, has also contributed to the growth of anti-Islam and, in general, xenophobic feelings in Italy.

In fact, for the first time, a party, the Northern League, has decided openly to use the Muslim presence to advance its political goals. Examples of the league's anti-Muslim activities include a campaign against the project of building a small mosque in the city of Lodi, near Milan (in October 2000, during a rally to protest against this effort, banners were boasting of having shed pig's urine on the ground indicated as the possible place for the mosque); a daily misinformation campaign in the party's daily newspaper, *La Padania*; a rally called "Stop Islam" in Verona, during which the party intended to insult Muslims by portraying Muhammad as vicious and lascivious (the rally was cancelled at the very last moment because of the insistence of the league's political ally, Silvio Berlusconi); and the initiative taken in November 2000 by a league mayor in Rovato, near Brescia, to prevent non-Catholics from approaching the churches beyond fifteen meters, in "response" to the impossibility of non-Muslims entering mosques in some Muslim countries—both an illegal and an inapplicable initiative, but a good symbol of this campaign. Later, this act was denounced and declared to be in violation of national laws.

INVOLVEMENT IN THE POLITICAL PROCESS

The level of the Muslim community's involvement in the political process, at both the local and the national levels, is extremely low, largely because of the small number of Italian citizens of Muslim faith—perhaps a total of no more than 50,000 people. Some Muslim activists, mostly converts, have tried to become more involved in local politics, especially in Milan. But so far, their activities have not gone much further than making statements to the press, declaring a desire to found an Islamic party, or asking for a mosque in exchange for the Muslim vote—a Muslim vote that practically does not exist; and there is no institution that can prove that it can influence that vote if it indeed existed. In fact, the principal political activity of the Muslim community at the national level is focused on reaching the *intesa* with the Italian government and then lobbying for it. At the local level, the main objectives are concerned with primary needs such as obtaining places of worship and some form of cultural recognition.

THE MUSLIM COMMUNITY'S LINKS WITH THE ISLAMIC WORLD

As in most other European countries, Muslims in Italy have different kinds of links with their countries of origin as well as with other Muslim countries and some transnational Muslim institutions. However, in general, Italian Muslims' level of involvement in the politics of their countries of origin is less intense than that of other European Muslims, partly because of the lack of a long colonial relationship between Italy and Muslim states.

A number of groups viewed as extremist, particularly from the Middle Eastern and North African countries, have some sympathizers within Italy's Muslim community. However, their numbers are not significant, and their influence over the Muslim population is highly exaggerated. Meanwhile, Italian Muslims do not seem to have much influence on the character and direction of Italy's policies toward Islamic countries.

CONCLUSION AND OUTLOOK

Despite the fact that issues related to Islam's political and legal position in Italy generate the most passionate reactions and debates on the part of both the Muslim leadership and professional observers, it is the social and cultural implication of Islam's presence in Italy that is becoming increasingly important for Italian society.

As shown in this chapter, Islam in Italy is still a recent phenomenon. But owing to media coverage and its perception by the public, it is rapidly becoming an important element in the country's social, cultural, religious, and political life and is affecting debate on these issues. In a sense, these reactions to Islam oblige the Muslims to become more active in the public space than they are either willing or able to be. Thinking about the Muslims' role is still in its initial stages, but new developments are visible. In particular, it is becoming apparent that the second generation of Muslims, who are becoming more active in Muslim associations, will play an important role in shaping public attitudes toward Islam. Indeed, it is this new generation that seems to have the ability to change the widely held view of Islam as an alien factor external to Italian realities. Because this second generation, together with the Italian converts, plays such a central role in the Muslim cultural process, in the next few years, it may cause a dramatic evolution of Islam and of how it is viewed.[16]

NOTES

1. See Felice Dassetto and Albert Bastenier, *Europa: nuova frontiera dell'Islam* [Europe: The new frontier of Islam] (Rome: Edizioni Lavoro, 1988).

2. See Gilles Kepel, *Les banlieues de l'islam* [The suburbs of Islam] (Paris: Seuil, 1987).

3. Jørgen Nielsen, *Muslims in Western Europe*, 2nd ed. (Edinburgh: Edinburgh University Press, 1995); and Felice Dassetto, *La construction de l'islam européen. Approche socio-anthropologique* [The construction of European Islam. A socio-anthropological approach] (Paris: L'Harmattan, 1996). For a synthesis and an interpretation, see also Wasif Shadid and Sjoerd van Koningsveld, *Religious Freedom and the Position of Islam in Western Europe* (Kampen: Kok Pharos, 1995). For recent collections of essays on different situations, see Wasif Shadid and Sjoerd van Koningsveld (eds.), *Muslims in the Margin: Political Responses to the Presence of Islam in Western Europe* (Kampen: Kok Pharos, 1996); Gerd Nonneman, Tim Niblock, and Bogdan Szajkowski (eds.), *Muslim Communities in the New Europe* (Reading: Ithaca Press, 1996); and Steven Vertovec and Ceri Peach (eds.), *Islam in Europe: The Politics of Religion and Community* (London/New York: Macmillan/St. Martin's Press, 1997).

4. Stefano Allievi (ed.), *L'occidente di fronte all'islam* [The West faces Islam] (Milan: Franco Angeli, 1996).

5. Georg Simmel, *Sociologia* (Milan: Edizioni di Comunità, 1989), 580.

6. It has been calculated that since Italy's unification (1861), almost 30 million people have migrated abroad, and still 5 million Italian citizens live outside the country.

7. Stefano Allievi and Felice Dassetto, *Il ritorno dell'islam. I musulmani in Italia* [The return of Islam. Muslims in Italy] (Rome: Edizioni Lavoro, 1993).

8. See Francesco Gabrieli, *Storici arabi delle crociate* [Arab historians of the Crusades] (Turin: Einaudi, 1987).

9. See Allievi and Dassetto, *Il ritorno dell'islam*, 114.

10. The estimate of Caritas (Caritas di Roma, *Immigrazione. Dossier statistico 2000*, Rome: Anterem, 2000) is that these two categories represent 19 percent of the total presence, which should be added to the previous number.

11. See Stefano Allievi, *Les convertis à l'islam. Les nouveaux musulmans d'Europe* [The converts of Islam. The new Muslims of Europe] (Paris: L'Harmattan, 1998), 66. Muslim and journalistic sources give a higher number.

12. See Ottavia Schmidt di Friedberg, *Islam, solidarietà e lavoro. I muridi senegalesi in Italia* [Islam, solidarity and work. The Senegales Mourids in Italy] (Turin: Fondazione Agnelli, 1994).

13. Allievi, *Les convertis à l'islam*, and "Social Compass," in *Conversions to Islam in Europe*, Vol. 46, no. 3, 2000.

14. Stefano Allievi, David Bidussa, Paolo Naso, *Il libro e la spada. La sfida dei fondamentalismi* [The book and the sword. The challenge of fundamentalisms] (Turin: Claudiana, 2000).

15. On the question of the *intesa* and the juridical problems linked to it, see particularly Stefano Allievi, *"Un'intesa per l'islam italiano?"* [An agreement for Italian Islam?], *Il Mulino* 5 (1996): 985–998; Stefano Allievi, "Muslim Organizations and Islam-State Relations: The Italian Case," in Shadid and van Koningsveld, *Muslims in the Margin*, 182–201; Silvio Ferrari (ed.), *L'islam in Europa. Lo statuto giuridico delle comunità musulmane* [Islam in Europe. The juridical condition of Muslim communities] (Bologna: Il Mulino, 1996); and Silvio Ferrari (ed.), *I musulmani in Italia. La condizione giuridica delle comunità islamiche* [Muslims in

Italy: The juridical condition of the Islamic community] (Bologna: Il Mulino, 2000).

16. All the Muslim reviews, and efforts to create one, have been made by converts. Their role is decisive in publishing and translating Muslim books, including the Qur'an.

5

Islam in the Benelux Countries

Nico Landman

INTRODUCTION

In May 2000, the Dutch Minister of Metropolitan Affairs, Rogier van Boxtel, announced the introduction of a training program by Dutch educational authorities for imams coming from Islamic countries to serve Netherlands' Muslim communities. The program lasts six months and includes instruction in Dutch language, social and political institutions, and way of life. The training will be obligatory for all imams who apply for residence and work permits. This initiative is a significant stage in the evolution of Dutch Islam because it aims to reduce its "alien character."

During the last twenty-five years, Muslims have built mosques and Islamic centers whose religious leaders and instructors have come mostly from each community's country of origin. During this period, an increasing number of Muslims have been born in the Netherlands and have Dutch as their mother tongue, while the community's religious leadership still lacks an adequate knowledge of the Dutch language, culture, and society.

The Dutch authorities view this situation as anomalous and believe that religious leaders should come from within the Dutch Muslim communities and be trained locally.[1] Meanwhile, imams recruited from abroad should be made familiar with Dutch language and society. Many second-generation Muslims, too, do not favor "imported imams" with whom they can communicate only through an interpreter and who are not educated enough to answer their specific questions related to their situation as a Muslim minority living in a secular environment. The established Muslim organizations, however, are skeptical about the government's real intentions.

Debate about the necessary qualifications of religious leaders reflects two facts (1) the change, at the turn of the twenty-first century, of Islam in the Netherlands from the religion of an immigrant community to the religion of Dutch citizens; (2) the dual nature of Dutch Islam, characterized by a generation born and raised in the Netherlands and developing a new form of Islam influenced by the realities of the Dutch society and an old religious infrastructure that retains a foreign flavor.

The same process is observable in Belgium. Through an ongoing process of adaptation and naturalization, a "transplanted Islam" is becoming an "implanted Islam." Here, too, this change is the result of the emergence of a new generation of Muslims who are self-educated in Islamic issues and are critical of the old institutions.[2] In short, Muslim communities in Holland and Belgium are experiencing generational and other forms of transformation as a result of interaction between their inherited cultures and identities and their secular environments.

IMMIGRATION, ETHNIC, AND ECONOMIC PROFILE

In the first half of the twentieth century, some Muslims from the Dutch colonies in the Indonesian archipelago came to the Netherlands as students and domestic workers. In 1932, they established the Netherlands' first Muslim organization in The Hague, the Indonesian Islamic Association. After the Indonesian independence, more Muslims from the archipelago, including seventy families from the Moluccas, settled in the Netherlands.[3]

The Surinamese Muslims came in the 1950s. Their numbers increased in the 1970s after the Dutch government announced that the colony would become independent. By the end of 1975, there were 188,000 Surinamese in the Netherlands. Surinamese Muslims' ethnic roots are to be found in the Indian subcontinent and in Java. These groups were overrepresented in the migration wave of 1974 and 1975.

The largest wave of Muslim immigration to the Netherlands occurred in the 1960s and consisted of workers from Turkey and Morocco. Unlike the Surinamese immigrants, who came with their families, the first wave of Turkish and Moroccan immigrants were single male laborers, because they expected to return home after a short stay. By the early 1970s, many of these workers decided to prolong their stay and were joined by their families, a fact that rendered the option of returning home less attractive. Presently, most Turkish and Moroccan immigrants return home only to be buried.

Table 5.1
Ethnic Profile of Muslims in the Netherlands

Country of origin	Immigrant population	Percentage of Muslims	Number of Muslims
Turkey	299,662	95	284,679
Morocco	252,493	98	247,443
Suriname	296,984	12	35,638
Iraq	30,002	95	28,502
Somalia	27,421	95	26,050
Iran	21,790	80	17,432
Pakistan	15,582	97	15,115
Afghanistan	15,811	95	15,020
Egypt	13,635	90	12,272
Other			48,000
Total			**730,150**

Source: National Office of Statistics, http://www.cbs.ne.

The third wave of Muslim immigrants consisted of political refugees fleeing revolutions and civil wars. After the 1979 Islamic revolution in Iran, members of opposition movements successfully acquired asylum. Other refugees came from Lebanon, Iraq, Afghanistan, the former Yugoslavia, and Somalia. These refugees initially hoped to return home, but continued strife and bleak economic prospects in their countries of origin have reduced their chances of return. Another type of Muslim immigrant is the student who stays in the Netherlands after completing his or her studies and often obtains residency permit by marrying a Dutch citizen. Finally, there is a group of Dutch converts to Islam, whose number is estimated at 5,000. This group is highly visible because some of its members play important roles in Muslim organizations, especially as facilitators in communication between Muslim organizations and Dutch authorities. The first Dutch were converted to Islam in the 1950s and 1960s by the Ahmadiyya sect. Later, conversions have resulted from friendships and marriages with Muslims.

The total number of Muslims in the Netherlands is estimated at more than 700,000, the overwhelming majority of whom are of Turkish or Moroccan origin (see Table 5.1). This number would be higher if the third-generation Muslims were included in the estimate. But the National Office for Statistics does not include this group, because it continues to base its calculations on the country of birth of parents or grandparents.

Table 5.2
Ethnic Profile of Muslims in Belgium

Country of origin	Muslims in Belgium, 1990
Turkey	99,000
Morocco	164,900
Algeria	12,400
Tunisia	8,300
Pakistan	1,500
Other	3,300
Total	**289,400**

Source: Felice Dassetto, ed., Islam en Belgique et en Europe: Facettes et questions. Facettes de l'islam belge (Louvain-la-Neuve: Academia Bruylant, 1997).

Nor does it include Dutch converts, because it assumes that the number of converts equals that of those who stop being Muslim.[4] Based on this method of calculation, in 1999, the total number of Muslims in the Netherlands was estimated to be 730,000, or 4.6 percent of the total population. The real figure could be much higher for two reasons: (1) The third generation is not included if both parents were born in the Netherlands; (2) the percentage of Muslims among the Surinamese, estimated to be 12 percent, may be as high as 21 percent. Thus, a figure of 800,000 for Muslims is not unrealistic.

In Belgium, too, labor migration from Morocco and Turkey in the 1960s is the main source of Muslim presence. The ethnic profile of Belgium's Muslim population is less heterogeneous (see Table 5.2). The Moroccans are more numerous than the Turks, and together they constitute 81 percent of the Muslim population. Other Muslims originate from other Maghreb countries and from Pakistan. According to Dassetto, in 1990, the number of Muslims in Belgium was around 289,400.[5] Owing to natural growth and net external migration, this number may have risen to about 350,000 in 2000, and some sources put the number at 400,000.[6]

GEOGRAPHIC DISTRIBUTION AND SOCIOECONOMIC PROFILE

As immigrant workers, the Moroccans and Turks in the Netherlands and Belgium have similar socioeconomic profiles. They live predominantly in industrial areas in and around large cities. More than 42 percent of Muslims in Belgium live in Brussels and other French-speaking industrial cities of the south. Recently, significant numbers of Turks have been settling in the Flemish cities of Antwerp and Gent and in regions like Limbourg. In the Netherlands, Amsterdam, Rotterdam, and The Hague have the largest concentration of Muslims.

The educational level of the immigrants is low. Of the Moroccan immigrants in the 1970s, almost 50 percent were illiterate, only 11 percent had finished primary school, and only 4 percent had received secondary education. Even if they were better educated in their countries of origin, this was hardly noticed because they were recruited for unskilled work in factories and in agriculture. In the 1980s and 1990s, when the process of mechanization of the Dutch and Belgian industries drastically reduced the need for unskilled workers, these immigrants were among the first to lose their jobs. Also, a large number of them stopped working for health reasons. The social security system provides them with an income, but they clearly belong to the poor classes and are overrepresented in depressed urban neighborhoods.

Nevertheless, an increasing number of "ethnic businesses," like Islamic butchers, groceries, travel agencies, etc., have arisen and have created new economic opportunities for these communities. The second generation of Muslims educated in Dutch and Belgian schools entered the labor market better equipped. Still, the number of Muslims in managerial positions and in professions that require advanced studies, such as medicine, is low. Of more concern to the host countries are young male Moroccans and Turks who leave school without a diploma or any technical skills and limited employment prospects. A combination of unfinished training, inadequate language skills, and religious and racial discrimination makes their economic prospects rather bleak, leading many of them to become involved in criminal activities.

Yet, many Turkish and Moroccan Muslim youngsters in the Netherlands do complete their studies and achieve social and economic success. The same also applies to young Muslims from other ethnic communities like the Surinamese and Moluccans. The unemployment rate for the non-Western immigrant population was 14 percent in 1999, which is much higher than the Dutch average of 4 percent. Also, the younger generations from immigrant families lag behind: Whereas 7 percent of the Dutch population between fifteen and twenty-four was unemployed in 1999, the figure for non-Western immigrants was 12 percent. Nevertheless, compared with the previous year, when unemployment among this group was 18 percent, there was a remarkable improvement, which can be explained only partly by the general reduction in unemployment.[7] Examination results of non-Western immigrant children in Dutch secondary schools point in the same direction. They still score below the national average, but their results are gradually improving. In 1999, 78 percent of the immigrant children, against 90 percent of other children, in high schools passed the A-level examination, which gives access to university studies.[8] Although this is a score far below the average, the results were two points better than the year before. Muslims are gradually finding their way into higher education in the Netherlands and in Belgium. This is making the social profile of Muslims more diverse.

MUSLIM COMMUNITIES AND ORGANIZATIONS

In Belgium and in the Netherlands, the Muslim population constitutes a highly complex mosaic of communities and organizations. This complexity is the result of their diverse history of immigration, ethnic and socioeconomic characteristics, and expectations about the future. Thus, it is misleading to speak of "the Muslim community," especially since some immigrants from Muslim countries do not see themselves primarily as Muslims, nor do they organize themselves along religious lines. Many Iranians in the Netherlands openly call themselves atheist or agnostic. For many of them, the most visible expression of their group identity is not mosque or Islamic center, but leftist political organizations. The Kurds from Turkey are organized along political lines, and politics rather than religion is the focus of their activities.

Even those communities and organizations that call themselves Islamic and are involved in religious activities are divided along ethnic, sectarian, and political lines. The ethnic divisions are obvious in the mosques. In the Netherlands, most of them are controlled by Turks, Moroccans, or Surinamese. In Belgium, Moroccans and other Maghrebi Muslims built the first mosques in Brussels in the early 1970s. The Turks established their own mosques soon afterward. Core activities like the daily prayers may be almost identical in the mosques of various ethnic communities and can be attended by Muslims from different backgrounds. But the social and cultural activities usually have one specific ethnic community as their target, and the dominant language in the mosque is that of that particular community. In the Netherlands, the language of the *khutba* is Arabic in Moroccan mosques and Turkish in Turkish mosques. Suriname mosques often have Urdu-speaking imams from Pakistan. Only in a limited number of mosques is Dutch becoming the predominant language. Smaller Muslim communities, like Egyptians or Iraqis, tend to form their separate networks, but they usually join those larger mosque communities where language and cultural barriers are the lowest. Therefore, Muslims from the Arabic-speaking world join Moroccan organizations, and Indians or Pakistanis join the Surinamese institutions.

Within different ethnic groups, religious and political movements from home countries are active and often create their own networks of local organizations. International Muslim organizations have also opened offices in Belgium and the Netherlands. The Muslim World League exercises influence through the Islamic Cultural Center in Brussels. The Libyan-based Islamic Call Society opened an Islamic Center in the Dutch town of Utrecht. The Jama'at-al-Tablig first established a foothold in both countries in the early 1960s and was particularly successful in Belgium, where the movement founded twelve mosque associations between 1975 and 1985.[9] Among the Surinamese Muslims, the Barelvi movement of the Indian subcontinent controls many of the mosques. This variety of actors from different parts of the Muslim world, with different cultural backgrounds, political agendas, and loyalties, adds to the complexity of the process of Muslim community building and institutionalization in the Benelux countries.

Yet, Muslim communities share a common religious identity, a common orientation toward Islamic religious sources, and a sense of belonging to a worldwide Islamic community, the *ummah*. They are faced with similar problems and challenges in the host societies, such as racial hostility, discrimination, and socioeconomic disadvantages, plus how to remain a Muslim in a non-Muslim environment and how to respond to anti-Islamic sentiments of European societies. These shared problems tend to consolidate a sense of solidarity, which is stronger in the case of second-generation Muslims. Nevertheless, ethnic and sectarian differences still divide the Muslims and shape the character of their communities and organizations.

MUSLIMS FROM DUTCH COLONIES

The Moluccan Muslims, who came to the Netherlands in 1951, lived together in an isolated camp in the province of Friesland. In the 1960s, they moved to the small towns of Ridderkerk and Waalwijk, where most of them still live in a few neighborhoods. The Moluccan Muslim communities of these towns each have their own mosque, which were recently built with the financial help of the Dutch government. The Moluccan Muslim community still retains its specific characteristics and its internal conflicts. Their Islam originally reflected the characteristics of the Muslim Moluccan villages in the Indonesian archipelago, which was heavily influenced by local non-Islamic traditions. Even today, some of the imams advocate the practice of this indigenous Islam. Since the 1970s, orthodox and/or reformist interpretations of Islam have become more influential among them, because the younger members of the community have studied at major centers of Sunni Islam, such as the Al-Azhar in Cairo, and have become influenced by mainstream Islam. Contacts with other Muslim communities in the Netherlands have also contributed to this process. Some of the Moluccan Muslims became pupils of the Turkish-Cypriot Sufi *shaykh* Nazim al-Haqqani and started a branch of his Tariqa.[10]

The Islam of the Javanese from Suriname also contained many pre-Islamic traditions, which are still observed. The practice of these traditions creates internal divisions between those who advocate a reformist or purer form of Islam and those who jealously guard Javanese culture against what they see as "Arab" influences. One source of dispute is disagreement about the direction of the prayers (*qiblah*).[11]

Those Surinamese Muslims whose roots are in the Indian subcontinent established their network of religious associations and Islamic centers during the second half of the 1970s. A possible explanation for this rapid religious institutionalization is the fact that in Suriname they lived as a religious minority and had their religious associations. Some Muslim associations from Suriname simply continued their existence after migration to the Netherlands. Today, they control about thirty Islamic centers, most of them in the big cities, especially in The Hague. The Taibah mosque in Amsterdam, which was opened in 1985, was the first purpose-built mosque of the Surinamese Muslim community and was symbolically important.

The Surinamese of Indo-Pakistani roots are divided into two distinct groups. The largest group is Sunni, and most of their organizations have a reference to the Ahl-e Sunna wal-Jama'at in their names. They are influenced by the teachings of the Barelvi movement, characterized by the veneration of saints, the annual remembrance of their death, and deep devotion to the Prophet Muhammad. Religious leadership is in the hands of Sufi *shaykhs* or *pirs*, most of whom do not live in the Netherlands but in India, Pakistan, or the United Kingdom. They regularly visit their disciples in Holland. These Surinamese Muslims share this Barelvi tradition with some of the Pakistani communities. The largest organization emerging from these communities is the World Islamic Mission in the Netherlands (WIMN), which is controlled by the pupils of *pir* Shah Ahmad Noorani, a Pakistani religious leader who is also an influential member of the Barelvi political party in Pakistan, the Jami'at Ulama-i Pakistan. His leadership over the WIMN and the mosques associated with it was formalized in the 1980s and 1990s.

Deobandi trends are also present among this group of Surinamese. Their principal organization is the Society for the Welfare of Muslims in the Netherlands, whose main center of operation is the Taiba mosque in The Hague.[12] Another group of Suriname Indo-Pakistani Muslims belong to the Ahmadiyya movement of Mirza Ghulam Ahmad. Although this missionary movement is viewed as non-Muslim by many Sunni Ulama and institutions because of Ghulam Ahmad's claim of being a prophet, their mission to Suriname was very successful. For many Surinamese, they represent a more liberal form of Islam. The Surinamese Ahmadis have their own network of local mosques and national organizations: the Federation of Ahmadiyya Anjumans in the Netherlands.

THE NON-COLONIAL MUSLIMS

Among the immigrant workers from Turkey and Morocco, the process of community building and institutionalization of Islam has been slow and arduous. In the Netherlands, at the local level, this process started in the early 1970s and in Belgium in the late 1960s and was linked to family reunifications. The presence of families emphasized the permanent nature of their residence and enhanced their awareness of the need for religious institutions for the preservation of their religious and cultural identity and the transmission of basic Islamic teachings to next generations.

The religious institutions created by Turkish and Moroccan immigrants reflected their weak socioeconomic position. Their mosques were former shops or residential houses, makeshift prayer halls rather than purpose-built mosques. Often, these buildings were unsuitable to accommodate large numbers, had no parking space, lacked adequate facilities to perform the ritual purification (*wudu'*), and were created without the permission of municipal authorities.

Despite these poor conditions, religious communities emerged around the activities organized in mosques: the daily prayers, Qur'an courses for the young, and the observance of annual religious holidays. Many Islamic centers also served as a meeting place, mainly for male adults of the first generation. By the 1980s and 1990s, the position of most local Muslim organizations had improved considerably. A growing number of these organizations are now located in newly constructed mosques or Islamic centers or in buildings that can serve their needs for several decades. In addition to religious ceremonies and Qur'an courses, they provide language and computer training.

In the Netherlands, the number of mosques is about 390. Of these, 200 are controlled by Turks, 120 by Moroccans, 40 by Surinamese, and 30 by other Muslims. About forty of these mosques are purpose built in Turkish or Moroccan styles or in a combination of both. In Belgium, in 1996, there were about 210 mosques: about 100 in Flanders, 60 in Wallonia, and 40 in Brussels. Moroccans controlled 61 percent of Belgian mosques, and another 34 percent were Turkish. In Belgium, the majority of mosques are located in preexisting buildings, but a small number of purpose-built mosques enhance Islam's visibility.

Since the late 1970s, most Turkish Muslim organizations have become members of national umbrella organizations, which are associated with various religious and political movements in Turkey. These Turkish umbrella organizations in the Netherlands and Belgium are similar to those in Germany and gradually have become almost branches of larger Turkish organizations headquartered in Germany.[13]

The largest of these organizations is usually referred to as Diyanet

(Directorate for Religious Affairs in Ankara), the institution that administers the activities of mosques in Turkey. The directorate controls a majority of Turkish mosques in the Netherlands (about 120) and in Belgium (about 55). Most of these mosques have an imam sent and paid by Diyanet, in other words by the Turkish government. In towns with more than one Turkish mosque, the Diyanet mosque is usually the biggest and attracts the largest community. Therefore, Diyanet mosques and the organizations controlling them are often able to present themselves as the mainstream Islam and portray rival groups as sectarian or extremist.

The Milli Görüs movement, the second largest Turkish umbrella organization, is close to the Welfare party (Refah) of Necmettin Erbakan and its successor, the Virtue party (Fazilet). (Note: The party was banned in 2001.) Although they are often labeled as fundamentalist, the mosques and Islamic centers belonging to this movement are among the most successful in terms of their social and cultural activities, especially for groups other than the first generation of male immigrants. The Amsterdam branch of Milli Görüs has a very trendy association of young women engaged in lively debates on a range of social issues with both Muslims and non-Muslims.

The Süleymanli movement is more focused on the transmission of religious knowledge and mystical practices within their own rather closed communities and Islamic centers.

While the Turkish mosques were drawn into large hierarchically organized structures, the Moroccan mosques tend to be more independent or only loosely connected to national networks. In a network analysis of Moroccan organizations in the Netherlands, carried out in 2000, 64 percent of these organizations were considered as "isolated" because they did not seem to have any formal ties with national organizations.[14] Nevertheless, a Union of Moroccan Muslim Organizations in the Netherlands (UMMON), which was founded in 1978, claims to represent most Moroccan mosques. The UMMON was loyal to the Moroccan authorities and expected the imams in their mosques to pray for the Moroccan king. The Moroccan authorities cooperate with the UMMON in sending preachers during the month of Ramadan and in the selection of imams. This loyalism led to strong condemnation by left-wing opposition groups and to attempts to found "independent mosques." By the second half of the 1990s, these tensions had subsided. Similar controversies occurred among the Moroccans in Belgium where the Moroccan embassy tried to exercise some influence in the mosques.

The Islamic Cultural Center of Brussels (ICCB) played a significant role in the institutionalization of Islam in Belgium. It is located in the Parc du Cinquentenaire, was opened in 1969, and has a library, mosque, and information service. The Saudi ambassador to Belgium chairs the center's board of trustees.[15] The ICCB gets most of its funding from the Muslim

World League, an international Muslim organization based in Saudi Arabia. Until 1990, the ICCB was treated by the Belgian government as the official representative body of the Muslim community.

Some of the immigrants from the Maghreb are members of Sufi orders, and some of these orders, like the Darqawi and the Alawi, have created an informal network of sympathizers in Belgium and the Netherlands.

Perhaps the most successful organization among the Maghrebi Muslims in Belgium is the Jama'at al-Tablig, which is also active in the Netherlands. This international Islamic movement was founded between 1920 and 1940 in northern India and has its center in Nizam ud-Din near Delhi. The movement is distinguishable by its missionary method. Itinerant groups of preachers approach local Muslims, teach them basic knowledge of Islam, and prompt them to follow Islamic rules in their daily life. In Belgium between 1975 and 1985, the Jama'at al-Tablig opened twelve mosques. More importantly, their preachers visited most of the other mosques and created a large group of sympathizers, mainly among Maghrebian Muslims. The Jama'at al-Tablig was the force behind the Federation of Mosques and Islamic Associations, which was founded in 1986, prompted partly by a desire to balance the power of the ICCB.[16]

Finally, a wide variety of Muslim organizations in Belgium are associated with Islamist movements from all over the Muslim world. Some of them focus on cultural activities like charity work, education, and sports. Others publish or distribute periodicals, books, or audiocassettes, some in Arabic, and some in French. A recent study of radical Islamist publications distributed in Belgium listed publications from the Afghan Mujahidin, Hamas, the followers of the Egyptian *shaykh* Umar abd ul-Rahman, the Algerian Islamic Salvation Front and its more militant factions, and several other movements. The most important Islamist associations among the Moroccans in Belgium is al-Adl wa'l-Ihsan, led by the Moroccan *shaykh* Abd al-Salam Yassin.[17]

Religious infrastructure of Muslims in the Benelux reflects the diverging migration patterns of these communities and the internal controversies that they brought into their new countries. In recent years, however, conditions in the host societies have increasingly tended to shape the Muslims' individual lives as well as the character of Muslim organizations and the dynamics of intra-Muslim relations. Principal reasons for this shift have been the following: (1) The importance of ethnic divisions among Muslim communities has been reduced because for the second generation of Muslims, Dutch—or, in the case of Wallonia and Brussels, French—has become their native language; at school they interact with children from a variety of ethnic groups, using Dutch (or rather the Amsterdam or Rotterdam dialect).[18] (2) Various Muslim organizations, notably the Milli Görüs, have been trying to appeal to diverse ethnic groups. The Milli Görüs message focuses on being a Muslim in a Western society rather than being a Turk, and it points out that its focus is on Europe rather than on Turkey. Yet, ethnic divisions remain important. Thus, despite the efforts of the Milli Görüs, the number of non-Turkish Muslims in its rank and file has remained very limited. Moroccan, Turkish, and Surinamese youth continue to form their own groupings and develop their own life styles. Therefore, even today, those Muslim organizations that attract the younger generation are those that originated in the ethnically divided religious infrastructure of the first generation. In short, Islamic identity has not yet eliminated ethnocentric identities.

INTRA-MUSLIM INTERACTION

Muslims from various ethnic communities and their organizations do interact in many fields, sometimes as rivals for resources and recognition and sometimes as coalition partners. In the Netherlands, attempts to create a representative council of Muslim organizations started in the 1970s but so far has been unsuccessful. In the 1990s, two Islamic councils claimed to represent the Dutch Muslim communities. The first was the Islamic Council of the Netherlands, in which the Turkish Diyanet, together with the Moroccan UMMON and the Surinamese WIMN, participated. The second was the Dutch Muslim Council, which combined most of the other existing umbrella organizations.[19] In recent years, two more Muslim councils have come into being, namely, the Council of Mosques in the Netherlands and the Netherlands Islamic Council. Though intended to succeed the two existing councils and to overcome intra-Muslim rivalry, these new initiatives seem to have only increased the confusion about Muslims' representation in the Netherlands.

The mere existence of two—and now four—Muslim councils claiming to represent the Muslims was a reason for the Dutch authorities to refuse all of them a status as spokesmen for Muslims. The Dutch state does not formally recognize religions. The constitution merely mentions the freedom of religion and forbids discrimination on the basis of religion. There is no state church, nor are there any formal ties between the state and specific religious communities. However, even without formal ties, many forms of cooperation between the state and religious organizations exist. For example, this is the case when religious communities do social work that the state wants to support and when specific religious needs must be met in state-controlled institutions like prisons. In these cases, the state does need a party to negotiate with. In practice, the absence of an organization that can speak on behalf of all Muslims constitutes a serious hindrance for its institutionalization in some fields. An example is the appointment of imams in hospitals. Hospital boards are willing to appoint imams only if they are "sent" by a religious organization that can guarantee the candidate's religious credentials. Obviously, they demand that the sending organization itself enjoy sufficient legitimacy. Although some hospital boards have shown a willingness to find pragmatic solutions, the presence of two or more Islamic councils that dispute the legitimacy of the others does not create an ideal climate for establishing a better working relationship between Muslim communities and Dutch authorities.

Broadcasting is another field that is affected by complicated interaction and rivalry between various Muslim groups. The broadcasting time, which the Dutch media authorities have allotted to the Dutch Muslim Council, has for years been challenged by its rival, the Islamic Council in the Netherlands, in several court proceedings. Also, internal strife within the Dutch Muslim Council has risked the loss of broadcasting time allotted to them.[20]

In some Dutch towns, local councils of mosques have been more successful in making coordinated efforts to communicate with the authorities. The Platform of Islamic Organizations in Rotterdam has long been recognized by the municipality as an important body with which the municipality can deal effectively in order to solve problems. Areas of cooperation include town planning that involves mosques, appointment of imams in prisons in Rotterdam and its surrounding areas, and regulation of Islamic religious education in Rotterdam's public primary schools. Dutch converts have played a crucial role in attempts to overcome ethnic divisions and bring Muslims together. They usually make a strong distinction between religious and cultural aspects of the Muslim immigrants' legacy and try to find the common Islamic ground for different ethnic and cultural communities. To play such a mediating role, they need excellent diplomatic skill because a too-critical attitude toward ethnic immigrant cultures can isolate them from these communities.

In Belgium, the question of representation of Islam got a different answer. The Belgian state does officially recognize religions. The consequence of the recognition of a religious community is that the children of that community get religious instruction in public schools by teachers appointed by representatives of the religious community and who are paid by the state. The state also takes care of the salaries of religious ministers. As early as 1974, the Belgian authorities formally recognized Islam and gave the Muslim religion the same juridical status as Catholic and Protestant Christianity and Judaism. However, because Muslim communities in Belgium lacked a single institution that could speak on their behalf, the recognition led to a struggle about representation. Until 1990 the government treated the ICCB as the main representative of Muslim communities. The ICCB was allowed to recommend teachers and imams who would then be appointed by the authorities. However, the ICCB was not an institution that had grown out of the Muslim communities living in Belgium, but rather it was a creation of Muslim governments, in particular Saudi Arabia. During the 1980s, growing opposition within Belgium's Muslim communities to the ICCB cast serious doubts on its legitimacy and frustrated the effective fulfillment of their tasks.[21] In 1994, after a long and arduous process of negotiations with different Muslim organizations, the Belgian government appointed a committee of seventeen Muslims, the Executives of the Muslims in Belgium, who had the task of appointing teachers of the Islamic religion in public schools and imams in hospitals and prisons. Moreover, the committee was involved in the preparation of elections leading to the establishment of a Central Body for the Islamic Religion in 1999.[22] This organization has sixty-eight members (fifty-one are directly elected and they then appoint seventeen others) and is now recognized as the formal representative organization of Muslims in Belgium, under whose authority the religious instruction at schools and the appointment of imams are organized.

POLICIES OF INTEGRATION

The response of the Dutch and Belgian authorities to the emergence of Muslim communities and organizations in their respective countries was not shaped solely by local laws and policies on religious life or by the existing relations between the state and Christian churches. Rather, because the presence of Muslim communities was the result of waves of immigration, policies concerning immigration in general and how to integrate newcomers within the society also influenced the authorities' reaction to the cultural and religious needs of Muslims.

In 1983, the Dutch Parliament adopted a minorities policy, which was designed as a coordinated effort to integrate newcomers into the host society. According to this policy, an open multicultural society was to be created, in which immigrants, individually and as a group, would enjoy equal rights and opportunities with the native population. The key word of the Dutch minorities policy was "integration." The concept was defined as a process of making the immigrants an accepted part of the society while retaining their cultural identities. In debates about the nature of multicultural society, the concept of integration has a more ambivalent and vague meaning: It is associated with the immigrants' acceptance of dominant norms and values and therefore with partial abandoning of their cultural traditions, hence the ambiguity of its implications for the immigrants' collective identity.

However, it is possible to distinguish between a pluralist and an assimilationist approach to the integration of minority groups.[23] The *pluralist* approach regards society as culturally heterogeneous and allows, or even encourages, cultural and religious communities to create their own organizations and institutions. Pluralism was a strong tradition in

Dutch society especially in the 1950s, when major religious and cultural communities had their own separate institutions. Since the 1960s, this institutional communalism has been eroded, although in some social sectors, such as parochial schools, it has remained intact. From this communalist perspective, Christian Democrat politicians have argued that integration policies should give the minority communities and their organizations a role in the process of integration, because this strategy can lead to the immigrants' collective emancipation. The *assimilationist* approach stresses the equal rights and opportunities of individual citizens in the public space. Separate cultural identities are accepted but are seen as part of private life. According to this approach, separate social institutions for different cultural groups are undesirable and, in some cases, a hindrance for individual emancipation, especially in the case of women. The Dutch Liberal and Social Democrat parties support this view.

The Dutch government's policies toward minorities have elements of both approaches. Communalist elements are reflected in the following examples: Turkish and Moroccan children receive lessons in their own language and culture in primary schools; national and local authorities fund welfare institutions for immigrants; and the government financially supports the activities of immigrant organizations and accepts councils formed by these organizations as mediators between the authorities and immigrant communities. However, Dutch policies toward minorities have focused mainly on individual immigrants and on providing opportunities for them in education and in employment, regardless of their cultural background. This attitude reflects the assimilationist dimensions of the government's policies.

Since the 1990s, this focus has become stronger. However, the word "assimilation" is not used in public discourse; politicians refer to "integration."

These opposite positions are clearly observable in debates about Islamic schools. Since 1988, thirty-two Islamic primary schools have been established, which attract about 6 percent of Muslim children. In August 2000, the first Islamic secondary school was opened. The Liberals and Social Democrats have criticized this process, although they agree that the state cannot deny permission for establishing Islamic schools if legal requirements are met. They maintain that these schools are a hindrance to the immigrants' integration into the multicultural Dutch society. Their schools do not interact sufficiently with children from other cultural and religious groups. They also maintain that these schools will be "black schools," in other words schools with predominantly immigrant students. In their view, the concentration of children from weak social groups, who do not speak Dutch as their mother tongue, is a serious handicap for successful education.

Advocates of Islamic schools point out that Islamic schools are established in quarters where many schools are already "black," either for demographic reasons or because "white" families send their children elsewhere. Islamic schools are, according to them, in a better position to address specific problems of Muslim children because they provide a safe and culturally homogeneous environment in which they can develop their own identity.

Because of the paucity of objective data, it is difficult to assess the respective merits of each argument. Nevertheless, recent studies suggest that the results of Islamic schools are similar to public schools in the same quarters with similar conditions.[24] Thus, it seems that the debate on Islamic schools is essentially ideological and concerns the respective merits and disadvantages of assimilationist and communalist approaches to the integration of Muslim minorities. Currently, the assimilationist approach is dominant, and therefore if Islamic schools exist, it is despite government policies.

A study of Dutch responses to the institutionalization of Islam shows that government agencies do not have a uniform reaction to Muslim claims and community needs.[25] Pragmatic attitudes among civil servants lead to different responses in different cities or in different social fields. However, there is a tendency to combine considerations of neutrality of the state in religious matters with the assimilationist tendencies of the minority policies. Consequently, the government is sometimes more involved in the religious life of Muslim minorities than the official separation between state and church would suggest.

In Belgium, too, the state's response to Muslim cultural and religious needs is influenced by the existing relations between church and state and by public debates on immigration and multiculturalism. The multiculturalism debate in Belgium cannot be separated from the nationalist and regionalist struggles between Belgium's Dutch- and French-speaking populations. A constitutional revision in 1993 transformed the unitary Kingdom of Belgium into a federal state consisting of three regions (Flanders, Wallonia, and Brussels), with a high degree of autonomy. In Flanders, a nation-building process is taking place, in which a "Flemish people" is being created and its cultural and linguistic unity emphasized. Accordingly, the debate on multiculturalism and integration here tends to portray cultural and religious "otherness" of the immigrants as a problem. The extreme right Vlaams Blok (Flemish Block), which openly expresses its xenophobic attitudes with the slogan "eigen volk eerst" (first our own people), has been the largest political party in Flanders since 1994. In Wallonia, the cultural and linguistic identity is not as strongly stressed, and integration debates emphasize socioeconomic problems rather than cultural differences.[26]

Belgian national minority policies have since 1989 been formulated and coordinated by the Royal Commissariat for Migrant Policies, which in 1993 was replaced by the Center for Equal Opportunities and the Fight against Racism. As in the Netherlands, attempts were made to improve the position of migrants in the labor market by training programs and by improving the educational performance of their children. As in Holland, "integration" became a guiding principle for the minority policies. In Belgium, too, the ambiguity of this concept leaves room for either assimilationist or communalist interpretations. Critics of the integration policy have claimed that its implementation is highly assimilationist, especially in Dutch-speaking Flanders. For instance, the procedure to acquire Belgian nationality involves an investigation of the "will to integrate." Insufficient competence in Dutch, the absence of Dutch books or the presence of Turkish newspapers in the applicants' house, watching of Turkish television, or wearing a headscarf can lead to the rejection of the application.[27]

Paradoxically, the laws regulating relations between religion and state encourage cultural and religious communities to create their own organizations and institutions and even provide financial help from the government. Thus, in regard to religious life, the Belgian system is communalist. It recognizes the Roman Catholic Church, the Reformed Church, the Anglican Church, the Jews, and, since 1974, Islam.

Because of this system, private (free) schools are confessionally based and mostly Roman Catholic. Muslim children mostly attend public schools, but a number also go to private schools, notably those run by Catholic churches. Private schools have adopted a variety of approaches toward the question of religious education for Muslim children, ranging from exempting them from Catholic religious instruction to arranging for Islamic instruction.[28] An amendment to the Education Laws in 1978, referred to as the "Scholastic Pact," provided for religious instruction for Muslim children in public primary and secondary schools. The cost of this education is covered by the government. From 1978 to 1990, the teachers were selected by the ICCB, which was also responsible for the curriculum of Islamic instruction. Presently, the newly established Central Body for the Islamic Religion appoints the teachers. The availability of Islamic instruction in public schools may have reduced the need for separate Islamic schools in Belgium. The first and, until now, only Islamic primary school in Belgium, the Al Ghazali School, was established in 1989 by the ICCB. This initiative was in reaction to the refusal of two municipalities of Brussels to offer Islamic religious instruction. In public debates that followed, views similar to those expressed in the Netherlands were voiced. The state secretary for migrants in the region of Brussels, Vic Anciaux, declared that Islamic schools were an obstacle to Muslims' integration into the Belgian society. Interestingly, the extreme rightist Vlaams Blok did not object to Islamic schools but rather opposed the introduction of Islamic instruction in public schools. In their view, a separate Islamic school would prepare Muslim children to return to their ancestral countries.[29]

Both the Dutch and the Belgian models allow for an institutionalized religious pluralism. However, in the case of Muslims, this institutionalized pluralism is counteracted by assimilationist tendencies of the minorities policies.

INVOLVEMENT IN LOCAL POLITICS

A majority of the foreign-born Muslims now have Dutch citizenship (figures for 1999 were 66 percent of the Turks and 50 percent of the Moroccans). Their percentage has been rising since the early 1990s, when, as part of a new policy on citizenship, the procedures for naturalization were simplified. Citizenship enables Muslims to participate in municipal and national elections and to run for office. Noncitizen immigrants who have resided in the Netherlands for at least five years can also vote in municipal elections and be elected to municipal council.

In Belgium, too, the rate of naturalization has risen in the 1990s, as a result of a modification of naturalization laws. The Belgian election system does not, however, allow voting rights to non-Belgian residents.

In the last two decades, Muslim immigrants have become involved in Dutch and Belgian politics and have been elected to municipal councils and to Parliament. Because of the voting rights for non-Dutch citizens, Muslim immigrants constitute a substantial part of the electorate in some Dutch towns. In Belgium, where voting rights are restricted to Belgian citizens, this is not yet the case, but as more and more Muslims acquire Belgian citizenship, they are gradually becoming a more important electoral bloc.

In both countries, religious parties have long played a prominent role in politics. Yet, it is interesting to note that, so far, there have been no serious attempts to establish a Muslim political party. The attempts that were made were not very successful. Only in the Netherlands did a Muslim party (the Muslim Democratic party) manage to obtain one seat in a local council in a district located in the southeastern part of Amsterdam. This district has a concentration of Surinamese Muslims, and the largest mosque of the WIMN is located there. Surinamese Muslims close to the WIMN founded the party and succeeded in electing their candidate. However, this was an exceptional case. The general pattern is that immigrants with political ambitions, including Muslims, try to achieve their goal by working through the established political parties. For example, a Moroccan Muslim, Muhammad Rabbae, is a prominent member of the Dutch Green party and a member of Parliament (MP) since 1994. A Turkish Muslim, Coskun Cörüz, was an MP for the Christian Democrat party in the Netherlands. Another Moroccan, Oussama Cherribi, is a Liberal MP. Most of the other parties have their own Muslim candidates, both in national and in local councils. In Belgium, too, Muslims are gradually finding their way to the highest representative bodies. Fauzaya Talhaoui, a young woman born in Morocco, has since 1999 represented the Flemish Green party Agalev in the Belgian Parliament.

Muslim candidates are placed on the party's lists in order to attract minority votes and are seen by the general public as spokespersons for particular minority communities, even if most of them refuse to limit themselves to "minority issues." They generally do not have close links to Muslim networks. They advocate the cause of minorities within the parameters of the party's ideology and support its economic and social philosophy. The Liberal MP Cherribi has shown himself highly critical of the established Moroccan Muslim organizations and their imams.[30] The Christian Democrat Cörüz is closer to Muslim organizations and is a strong supporter of Islamic schools and state funding for the activities of Muslim organizations. However, his views are in line with the communalist ideas of the Christian Democrat party.

In short, Muslim individuals have started to participate in Dutch—and, to some extent, in Belgian politics, but they do so as individual citizens with diverse political affiliations and not as representatives of the overall Muslim community or of ethnically based Muslim groups.

LINKS TO COUNTRIES OF ORIGIN AND THE ISLAMIC WORLD

In debates regarding the integration of immigrant groups in Holland and Belgium, a recurring theme is that of the ties that the immigrants and their organizations maintain with their countries of origin. The most prevalent political view is that maintaining such ties is acceptable for the first generation of immigrants but should be reduced and ultimately eliminated in the case of succeeding generations. From an assimilationist perspective, such links are a priori undesirable because they imply a group identity, which distinguishes an ethnic community from the rest of the society. But even those sympathetic toward Muslim community-building efforts believe that these communities should become rooted in the Dutch or Belgian societies rather than being a branch of a tree that is rooted elsewhere. This view is clearly behind the continued attempts of the Dutch government to control the influx of religious leadership from the countries of origin and to create a local infrastructure to train imams.[31] In Belgium, similar concerns have led the authorities to closely supervise the emergence of the Central Body for the Islamic Religion and to refuse some candidates who were close to the Turkish Milli Görüs movement or to the Muslim brotherhood to be elected to its governing organs.

The Dutch and Belgian public is also highly distrustful of foreign influences on the Muslim communities, especially when these influences come from countries with a poor record in democracy and human rights. The authorities are justifiably afraid that violent political conflicts in the countries of origin could spill over into the Netherlands or Belgium. Moreover, developments in the Islamic world, such as the Iranian revolution, civil war in Lebanon, or the rise of the Taliban in Afghanistan, plus the reaction of some members of the Muslim community to aspects of Western—especially US—policy toward Muslim countries, adversely affect the public perception of Islam and Muslims. To illustrate, on 20 April 1986, there were demonstrations in Brussels against the US bombing of Libya. According to some analysts, the demonstrations were "a strong public statement of Islamic identity."[32] Slogans like "No to America's war politics" and "Yes to peace, no to terrorism" showed the anger of the predominantly Arab demonstrators. The media, however, focused on some small radical groups among the demonstrators, including Iranians carrying portraits of the Ayatullah Khomeini, and presented the demonstrations as proof of Islam's "fanatical" and "fundamentalist" nature.[33]

No doubt, there is a strong connection between political developments in the immigrants' countries of origin and the immigrant communities in the Netherlands and Belgium. The Turkish-Kurdish confrontation has for many years preoccupied Turkish immigrants. Political refugees from countries like Iran, Iraq, and Afghanistan carefully follow developments in their home countries. Radio, satellite television, and the Internet make it very easy to do so on a daily basis.

In some cases, political militants from Muslim countries try to collect financial support for their struggle and distribute propaganda. The Afghan resistance against the Soviet invasion in 1979 was supported financially by Muslim communities in Western Europe. Even young militants joined the rebels. In the 1990s, the struggle in Algeria was echoed among the Muslims in Belgium by a series of conferences, collections, distribution of pamphlets, and audio and video cassettes with speeches of the leaders of the Islamic Salvation Front. These activities and links are closely monitored by the Dutch and Belgian security services.

Some Muslim organizations in the Netherlands and Belgium depend ideologically and organizationally on parties or institutions in their countries of origin. This is particularly so in the case of Turkish community. The link between the Milli Görüs movement and the Turkish Welfare party and its successor, the Virtue party, has already been mentioned. A radical wing of the Milli Görüs movement, the Union of Islamic Associations and Communities led by Cemalettin Kaplan in Germany, broke away in 1983 and tried to use its West European base to create an Islamic state in Turkey. Kaplan himself was declared head of the new government in exile. He was succeeded by his son, Metin, in 1995. Kaplan's movement has its sympathizers both in the Netherlands and in Belgium. The institutions of "mainstream" Turkish Islam depend financially on the Directorate of Religious Affairs (Diyanet). The ideological dependence of the Diyanet network in the Netherlands could be observed in their protests against an Armenian initiative to create a monument in the Dutch town of Assen in commemoration of the Armenian genocide of 1915.

The ideological and organizational links between immigrant Muslim organizations and political institutions in the country of origin are less strong in the case of Moroccan Muslims, because many of them come from marginal regions in Morocco, like the Rif Mountains, and are not very interested in Moroccan politics. The Moroccan state continues to play a role in the religious life of Moroccan citizens in the Benelux, and many Moroccan mosques continue to mention the Moroccan king during the Friday prayers.

Second-generation Dutch and Belgian Muslims may be expected to be less involved in the politics of their ancestral countries. Nevertheless, the combination of home life, where ancestral culture is kept alive, and the communications revolution tends to preserve feelings of affiliation with ancestral lands and with events there. Therefore, some Dutch towns have witnessed clashes between Turkish and Kurdish youngsters who have spent all their lives in Holland. Activist elements are also deeply interested in the Muslim world. In Belgium, Islamist movements from Egypt, Algeria, and Morocco attract young Maghrebi Muslims with a message that combines protest against their own social deprivation with involvement in the global struggles of Muslims. Thus, links to political groupings in the countries of origin exist not only the case of the first generation but also succeeding generations of immigrants.

CONCLUSION

In the last decades of the twentieth century, Muslim immigrants from Turkey, Morocco, and several other Muslim states settled in the Benelux countries and created a network of Muslim organizations. These organizations were characterized by the cultural outlooks of these immigrants and reflected the expressions and forms of Islam in their countries of origin. They also bore the marks of their weak socioeconomic position, hence Islam's association in the Benelux with marginal, poorly educated groups with insufficient knowledge of local language, culture, and society.

More recently, a second generation of Muslims has begun to shape the face of Islam in the Benelux. This generation is far better educated and socially and economically more successful. Their orientations are shaped not only by their parents' culture but also by the Dutch and Belgian schools where they are educated and by their dealings with non-Muslims at schools and at work. Regrettably, in some cases, their orientations are formed by experiences of discrimination and rejection by the host society. This at times makes them receptive to radical ideas or leads them to reject the culture of their adopted country, which enhances prejudice against them, thus perpetuating the cycle of rejection and alienation.

There is shift from an "Islam of parents" to an "Islam of children." But it is still not clear what forms this Islam will take and how localized its expressions will be. It seems likely that several expressions of Islam will coexist simultaneously. Some will continue to depend on institutions in the countries of origin, while others will become more independent and culturally closer to Dutch and Belgian societies. But it is unrealistic to expect that Islam in European countries will become isolated from the rest of the Muslim world. Both Islam's character as a world religion and the advanced means of communication ensure that local expressions of Islam in the Benelux countries will be linked to the global Islamic *ummah*. However, the interaction is likely to be more intricate and complex, with the Muslim diaspora in Europe increasingly influencing intellectual and other trends in the Islamic world.

NOTES

1. Nico Landman, *Imamopleiding in Nederland: kansen en knelpunten* [Training imams in the Netherlands: chances and problems] (Den Haag: SDU, 1996), 7–9; also, Wasif Shahid and Sjoerd van Koningsiveld, "Beeldvorming over de imam in Nederland" [Images of the imam in the Netherlands], in *Religie, cultuur en minderheden: historische en maatschappelijke aspecten van beeldvorming*, ed. Wasif Shadid and Sjoerd van Koningsveld (Tilburg: Tilburg University Press, 1999), 55–77.

2. Felice Dassetto, *Islam en Belgique et en Europe: facettes et questions*, [Islam in Belgium and Europe: aspects and questions], in *Facettes de l'islam belge* (Louvain-la-Neuve: Academia Bruylant, 1997), 18–35.

3. Dieter Bartels, *Moluccans in Exile: A Struggle for Ethnic Survival* (Leiden: COMT, 1989), 13ff.

4. See *Maandstatistiek voor de Bevolking* [Monthly Population Statistics], 1994/2, and 1992/12.

5. Dassetto, *Islam en Belgique et en Europe*, 18–35.

6. Herman de Ley, *Gent: een stad waar ook moslims zich thuis kunnen voelen* [Ghent, a city in which also Muslims can feel at home] (Ghent: Center for Islam in Europe, 1998), 3.

7. National Office for Statistics, *Allochtonen in Nederland 2000* (The Hague: 2000), 30.

8. Ibid., 21.

9. Felice Dassetto, "The Tabligh Organization in Belgium," in *The New Islamic Presence in Western Europe*, ed. T. Gerholm and Y.G. Lithman (London: Mansell, 1988), 159–173.

10. Antje va der Hoek, *Religie in ballingscha. Institutionalisering en leiderschap onder christelijke en islamitische Molukkers in Nederland* [Religion in exile. Institutionalization and leadership among Christian and Muslim Moluccans in the Netherlands] (Amsterdam: VU Uitgeverij, 1994), 205ff.

11. M. Nur Ichwan, "Continuing Discourse on Keblat: Diasporic Experiences of the Surinamese Javanese Muslims in the Netherlands," *Sharqiyyat* 11 (1999): 101–119.

12. Ruud Strijp, "Moslims in Nederland en België," in *Het huis van de islam*, ed. Henk Driessen (Nijmegen: SUN, 1997), 405–426.

13. Nico Landman, *Van mat tot minaret: de institutionalisering van de islam in Nederland* [From prayer rug to minaret: the institutionalization of Islam in the Netherlands] (Amsterdam: VU Uitgeverij, 1992), 77–148; Ural Manco, "Les organisations islamiques dans l'immigration turque en Europe et en Belgique," in Dassetto, *Facettes de l'islam belge*, 143–158.

14. Anja van Heelsum, *Marokkaanse organisaties in Nederland. Een netwerkanalyse* [Moroccan organizations in the Netherlands. A network analysis] (Amsterdam: Instituut voor Migratie-en Etnische Studies Universiteit Amsterdam, 2000), 23.

15. Jørgen Nielsen, *Muslims in Western Europe*, 2nd ed. (Edinburgh: Edinburgh University Press, 1995), 68.

16. Dassetto, "Tabligh Organization in Belgium," 159–173.

17. Alain Grignard, "L'islam radical en Belgique à travers la littérature de propagande: une introduction," in Dassetto, *Facettes de l'islam Belge*, 167–178.

18. Thijl Sunier, "Islam among Turkish Youths in the Netherlands," in *L'islam en Europe. Aspects religieux*, ed. J.D.J. Waardenburg (Lausanne: Université de Lausanne, 1994), 85–91.

19. Abdulwahid van Bommel, "The History of Muslim Umbrella Organizations," in *Islam in Dutch Society. Current Developments and Future Prospects*, ed. Wasif Shadid and Sjoerd van Koningsveld (Kampen: Kok Pharos, 1992), 124–143.

20. Nico Landman, "The Islamic Broadcasting Foundation in the Netherlands: Platform or Arena?" in *Islam in Europe: The Politics of Religion and Community*, ed. Steven Vertovec and Ceri Peach (New York: St. Martin's Press, 1997), 224–243.

21. Johan Leman and Monique Renaerts, "Dialogues at Different Levels among Authorities and Muslims in Belgium," in *Muslims in the Margin. Political Responses to the Presence of Islam in Western Europe*, ed. Wasif Shadid and Sjoerd van Koningsveld (Kampen: Kok Pharos, 1996), 164–181.

22. Pierre Blaise and Vincent de Coorebyter, "La reconnaissance et la représentation de l'islam en Belgique," *Nouvelle Tribune* 18 (January 1998): 14–18.

23. Jan Rath, Rinus Penninx, Cees Groenendijk, and Astrid Meyer, *Nederland en zijn islam: een ontzuilende samenleving reageert op het ontstaan van een geloofsgemeenschap* [The Netherlands and its Islam: a depillarizing society responds to the emergence of a faith community] (Amsterdam: Het Spinhuis, 1996), 18–19.

24. Geert Driessen, "Islamic Primary Schools in the Netherlands: The Pupils' Achievement Levels, Behaviour and Attitudes and Their Parents' Cultural Backgrounds," *Netherlands' Journal of Social Sciences* 33 (1997): 2–66.

25. Rath et al., *Nederland en zijn islam*, 243.

26. Jan Blommaert and Marco Martiniello, "Ethnic Mobilization, Multiculturalism and the Political Process in Two Belgian Cities: Antwerp and Liege," *Innovation: The European Journal of Social Sciences* 9, (1996): 51–73.

27. Ibid.

28. Nielsen, *Muslims in Western Europe*, 73.

29. Johan and Renaerts, "Dialogues," 164–181.

30. See his Ph.D. dissertation: Oussama Cherribi, "Imams d'amsterdam: à travers l'exemple des imams de la diaspora marocaine" [Imams of Amsterdam: About the example of the imams of the Moroccan diaspora] University of Amsterdam, 2000.

31. H. Beck and Ljamai, "De imam en zijn opleiding in pluralistisch Nederland" [The imam and his training in the pluralistic Netherlands], in *De passie van een grensganger. Theologie aan de vooravond van het derde millenium*, ed. K.W. Merks and N. Schreurs (Baarn: Ten Have, 1997), 302–315.

32. Nielsen, *Muslims in Western Europe*, 72.

33. Felice Dassetto, *La construction de l'islam européenne: approche socioanthropologique musulmans d'Europe* (Paris: L'Harmattan, 1996), 32–36.

6

Islam in Scandinavia

Lief Stenberg

INTRODUCTION

The Muslim presence in the Scandinavian countries is a recent phenomenon and the consequence of the same factors that have led to the establishment of Muslim communities in other European countries.[1]
According to the census of 1930—the last year during which the Swedes
were asked to specify their religion—fifteen people identified themselves
as Muslims.[2] The numbers for Norway and Denmark were probably less.

Today, there are an estimated 250,000 Muslims in Sweden, 122,000 in
Denmark, and 74,000 in Norway. In reality, these estimates may be low.
Certainly, representatives of Muslim communities tend to cite higher
numbers. They put the number of Muslims in Sweden at around 300,000
to 350,000 or even 400,000.

A major problem in providing exact figures is disagreement regarding
the definition of who is a Muslim. Some experts consider as Muslims
only those who are strict observers.[3] Some governmental organizations
also use a similar method by focusing on those Muslims who are connected with Muslim organizations affiliated to the Commission for State
Grants to Religious Communities (*Samarbetsnämnden för Statsbidrag till
Trossamfun*). Calculated on this basis, in 1998, only 90,000 qualified as
Muslims in Sweden.[4] What is clear is that currently Islam is the second
largest religion after Christianity in all Scandinavian countries. Muslim
communities in the three Scandinavian countries have common characteristics as well as differences. There are also similarities and differences

in their respective governments' approach toward new immigrants, especially in terms of their integration within existing social and political structures.

HISTORICAL BACKGROUND

The first group of Muslims who arrived in Sweden toward the end of the Second World War were of Tatar origin, who had been living in Finland since the nineteenth century, when Finland was part of the Russian Empire.[5]

In Denmark, Muslim presence dates to the 1950s. These early Muslims belonged to the Ahmadiyya sect and by 1958 had already built a mosque in a suburb of Copenhagen.[6] In short, there were only very few Muslims living in Scandinavian countries prior to the labor migrations of the 1960s and 1970s and the more politically driven migrations of the 1980s and the 1990s.

In Sweden, labor migration involving Muslims began in the late 1950s and early 1960s and in Denmark and Norway in the late 1960s and early 1970s. Initially, immigration policies of Scandinavian countries were rather liberal. By the mid-1970s, the need for immigrant labor was reduced because of Europe-wide economic stagnation. Consequently, legislation was enacted to restrict immigration. In the following decades, most of the immigrants came to the Scandinavian countries as part of family reunification or as political refugees (see Tables 6.1 to 6.3).

SECTARIAN PROFILE

The majority of Muslims living in the Scandinavian countries adhere to Sunni Islam. One exception in Sweden's case was a group of Shi'as of Indian origin that had arrived there in 1973 following Idi Amin's government policy of expelling Asians from Uganda. They settled in a small town in the western part of Sweden named Trollhättan. In 1976, they formed a congregation, and in 1986, they built a mosque. It appeared that the group had integrated fairly well into the society in terms of its members' access to jobs and education. Suddenly, however, these perceptions were challenged, when in 1993 their mosque was burned down. However, it appears that this was not the act of anti-Islamic or racist groups but rather that of criminal youths who acted with no obvious motive. The mosque was rebuilt with the help of the entire community. During the 1980s and 1990s, with the influx of large numbers of Iranians, Iraqis, and Lebanese, the number of Shi'as increased. However, it is important to note that not all Iranians are Shi'a or even Muslim. Rather, a portion of them are Baha'is, some are nonobservant, and others describe themselves as secular. Nevertheless, most of them view them-

Table 6.1
Ethnic Profile of Muslims in Sweden

Country of origin	Number in 2000
Afghanistan	3,100
Algeria	1,300
Bangladesh	1,500
Bosnia	60,000
Egypt	1,500
Ethiopia	5,000
Gambia	1,200
Iran	48,000
Iraq	37,000
Kosovo/Albania	8,500
Lebanon	17,000
Morocco	4,000
Pakistan	2,700
Somalia	12,000
Syria	5,000
Tunisia	2,500
Turkey	30,000
Uganda	1,500
Others	9,000
Total	**250,800**

Note: Numbers not including Muslims holding Swedish citizenship.

Source: Author's estimates.

selves as Shi'as in a cultural sense. The same is true of the Lebanese and Iraqis, some of whom are Christians or Sunni Muslims.

Currently, there are about 60,000 Shi'as in Sweden, 8,000 in Denmark, and 15,000 in Norway. Most of these Shi'as adhere to the Twelver branch of Shi'ism, but other groups, like the Ismailis, are also present in all three countries. The Shi'as, like the Sunnis, tend to organize along ethnic lines, but there are also centers like the Islamic Center in Copenhagen that serves a variety of Shi'a Muslims in the greater Copenhagen area.

Table 6.2
Ethnic Profile of Muslims in Denmark

Country of origin	Estimated numbers
Bosnia and former Yugoslavia	26,000
Iran	4,000
Iraq	11,000
Lebanon and other Middle East	7,800
Morocco	3,600
Pakistan	7,100
Palestine	8,700
Somalia	13,000
Turkey	38,000
Others	3,000
Total	**122,200**

Note: Numbers not including Muslims holding Danish citizenship, which are estimated to add another 20,000 to the figures noted.

Source: Author's estimates.

SOCIAL AND ECONOMIC PROFILE

In the Scandinavian countries, too, Islam is an overwhelmingly urban phenomenon. Most Muslims have settled in a few large cities because of the greater availability of jobs in urban areas and the existence of earlier immigrant communities. In Sweden, major centers of Muslim concentration are Stockholm and its suburbs, Gothenburg and Malmö. According to some estimates, half of Sweden's Muslim population lives in Stockholm. No single ethnic group dominates any of Sweden's larger cities. The Turks are almost evenly divided among major cities. Malmö, in southern Sweden, however, has traditionally had a concentration of immigrants from the former Yugoslavia.

The government has encouraged municipalities located outside larger cities to receive more recent immigrants and asylum seekers and to actively help them in order to encourage them to settle permanently in these areas. This is generally done through a contract formed between the board of immigration and the municipality. Given the difficult economic conditions of many local municipalities, many of them have been willing to receive asylum seekers and refugees for financial reasons. Yet often, as soon as immigrants placed in a rural area or small towns receive

Table 6.3
Ethnic Profile of Muslims in Norway

Country of origin	Estimated numbers
Bosnia	10,000
Iran	9,000
Iraq	5,000
Kosovo	6,000
Lebanon and other Middle East	3,000
Morocco	4,500
Pakistan	5,000
Somalia	7,000
Turkey	21,000
Others	3,500
Total	**74,000**

Note: Numbers not including Muslims holding Norwegian citizenship.

Source: Author's estimates.

their residence permits, they move to larger cities, following a nation-wide trend of urbanization.

In Denmark, the majority of Muslims are concentrated in the greater Copenhagen area, plus cities like Aarhus, Aalborg, Odense, and Ros-kilde. In Norway, the majority of Muslims live in and around Oslo and Akershus, plus Bergen, Drammen, Stavanger, and Trondheim. Most of the Pakistanis live in Oslo, whereas the Turks are more evenly distrib-uted among major cities.

The Muslim communities of the Scandinavian countries are still in a much lower socioeconomic position compared with the natives or im-migrants from Europe and North America. Because education is crucial in terms of increasing opportunities for upward social and economic mobility, it is important to assess the present educational situation of Muslims. In general, Muslims are less educated than the native popu-lation. A report by the Swedish Ministry of Finance, whose principal purpose was to ascertain whether there were any differences between native Swedes and those with a foreign background in terms of educa-tion and employment, found that the percentage of foreign students dropping out of high school was higher than for native Swedes: 20 com-pared with 10 percent.[7] The report also indicates that even those foreign students who perform well at school still do less well on the job market.

An interesting aspect of the report is the finding that among people born outside Sweden, students from countries in Africa, Asia, and Latin America generally have higher grades than those born in a European country. Despite this difference in grades, the non-European youth face a higher risk of becoming unemployed after finishing their education. One possible explanation is that they are subject to ethnic and religious discrimination.

The report indicates that, partly because of the following reasons, young immigrants have motivational problems that set them back in their studies. In Sweden, degrees obtained in countries outside Europe and North America are considered less worthy. Consequently, many educated immigrants have to accept low-level jobs. Therefore, the presumably well-educated father or mother of young foreigners works in factories, cleaning services, health care, and the catering trade. This situation seems to convince their children that education is neither an advantage nor a necessity for a better life. The report sees a direct link between uneducated parents or educated parents working in less skilled jobs and low school grades and high unemployment levels among young immigrants. The report concludes that there is a tendency in the Swedish society to create a vicious circle that traps immigrants in a chain of less education and unemployment.

Similar patterns, including discrimination, exist in other Scandinavian countries. In Denmark, a study of new Danish men and women between the ages of thirty and thirty-five, originally from former Yugoslavia, Turkey, and Pakistan, shows that their level of education is lower than that of native Danes.[8] In general, Danish statistics reveal that the number of students dropping out of various types of education is higher among students with a foreign background. Foreign-origin students of vocational schools have problems finding opportunities for training because employers do not accept trainees coming from an ethnic minority. Norwegian statistics also show that immigrants from Muslim countries have a lower level of education than both other migrants and native Norwegians. Thirteen percent of Moroccan and 8 percent of Pakistani women in Norway have no education, while among native Norwegian women, the number is 0.

In Sweden, Denmark, and Norway, official statistics also reveal that immigrants from Kosovo, Morocco, Pakistan, Somalia, and Turkey have a low level of higher education: Only 1 to 2 percent of the immigrants from these countries have finished a long-term higher education (at least three years of college or university). Of immigrants from Iraq and Lebanon, only 3 to 5 percent have completed a higher education. The most well-educated groups of migrants are the Bosnians. In Norway, almost 9 percent of them have finished higher education. The level of education among Iranian immigrants is also relatively high. In Norway, almost 7 percent of them have completed higher education. But even higher education does not guarantee appropriate employment. In an article dealing with the problems of Turkish immigrants in Denmark published in the *New York Times*, a young Turk, Bunyamin Simsek, related that he had to work as an airline steward because he could not find a job as an architect even though he was educated in Denmark. Another young Turkish woman related that when she applies for jobs and they see her name, they ask where she is from before declining to interview her.[9] In both Norway and Sweden, similar examples are related in the press.

Most Muslims in the Scandinavian countries work in the service sector, that is, catering, hotels, health and social services, cleaning companies, transportation, and the industrial sector. The percentages of those who are self-employed, own businesses, or work at managerial and other professional jobs differ among ethnic groups. In Sweden, the proportion of small-business owners is three times higher among Turks and Lebanese immigrants than among native Swedes; compared with Somali immigrants, it is more than twenty times higher. In most Scandinavian cities, migrants own small businesses like food stores and restaurants. Yet, the rate of unemployment is higher among Muslims than in the native population. In Sweden, the level of employment among Turkish immigrants is 42 percent, followed by Iranians at 40 percent, Lebanese at 31 percent, Iraqis at 21 percent, and the lowest level of employment among Somalis at 12 percent. The average rate of employment among all Swedes including immigrants is 74 percent. These figures are from 1998. In 1999, 15.1 percent of migrants born outside Sweden were unemployed compared with to 4.7 percent for native Swedes.

INVOLVEMENT IN POLITICAL LIFE

Presently, an estimated 15 to 30 percent of Muslims in Sweden, Denmark, and Norway are naturalized citizens. Yet, their level of political participation at both local and national levels is very low. In Sweden, of 349 members of Parliament, only 3 or 4 are Muslims. The level of participation at the national level is higher in segregated neighborhoods with high concentrations of Muslim population, such as Rosengard, and similar ones in Stockholm and Gothenberg. Immigrants are interested in politics, but they feel that they are unable to change their own conditions and those of the society by acting through the existing political systems. The level of immigrants' participation in labor unions and other associations is lower than that of Swedes. Thus, although in the last decade the rate of participation of native Swedes in politics has declined, the gap between them and the immigrants has widened. However, many of the smaller ethnic and Muslim organizations are involved in local politics.

Despite the present low level of their participation, Muslims can potentially become a significant political force. Already, some Muslim organizations try to influence politicians in regard to issues of concern to their community. For example, the head of the Muslim Council of Sweden (SMR) wrote open letters to Swedish political parties before elections in the 1990s, presenting the demands of the Muslim community. The letters indicate that political parties can obtain the Muslims' votes if they fulfill a set of requests, the most important being granting of financial and political support to build Muslim cultural centers in Stockholm and Gothenburg, assistance to Muslim schools, observance of Muslim holidays, time off from work for Friday prayers, permission to slaughter animals according to Muslim law and to have Muslim burial grounds, and support for the establishment of courses to educate imams at Swedish universities.[10] At local levels, Muslim leaders have made similar requests. However, the picture is not all bleak. In a forthcoming report written by political scientists Per Adman and Per Strömblad on behalf of the board of integration, the results of which were mentioned in the Swedish daily *Dagens Nyheter* on 8 October 2000, it is indicated that in the 1999 election to the European Parliament, young people with a foreign background born in Sweden participated at a higher rate than ethnic Swedes in general. This finding could mean that (1) there has been a shift in the attitude of young people with a foreign background and (2) the problem of low participation may be a phenomenon related to the age and experience of immigrants.

In terms of political affiliation, older immigrants tend to be attracted to leftist parties. Thus, within the membership of the trade unions and in the Social Democratic and other Leftist parties, there are Turks who arrived in Sweden in the 1960s and 1970s. Some Muslims are active in right-wing parties, despite the latter's antiimmigrant and anti-Muslim tendencies. These Muslims are primarily of Arab and Iranian origin and are small businesspeople and shopkeepers. They seem to be attracted by the classic right-wing messages about lower payroll taxes, lower taxes in general, a reduction in the power of the labor unions, and other conservative values. If this trend is correct, it suggests that, as the process of Muslims' integration progresses, in their voting pattern the majority of Muslims will give priority to social and economic factors. It is also possible that "Islam" will be interpreted in a way that justifies specific political positions of Muslims.

The general trends presented above can be observed in Norway and Denmark too. One member of the Parliament in Norway and one in the Denmark have Arab names. The level of political involvement among Muslims in these countries, too, is focused primarily at local activities. Muslims of Scandinavia have many points in common in terms of their conditions and challenges they face, but there are also differences. In

Denmark, negative views of Muslims are more severe than in Sweden and Norway. In 1999, the public attitudes shifted, and it became acceptable to state arguments usually used by the right-wing fringe.

MUSLIM ORGANIZATIONS

Muslims in various Scandinavian countries have established a number of organizations, councils, associations, and congregations. In Sweden, it is estimated that about 115 congregations are attached to one of the national organizations.

The formation of Muslim organizations in Sweden has resulted from the desire of the state to organize Islam in the same way that Christianity is organized through the medium of Free Churches. In order to receive state funds administered by the Commission for State Grants to Religious Communities, Muslim associations are required to organize themselves along the lines of other national movements/popular associations (*folkrörelser*). This means that they must have a board, a chairman, a secretary, a treasurer, and a list of their members. The commission has introduced a system of subsidies in order to help Muslims set up such organizations, and it arranges courses to prepare individuals to act as treasurers and secretaries in them. The commission distributes three kinds of funds: (1) General funds support the daily activities of organizations whose expressed intention is to enable Muslim congregations to exist; (2) Other funds are directed to specific activities, especially religious instruction. Until recently, only Christian colleges and seminaries for the education of priests received this funding. In spring 2000, a Swedish Islamic Academy was established with the aim of developing a system of education in Islamic sciences at a high academic level. This is the first step toward creating the kind of educational infrastructure that would provide Muslim congregations with properly educated religious functionaries, notably *imams*; and (3) Start-up funds help support congregations in their initial phase of development.

At the national level, the following organizations have been receiving funds from the commission: the United Islamic Congregations in Sweden (FIFS), established in 1974; the Swedish Muslim Federation (SMuF), founded in 1982; and the Union of the Islamic Cultural Centers in Sweden (IKUS), founded in 1984. They all distribute funds and organize a number of local congregations. Through the umbrella organization, SMR, which was formed in 1990, SMuF and FIFS cooperate at the national level. Most activities at the national level are conducted by SMR and its sister organization, the Islamic Information Association. The latter provides information about Islam, and its activities target both Muslims and non-Muslims.

There are three other organizations that are striving to be recognized as national movements in order to receive state grants, namely, the National Islamic Federation of Bosnia-Herzegovina in Sweden, founded in 1995; the Islamic Shi'a Congregations in Sweden, established between 1992 and 1993; and the Islamic National Federation in Sweden (IRFS), started in 1995. IRFS organizes about sixteen congregations and is dominated by immigrants from Somalia. The National Islamic Federation of Bosnia-Herzegovina allows its congregations to be affiliated with SMuF and FIFS in order to receive state grants. The Ahmadiyya congregations do not receive any state grants, although the Ahmadiyya has been active in Sweden since 1956.

FIFS, IKUS, and SMuF form the Islamic Council for Cooperation, which was established in 1988. The main purpose of the council is to advise the commission on the manner of distributing state grants among various Muslim congregations. The council also aspires to act as a cooperative link among various national Muslim movements. This form of organization has created a situation that enables established organizations to prevent other institutions from being recognized by the commission. The three recognized organizations have intensified their cooperation since they have been challenged by more recently created organizations, such as the National Islamic Federation of Bosnia-Herzegovina and the Islamic Shi'a Congregations. These already established organizations argue that, in order to maintain their influence, Muslims should not be further divided, especially along ethnic lines, although all three of the recognized national movements have their own specific ethnic character. IKUS organizes mainly early Turkish immigrants and is not part of the umbrella organization SMR. IKUS is also linked to the Süleymanli movement that aims to Islamize Turkish society through religious education. The Süleymanli has its roots in the Turkish Qur'anic School Movement and the Naqshbendi Sufi order.[11] It is also the only national movement that organizes exclusively Sunni congregations. The rift between IKUS and the other two national movements reflects a schism between the "early" Turkish immigrants of the 1960s that traditionally have represented Islam in Sweden and the "new" Muslims of primarily Arab and Iranian origins.

FIFS and SMuF organize primarily congregations dominated by Arab communities. The leaders of FIFS, SMuF, and the Muslim Council (SMR) as well as the editorial staff of the most well known Muslim journal in Sweden, the monthly *Salaam*, all have a connection to what can be loosely described as the "Salafi" interpretation of Islam.[12] This is an understanding of Islam close to the teachings of Hasan al-Banna and Sayyid Muhammad Qutb of the Ikhwan al-Muslimin (Muslim Brotherhood).[13] *Salaam*'s main focus has been on the following themes: the relationship between Muslims as a minority and the Swedish society; the need for mosques; the importance of "Islamic" education and upbringing; the "true" teachings of Islam (often in relation to the actual practice of Muslims); gender issues and the role of women; and how to be a good Muslim. Some articles are written by Swedish converts to Islam, but the bulk of the texts are translations of what can be characterized as globally spread material, along the lines of ideas expressed by the French Muslim convert Maurice Bucaille on Islam and science.[14] Indeed, as Jonas Otterbeck has noted, there is nothing innovative in *Salaam* material.[15] All Muslim national organizations are linked to international networks of Muslim organizations. The international aspect of their activities is reflected in Muslim bookshops attached to local mosques. Most of the material found in the bookshops attached to purpose-built mosques in Malmö, Uppsala, and Stockholm is ideologically close to "moderate Islamism" or "Salafi" reformism, and a large part of its "literature" is intended to teach Muslims about Islam. Some of the literature is translated into Swedish, some is in Arabic, but most of it is in English, including books published by the Islamic Foundation in Leicester, England, and the International Institute of Islamic Thought in Herndon, Virginia, USA. Recently, a Swedish convert translated the Qur'an into Swedish.[16]

LOCAL ORGANIZATIONS

Local Muslim organizations are formed mostly around the mosque or the Islamic center. The term "Islamic center" is not used in an ideological sense in this text, although among Muslims it is often affiliated with the Salafi movement. The mosque in this context means an apartment or a basement transformed into a prayer hall, while an Islamic center usually contains a purpose-built mosque plus classrooms, bookshop, and offices. Mosques in apartments and basements have been part of Muslims' life in Sweden since the 1950s, but their numbers grew only in the 1970s. The struggle to construct purpose-built mosques has been a main feature of Muslim organizations' work since the 1970s. It symbolizes the Muslims' efforts to establish an Islamic identity in Sweden and to become an acknowledged part of the Swedish society.[17] The resistance to this type of visible mosques has been strong among the general public, local politicians, and churches. Today, Sweden has five purpose-built mosques, three Sunni, one Shi'a, and one Ahmadiyya. The situation among Muslims in Sweden's third largest city, Malmö, can serve as an example of the roles that mosques and Islamic centers play in the country as a whole. Financed by Saudi Arabia and Libya, and with the approval of city planners, an Islamic center was inaugurated in 1984. Today, Muslims active at the center claim that they serve about 1,000 persons at Friday prayers. Muslims from former Yugoslavia are the most numerous, but the mosque's attendance is multiethnic. The *khutba* (sermon) is delivered both in Arabic and in Swedish, and sometimes a summary is given in

Albanian and Turkish. The speeches of the imam, who is from Albania, are generally short and largely nonpolitical and focus on ethical issues, especially how to live as proper Muslims in Sweden. Because of the linguistic diversity of the center's attendants, there is a problem of communication. Thus, the mosque officials want to make Swedish the language of intra-Muslim communication and an essential component of efforts to create a Swedish Islam recognized by the society. The Islamic center plans to open an elementary school and a medical clinic. The center holds separate Qur'anic schools for boys and girls on Friday evenings, Saturdays, and Sundays. It also arranges lectures on Islam. The lecturer can be an invited Muslim guest from Sweden, another European country, and the Middle East or Bosnia. At times, guest speakers cause problems and stir up emotions. Despite their extensive external links, the center's officials claim that they want to remain politically, theologically, and economically independent. The Islamic center also takes care of visitors from non-Muslim communities. According to its officials, the center receives about 85,000 non-Muslim visitors annually, and it has undertaken relief projects in Afghanistan and Bosnia.

The Islamic center in Malmö is located in a semiindustrialized area, next to the city's ring road. On the other side of the road is a large housing area called Rosengård. This area is characterized by its gray-colored and gloomy high rises, which are almost entirely populated by immigrants—Muslim and non-Muslim, first and second generation. In fact, 83.5 percent of the area's population was born outside Sweden or has a parent born abroad. The rate of unemployment is high compared with most other areas of the city.

In the south of Sweden, Rosengård has come to symbolize problems involved in integrating the immigrant population. Similar areas exist in Stockholm, Gothenburg, and some of the other larger cities. Most of them were completed in the 1960s in order to solve the housing shortage. Instead of becoming the symbol of the welfare state, they have become large areas for housing immigrants and other low-income groups.

This area in Malmö has five small mosques, which are intimately connected to specific ethnic groups. There is one Palestinian-Arab mosque in which the Friday sermon is delivered entirely in Arabic. In this mosque, the political message is very strong and the Friday *khutba* always discusses the political situation in Palestine.

The first Swedish Muslim school was established following the change in laws in 1992, which facilitated the establishment of such schools. The setting up of the school, officially called *Al Ulum ul Islamia* (Islamic Sciences), was the result of discussions concerning how to create a viable future for Muslim youth. From an analytical perspective, the establishment of the school can be interpreted as an initiative to maintain the "Islamicness" of the Muslim community and its Islamic and ethnic culture and identity. In 1998, about ten Muslim elementary schools existed in Sweden. Another ten were about to receive the permission to start or to expand their activities. All of them exist in larger cities and housing areas dominated by a Muslim or immigrant population. The schools are subsidized by the state and are controlled by the Swedish Board of Education in cooperation with local school boards. To get permission to start a Muslim school, the organizer must fulfill the same requirements applied in the case of municipal schools. The difference between Muslim schools and municipal schools is the former's emphasis on teaching Arabic and studying Islam. Muslim schools also stress the teaching of the Swedish language. Muslim schools must be open to non-Muslim children, but so far all the students have been Muslims. The founding of Muslim schools in Sweden has received much attention in the media, but it has also been discussed within the Muslim communities. The main question is whether such schools help the integration of Muslim children in the society.

Beneath the gloomy picture of unemployment and low incomes, this area is also a center for social and cultural movements with an "Islamic" character. There are a number of locally based associations, both Sunni and Shi'a, which are trying to develop patterns for Islamic life and identity. Social activities focus on the youth, in order to keep them away from what they pejoratively call the "Swedish culture" and protect them against drug abuse, sexual promiscuity, and criminality. Other activities focus on sports and education about Islam for women. In this area, young Muslims play Islamic music, a hybrid that may contain everything from hip-hop to "Islamic" translations of songs by a famous eighteenth-century Swedish poet. The purpose behind these activities is to maintain the authority of religious leaders over young Muslims and to accommodate new ideas to Islam and Islamize notions about equality and freedom of thought and action.

The examples of the mosque and the Islamic center in Malmö are typical of Muslim experience in the rest of Sweden. Their conditions reflect diverging attitudes toward integration and toward being a Muslim in Sweden. The older generation of immigrants and most of the representatives of Muslim organizations in Sweden see their presence in Sweden as permanent, and therefore want to be integrated at all levels of the society. Newly arrived refugees and immigrants see their presence in Sweden as temporary and tend to focus more on the situation in their countries of origin.

In terms of attitudes toward being a Muslim in Sweden, a recent tendency is a growing interest in Sufism. Consequently, in the last few years, Sufi orders have established themselves as religious organizations partly under the influence of refugees from Kosovo and Bosnia. The Naqshbendi order is most active and has followers among Turkish and

Pakistani immigrants in Norway and Sweden. An Iranian branch of the Nimatullahi order runs a Sufi house in a Stockholm suburb.[18]

This new interest in Sufism is a sign that more Muslims active in local mosques and organizations embrace a form of Islam that focuses on the individual, in terms of both ethics and religious rituals. It also reflects Muslims' efforts to solve the dilemma of how to find a viable Islamic framework in a non-Muslim environment.

Except for the Ahmadiyya congregation established in the 1950s, Muslims in Denmark began to organize in the mid-1970s. Today, there are a number of small mosques and a few Islamic centers in the country. The Islamic Cultural Center located in a suburb of Copenhagen was opened in 1976. The center serves primarily Arab and Pakistani Muslims. As in Sweden, the establishment of Islamic centers has been accompanied by the founding of small local mosques. One or a few ethnic and religious groups dominate most of the established congregations and organizations. The level of contact with the country of origin varies. Both the Diyanet and the Turkish opposition movement, Milli Görüs, are active among the Turkish Muslims of Denmark. Yet, the Islamic center in Copenhagen focuses on Muslim life in Denmark and meeting their religious needs. It serves the community of Muslims by offering, for example, a Qur'anic school for children. The center has extensive activities designed to serve Danish society, and it receives a large number of non-Muslim visitors. The first Muslim school started in Copenhagen in 1978. In the mid-1990s, there were eleven Muslim schools in the country. The debate concerning the necessity of such schools is similar to the one in Sweden.

Another active organization is one for Muslim students and academics. It tries to develop ideas on how to live a Muslim life in Denmark and to keep an Islamic identity in a non-Muslim environment. Other ethnically based organizations include the Minhaj al-Qur'an movement and the Barelvi, which attract primarily Muslim Pakistanis. The Turkish Diyanet is also connected to congregations on a national level and through the Turkish embassy provides them with educated *hojas* (imams), either regularly or on certain occasions such as religious feasts. Mosques and congregations can also be supported by global organizations like the Muslim World League. The league has been active in Denmark since 1974 and runs one mosque in Fredriksberg and another in Hesingør. It also financially supports a few imams. Both of the mosques sponsored by the Muslim World League attract Muslims from Albania and from the former Yugoslavia.

In Norway, the first Muslim congregation was established in the 1970s. By 1998, there were close to eighty registered and nonregistered congregations. In order to coordinate and improve relations between different Muslim organizations and between Muslim organizations and the state, the Islamic Council of Norway was founded in 1992. This initiative was followed by the establishment of the Islamic Information Association. This organization seems to have been inspired by its Swedish counterpart and, like the Swedish organization, is dominated by female converts. The Norwegian Muslim congregations are organized along ethnic and national lines. The largest group of Muslims in Norway is the Pakistanis, followed by Bosnians, Turks, and Moroccans. Because of the numerical superiority of Pakistanis, Islam in Norway is influenced by the Barelvis and Sufism. The Barelvis are divided into a number of organizations like the Minhaj al-Qur'an and Jamaat-e Ahl-e Sunna and the World Islamic Mission. The Sufi orders that are most visible are the Chistiyya, Naqshbendi, and the Qadiriyya. However, the Sufi orders are not connected only to Pakistani Muslims and include Turks and North Africans. Within the Turkish Muslims, Diyanet plus the Milli Görüs and the Süleymanli movements are strongly represented. Moroccan Muslims are divided into a number of movements, notably those that support the government in the home country and those that oppose it. One movement that attracts Muslims of different ethnicity is the transnational Tabligh movement.

Muslim communities in Denmark are not organized hierarchically as they are in Norway and Sweden. Yet, Muslim organizations in all three countries have certain common characteristics. Muslim organizations are divided along severe lines: an interest in the life of their members' countries of origin and life in Scandinavia. Some organizations are ethnically based, while others stress the common identity of Muslims; some focus on a law-oriented understanding of Islam; and some are more attracted by its mystical aspects. However, there are organizations such as the Barelvis who combine ethnic peculiarity with a particular understanding of Islam.

DEBATING MUSLIMS IN SCANDINAVIA

Since the early 1990s, questions concerning immigration and Islam have been subject to public debate in the Scandinavian countries. In general, the media and the public have a mostly negative view of Islam and of Muslim immigrants. Håkan Hvitfelt, who in 1991 conducted a survey about how Islam is portrayed in the Swedish media, refers to a survey in which Swedes were asked about their attitude toward Islam. According to this survey, only 2 percent of respondents expressed a positive view of Islam and 65 percent said they viewed Islam negatively. Hvitfelt's own research of the major Swedish news programs between 1991 and 1995 shows that nearly 45 percent of the newscasts dealing with "Islam" were about violence.[19] It can, of course, be argued whether linking Islam to violence, terrorism, and war is a reflection of an anti-Muslim bias or the consequence of a general trend in news reporting. Nevertheless, if one excludes Swedish tabloids, a more positive view of Islam and Muslims is reflected in most major newspapers, although there are examples of Islam being portrayed as a negative force. Some good examples of this attitude are articles that appeared in newspapers in Bergen, Norway, in the 1970s. In connection to political events like the overthrow of the Shah of Iran and the occupation of the US embassy in Teheran, *Bergens Tidende* (a daily local paper) contained a caricature portraying the Ayatullah Khomeini as an executioner holding a blood-stained sword in his hands above a copy of the Qur'an from which a stream of blood was running out. Muslims in the city protested this treatment of the Qur'an, but they did not object to the portrayal of Ayatollah Khomeini. The legal case brought forth by Muslims was dismissed. The newspaper in a commentary on the dismissal triumphantly called the Muslims "the friends of Ayatollah Khomeini" and compared their report to the police to the behavior of Nazis and Fascists in the 1930s who tried to take to court those newspapers that printed caricatures of Hitler and Mussolini. Since the 1970s, the situation has changed, but one can still argue that this type of portrayal of Muslims, although not as flagrant, is still prevalent in the media and elsewhere.[20]

Political groups often behave in a similar fashion. In 1991, a political party called New Democracy (*Ny Demokrati*) was established in Sweden. This party was critical of the government's policies on immigration, and its leaders presented a very stereotyped view of Islam. Today, the party has vanished, but its views regarding Islam, the cost of immigration for Swedish taxpayers, and their threat to Swedish culture are prevalent in the society. In sum, it appears that in Sweden, while the government is trying to portray the presence of immigrants as a positive force in the society, large portions of the Swedish public has a negative view of them. It must be noted, however, that not all immigrants or all Muslims can be lumped together. For example, while the general view of Islam and Muslims is negative, Muslim Bosnian immigrants have been characterized as "good" immigrants. A survey of attitudes during 1994 and 1995 among civil servants in the city of Malmö dealing with refugees shows how generalizations about "Bosnians" are made as part of a process of stratification of different groups of refugees within the administration itself. The bureaucratic rationalization of how different refugees were handled has created a stereotype of "Bosnians" that, compared with other groups, such as Iranians or Somalis, is more favorable to Bosnians.[21]

The opinion on Muslims and other immigrants in Denmark is even more negative than in Sweden. Indeed, compared with Denmark, the debate about Islam and Muslims in Sweden has been rather calm. To illustrate, in an opinion poll conducted in September 2000, one Danish political party, Dansk Folkeparti, that opposes immigration, received about 15 percent of votes. The high percentage of approval given to a right wing party known for its hostility toward immigrants may be one reason behind the suggestion made by Minister of Interior Karen Jesperson that criminal asylum seekers should be isolated on an island. Some political commentators think that the political debate concerning the referendum on the European Monetary Union that took place in late September 2000 was overshadowed by public discussions for and against migrants, Muslims, and Islam in Denmark.[22] Yet, despite heated debates and negative attitudes toward Islam, positive events do occur. Projects are developed to close the gap between different ethnic and religious groups in the society. One Swedish project that has received much attention is called "The Children of Abraham." It focuses on what is perceived as the common ground in Christianity, Islam, and Judaism and tries to establish mutual understanding among believers of different faiths. The activities of the project take place in suburban areas in Stockholm largely inhabited by immigrants. In Denmark and Norway, there are also examples of dialogue, such as the building of an Islamic and Christian Study Center in Denmark. The outreach activities in the main mosques can also be seen as one way of trying to present Islam to Scandinavians and to bridge the gap between people.

It is very difficult to predict the direction in which the public opinion regarding Islam in the Scandinavian countries will evolve. Currently, it appears that the public opinion in Denmark, Norway, and Sweden is caught between stereotypes of Islam, on the one hand, and a willingness to help people in a crisis situation, on the other. Negative attitudes toward Muslims and Islam also reflect broader social and identity-related problems of Scandinavian peoples in a changing world rather than mere xenophobic attitudes.

CONCLUSIONS

The process of the integration of Muslims in the Scandinavian countries takes place at different levels and through different means. This process takes place at four integrated levels:

1. The general integration of Muslims, in order to make Islam and Muslims an accepted part of the country's everyday life. Yet, so far, Muslims have not been integrated at this level. The persistence of communalism among Muslims plus segregation in housing and in the labor market symbolize this failure. Moreover, the public's and the media's perceptions of Islam remain negative, although such views are more common among the older generation. What makes integration difficult at this level is that it requires changes and adaptation not only from Muslims but also

from the native Scandinavians. Thus, Muslims have to reinterpret Islam in order to be able to live a life they consider to be
"Islamic" in a secular society, and Swedes also have to make
changes in order to accommodate Muslims. This latter process
is observable in the changes made in Swedish laws in order to
prevent ethnic discrimination in the labor market and in the
workplace. For example, the Swedish state is moving toward
acceptance of the headscarf as an expression of personal belief
and therefore is inclined to grant Muslim women the legal right
to wear headscarves at the workplace.

2. Political level. Integration at this level is low. Very few Muslims
   are active in the Scandinavian political life at a national level,
   and these are few who can be characterized as leaders or representatives of Islam and Muslims. The typical representative of
   Islam as portrayed in the media is a middle-aged man of Arab
   origin that supports the Muslim brotherhood or the Salafi movement. He views Islam as an all-encompassing order, and his aim
   is to live all aspects of his life in accordance with Islam. He
   works for a Muslim organization and actively tries to gain support from the state or the local municipality for his particular
   brand of Islam. He represents his favorite brand to non-Muslims
   and national and local authorities as the real and objective "Islam." He also tries to convince his fellow Muslims that his brand
   of Islam is the correct one. He does not consider involvement in
   Swedish political life necessary. The other prototype of Muslim
   is the female convert. She differs from the male prototype on
   two points: She discusses the women's position from a "femi-
   nist" and "Islamic" standpoint and is more interested in Scandinavian politics. However, most Muslims who are active in
   party politics in Scandinavia and are present on the public scene
   are basically secular. These two groups—secular and observant—
   differ on many issues, notably the position of women, and the
   issue of headscarves.

3. The level of religious rituals. For example, in Sweden, Muslims
   have to attacked the Freedom of Religion Act from 1951 because of
   restrictions on the Islamic way of slaughtering animals.

4. The ideological level. At this level, the situation for Muslims in
   Sweden is quite positive. Today, Muslim individuals and organizations more than before express the idea that they are part of
   the development of what they call Euro-Islam. They want to
   point out that they have distanced themselves from the political
   problems of the Middle East, Africa, and Asia and that they are
   willing and able to create a more "true" Islam in Europe.

In short, there is room for optimism at least on one point, namely, that the atmosphere of being Muslim in Scandinavian countries and Europe in general seems to be giving birth to new interpretations of Islam that will be interesting to follow. However, in the social, political, and economic sphere, the situation of many Muslims in the Scandinavian countries will remain difficult and the gap between Muslims and indigenous peoples can become wider. Differences at this level can also deepen within the Muslim community.

NOTES

1. Two good sources for information on Islam and Muslims in Denmark and Norway are www.sdu.dk/hum/timjensen/Rel/islam.html and www.olo.no/~leirvik/tekster/IslamiNorge.html.

2. Pia Karlson and Ingvar Svanberg, *Moskéer i Sverige. En religionsetnologisk studie av intolerans and administrativ vanmakt* [Mosques in Sweden. A study in the field of ethnology of religion on intolerance and administrative impotence] (Uppsala: Svenska kyrkans forskningråd, 1995), 14.

3. See Åke Sander, *I vilken utsträckning är den svenske muslimen religios?* [To what extent is the Swedish Muslim religious?] (Göteborg: Centrum for studier av Kulturkontakt och Internationell Migration, 1993), 72ff.

4. See the SST's yearbook 2000.

5. See Jonas Otterbeck, "The Baltic Tatars—The First Muslim Group," in *Sweden in Cultural Encounters in East and Central Europe* (Stockholm: Swedish Council for Planning and Coordination of Research, 1998); and Ingvar Svanberg, "The Nordic Countries," in *Islam outside the Arab World*, ed. David Westerlund and Ingvar Svanberg (Richmond: Curzon Press, 1999).

6. Jørgen Nielsen, *Muslims in Western Europe*, 2nd ed. (Edinburgh: Edinburgh University Press, 1995), 76.

7. Mahmood Arai, Lena Scröder and Roger Vilhelmson, *En svartvit arbetsmarknad—en ESO-rapport om vägen från skola till arbete* [A black and white labor market—an ESO report on school, work and immigrant background] (Stockholm: Ministry of Finance, ESO—*expertgruppen för studier I offentlig ekonomi*, 2000).

8. Garbi Schmidt and Vibeke Jakobsen, *2000: 20 år I Danmark. En undersogelse af nydanskeres situation og erfaringer* [Twenty years in Denmark. A study of the situation and experience of New Danes] (Köbenhavn: *Socialforskningsinstituttet*, 2000), 67ff.

9. See Roger Cohen, "For 'New Danes' Differences Create a Divide," *New York Times*, 18 December 2000.

10. For an example of such a letter, see Leif Stenberg, *The Islamization of Science: Four Muslim Positions Developing an Islamic Modernity* (Stockholm: Almquist and Wiksell, 1996).

11. Svanberg, "The Nordic Countries," 387ff.

12. From 1986 to 1994, *Salaam* was published every month, but since 1995, it has become a bimonthly journal. For an analysis of the contents of *Salaam*, see Jonas Otterbeck, *Islam på svenska. Tidskriften Salaam och islams globalisering* [Islam

in Swedish. The journal *Salaam* and the globalization of Islam] (Stockholm: Almquist & Wiksell, 2000).

13. Tariq Ramadan, *To Be a European Muslim* (Leicester: Islamic Foundation, 1999), 241.

14. For more details on Bucaille and his positions among Muslims in Europe, see Stenberg, *Islamization of Science*, 221–267.

15. See Jonas Otterbeck, "Islam på soenska—Tidskriften Salaan och islams globalisering," Lund University, Dissertation Abstract, http://www.lub.lu.se/cgi-bin/show_diss.pl?db=global&fname=hum_121.html.

16. The first complete translation of the Qur'an into Swedish was edited by Fredrik Cruseustalpe in 1843. A later translation was done in 1917 by K.V. Zettersteen, a professor of Semitic languages at Uppsala University.

17. For a more detailed discussion of the role of mosques in Sweden, see Pia Karlsson, "*Islam tar plats—moskéer och deras funktion,*" [Islam finds its position—mosques and their function] in ed. David Westerlund and Ingvar Svanberg *Blågul Islam? Muslimer i Sverige* [Blue and yellow Islam? Muslims in Sweden] (Nora: Nya Doxa, 1999).

18. See Svanberg, "The Nordic Countries," 390ff.; and David Westerlund, "Euro-Sufism—universaliser och konvertiter" [Euro-Sufism—universalists and converts], in Westerlund and Svanberg, *Blågul Islam?*.

19. See Håkan Hvitfelt, "*Den muslimska faran: Om mediebilden av islam*" [The Muslim threat: on the media image on Islam], in *Mörk magi I vita medier* [Dark thoughts in white media], ed. Yiva Brune (Stockholm: Carlssons, 1998).

20. Richard Johan Natvig, "*Islam på bergensk: Framveksten av muslimske organisasjonar I Bergen*" [Islamic Bergen: The growth of Muslim organizations in the city of Bergen], in *Religionsbyen Bergen* [Religions in the city of Bergen], ed. Lisbeth Mikaelsson (Bergen: Eide, 2000).

21. Fredrik Miegel, "*Administration av en konstruktion. Om mottagandet av bosniska flyktingar I Malmö*" [The administration of a construction. On the reception of Bosnian refugees in Malmoe], in *Integration—retorik, politik, praktik. Om bosniska flyktingar I Norden* [Integration—rhetoric, politics and practice. On Bosnian refugees in the Nordic countries], ed. Berit Bergand Carl-Ulrik Schierup (Köpenamn: Nordiska minsterrådet, 1999).

22. *Sydsvenska Dagbladet*, 18 September 2000.

7

Islam in Austria

Sabine Kroissenbrunner

INTRODUCTION

The Muslim community is one of the largest and most important religious communities in Austria today. With 300,000 followers, Islam ranks third after the Roman Catholic and Protestant churches in terms of its adherents.[1] Two features distinguish Islam in Austria from that in other European countries in its historical and current aspects: The first is the legal recognition of Islam granted by the Austrian state in 1874 on the basis of which the Islamic Religious Community in Austria (IRCA) was officially recognized as a legal, corporate body in 1979.[2] Second, the character of Islam in Austria has been shaped by the historic encounter of the Austria-Hungarian Empire with the neighboring Muslim world and the images created by this encounter.

The pattern of immigration from the former Yugoslavia and Turkey has also played a role in this process. These Muslims have contributed to the pluralist character and complex structures of Islam in Austria. They have challenged the established order and have contributed to it constructively.[3] The question for the future is to what extent and in what form Austria's Muslims will play a role in the development of a "European Islam."

ISLAM IN AUSTRIA: A HISTORICAL BACKGROUND

Since the Ottoman Turkish military advance toward Central Europe in the seventeenth and eighteenth centuries, Muslims have been present in the Austrian-Hungarian Empire. After 1730, a community of Muslim merchants was established in Vienna. This was made possible by the period of tolerance and enlightenment under Emperor Joseph II following his Declaration of Tolerance (Toleranzpatent) issued in 1781. A Turkish ambassador resided in Vienna, and the Ottoman Empire's embassy hosted a mosque and an imam. Oriental poetry and philosophy became fashionable in Austria's elite circles, and Islamic mystical groups are said to have existed.[4]

Periods of struggle between Austria and (Ottoman) Turkey have also left their mark.[5] A small booklet commemorating the two Ottoman sieges of Vienna (1529 and 1683) states: "We and the Turks—there hardly is a human problem that might not be treated in this context."[6]

Long before the emergence of Muslim neighborhoods in Europe, a space for Muslims in Austria had been delineated by the popular writer Johannes N. Nestroy (1801–1862). The Orient, he said, starts in the third district of Vienna. Today, Vienna's third district is home to immigrants from Turkey and the former Yugoslavia.

Fundamental Law on the General Rights of Citizens, passed in 1867, guaranteed freedom of belief and conscience and independence to all churches and religious communities that were legally recognized by the state regarding their "internal affairs," such as rites, religious education, and foundations. The first Law of Recognition (20 May 1874) defined legally recognized churches and religious communities as public corporate bodies with special privileges such as the right to practice one's religion in public, independence with regard to all "internal affairs," and protection of the community's property. Legally recognized churches and religious communities have been entitled to make use of the Law on Religious Education at School (first law enacted in 1868) and the Law on Private Schools and to apply for financial support from the state. Since then, legal recognition has been granted on the basis of the 1874 General Law of Recognition and on the bases of laws for the recognition of a specific religious community.[7] Islam was granted legal recognition by the Austrian state in 1874. In 1878, Austria officially incorporated the former Turkish provinces of Bosnia and Herzegovina. This act brought about 1 million Muslims under Austrian rule. The encounter with the Bosnians has left a diverse image of Islam in Austria.[8] The general recognition of Islam according to the Hanafi rite was confirmed and in some points expanded by the Law of Recognition of Islam of 15 July 1912. The Law of 1912 was crucial for the Muslims' later appeal for official recognition of the IRCA as a legal, public corporate body. This status was officially granted in 1979. During the first Austrian Republic (1918 to 1938), Muslims were organized in the Union for Islamic Culture. This organization was dissolved by the Nazis in 1939. During World War II and the period of Nazi regime in Austria, the Islamic Community of Vienna was set up, but it was dissolved in 1948 because of the pro-Nazi stance of some of its members. The following years saw the establishment of the Organization of Austria's Muslims (1951) and an office of the international humanitarian organization, Jami'at ul-Islam (1958 to 1962).

In 1964, the Muslim Social Service (MSS) was founded by Bosnian-origin Austrian citizens.[9] Its main objectives were the provision of adequate infrastructure (praying room and library) for Muslims in Austria and providing social assistance for Muslim refugees from Eastern Europe. In 1979, the first mosque (the Vienna Islamic Center) was opened near the United Nations Headquarters in Vienna. But the mosque's location and its links to Saudi Arabia have kept many Muslims away from it.[10] The MSS therefore established a second mosque in 1981.[11] The MSS and its founders had a comprehensive approach to Islam and saw themselves embedded in the long historic tradition of Islam in Austria and in the Balkans. Its publication, *The Straight Path* (*Der gerade Weg*), was multilingual (German, Bosnian, and Turkish) and argued in favor of official recognition of Islam as a religious community equal to the Catholic church. In 1971, the MSS, the Muslim Student Union, the Social Association of Turkish Workers of Vienna and Surroundings, and the Iranian Islamic Student Association applied for Islam's legal recognition. In May 1979, Islam was legally recognized as a religious community with its own constitution, its institutional body (IRCA, based in Vienna),[12] and four Islamic communities in Austria.[13]

The MSS consulted the Al-Azhar University in Cairo, the Turkish Directorate for Religious Affairs (Diyanet), and the Highest Council of the Muslim community in the former Yugoslavia for clarification of a number of issues related to Islamic law. The Austrian government also consulted the Diyanet on the question of various schools of Islamic law (*shari'a*). The Diyanet responded that all schools of Islamic law represented Islam in its totality, and therefore the traditional recognition of the Hanafi rite by the Austrian state amounted to the recognition of Islam. Consequently, the Diyanet believed the rights of Muslims would be sufficiently protected even if reference were made only to the Hanafi rite.[14]

The IRCA claims to represent the interests of Muslims in Austria and to promote and develop relations between the Muslim community and the Austrian state. The IRCA is an institution of crucial importance for Austria's Muslims and a legitimate representative of the Muslim community with which the Austrian state and other political and social institutions can deal on issues ranging from interreligious dialogue to the integration of Muslims in the Austrian society.

The constitution of the IRCA defines the wide range of its tasks: proclaiming Islam; caring for Islamic instruction and education of Muslims; fostering the humanitarian aspects of Islam; organizing religious lectures;

publishing and distributing Islamic journals and literature; establishing and preserving mosques, religious schools, and other religious and re- ligious/cultural infrastructure; conducting public and private religious services; offering funeral services; educating male and female teachers of Islamic religion, pastors, and religious personnel; and offering any other activities that could provide information about Islam.[15]

Among the IRCA's major responsibilities are to organize Islamic relig- ious instruction at state schools that was introduced in 1982, by issuing certificates for qualified teachers,[16] and the recruitment of and assistance to imams. There are seventy imams in Vienna and its surroundings who serve in the two big mosques and in more than fifty small prayer rooms.

Since 1979, the IRCA has had two presidents (Dr. Ahmed Abdelrahim- sai, 1979 to 1998; Dr. Anas Shakfeh, 1999 to present). It is unique in that it has tried to establish an administrative as well as religious hierarchy approved by its members. The IRCA is represented by three organiza- tional bodies: the Shura Council (the legislative body of the IRCA), the Higher Council (the executive body of the IRCA); and the Mufti or First Imam (the spiritual head of the IRCA). The Shura and Higher Councils are assisted by an advisory committee that hosts "the general secretaries of the big Islamic organizations in Austria." Representative bodies of each of the regional Islamic religious communities are the Community Assembly, the Community Executive Committee, and the Imam.

ETHNIC AND SECTARIAN PROFILE

Austria's Muslim community is ethnically diverse and divided along sectarian lines (see Table 7.1). According to one estimate, about 85 to 90 percent of the Austrian Muslims are Sunni and about 10 to 15 percent are Shi'a. There are also Alavites whose numbers in Vienna alone are estimated to be between 10,000 and 25,000.[17] The Iranian community be- longs to the Twelver branch of Shi'ism.

SOCIOECONOMIC PROFILE

An accurate picture of socioeconomic conditions of Muslims living in Austria is difficult to obtain. The only nationwide data available are based on the 1991 census, which does not reflect present conditions. Therefore, the situation of Muslims in Vienna will be examined.[18] Austria has a labor system for immigrants according to which three different categories of "work permits" are granted. The third category permit is granted after a minimum of five years of legal work in Austria. Presently, about 90 percent of immigrants from the former Yugoslavia and Turkey have obtained the third category permit, which offers the broadest and most flexible entry into the labor market. As far as Bosnian citizens are

Table 7.1
Ethnic Profile of Muslims in Austria and Vienna

Country of origin	Numbers[1] in Vienna	Numbers[2] in Austria
Turkey	43,950	134,210
Bosnia-Herzegovina	20,815	60,000–80,000
Kosovo Albanians	NA[3]	30,000
Egypt	4,696	5,000–6,000
Iran	6,976	7,000–8,000
Iraq	1,123	NA[4]
Lebanon	376	
Libya	533	
Morocco	220	
Pakistan	1,241	
Tunisia	925	
Syria	545	

[1]Figures for Vienna, December 31, 2000 (*Source*: Statistical Service of the Municipality of Vienna).

[2]Figures for Austria, January 1, 2001, only exactly available for Turkey (*Source*: Austrian Statistical Office). Remaining figures are rough estimates.

[3]Not registered as Kosovo Albanians. The figure for Austria is estimated by the Ministry of Interior.

[4]Giving figures here is not possible, but the overall number in Austria might vary only slightly from the figures given for Vienna since the majority of these citizens live in Vienna. The difference between the overall estimated number of Muslims in Austria (300,000 and more) and the figures given here can be explained by Muslims already having acquired Austrian citizenship and by Austrian converts.

concerned, only 43 percent of them have acquired this status. This is due to their relatively late arrival. In 1999, the great majority of foreign citizens, 72.6 percent, still consisted of blue-collar workers, and only 27.4 percent had obtained the status of white-collar workers. The great majority of these blue-collar workers are employed in restaurants and hotels, construction, and other services. Their income is at least 15 percent lower than the average income of Austrians in similar jobs. As far as unemployment is concerned, the general principle of "first fired—last hired" applies in the Austrian, or at least Viennese, context. In 1999, 68,385 persons were registered as unemployed. The situation in the housing sector is depressing as well, and data are more accurate: Eighty-five percent of former Yugoslavian and 88 percent of Turkish citizens live in houses that were built before 1918 and their infrastructures are poor. Only 1 percent of these immigrants live in houses built after 1980, and only 14 percent of former Yugoslavian and 11 percent of Turkish citizens live in houses that have full amenities. These figures show that the general socioeconomic situation of foreigners, including almost the entire Muslim population, is rather poor. However, well educated academics, doctors, and other professionals from different Arab countries and Iran have settled in Vienna and enjoy better social and economic conditions.

THE DYNAMICS OF INTRA-MUSLIM INTERACTION

Muslim communities in Austria distinguish themselves mainly according to their national and/or ethnic origin. Their frame of reference in terms of identity construction and reconstruction, relations to other organizations, and policy formulation is mainly their country of origin—and not Islam and Muslim communities. Any presentation of statistics according to nationality or ethnicity reflects neither actual belonging to Islam nor level of religious observance. Interaction of Muslim communities among each other and the ways and means they use to communicate with institutions of the Austrian society should be seen in a framework determined by the discourse and structures of their countries of origin, its politics, plus the politics of Islam, minority politics, and the policies of the host country. This means that there are many "Islams" not only in the Austrian society but within the Muslim society itself.[19] Another factor that shapes the character of different Muslim communities' interaction, their policies of integration, and involvement in Austria's politics comprises their organizational patterns and capacities.

The Muslim communities' politics, structures, and activities have become increasingly modernized[20] in order to live Islam in the diaspora more visibly, actively, and often more "traditionally" ("orthodoxly") than in their countries of origin.

The most important Muslim organizations in Austria tend to establish "parallel societies" to that of Austria.[21] They strive to provide their communities with Islamic organizations, interest groups (especially for women and youth), commercial associations, soccer clubs, cultural facilities, private schools and kindergartens, and scholarships that mirror the ones that exist in the host societies. Part of the goal of these efforts is to ensure upward social mobility.

Although the IRCA functions as a common center in terms of administration and is recognized by all Muslim organizations, it is not regarded as the only representative of Islam in Austria. Most Muslim organizations in Austria have their "headquarters" not only back home (mainly Turkey) but also in other European Union (EU) countries (e.g., Germany). Turkish-Muslim sociopolitical networks in Austria have developed along patterns similar to those in Germany.[22]

Some communities have very limited contact with the authorities of their home countries. For example, the majority of Iranian citizens or Austrian citizens of Iranian origin are refugees either from the Shah or from the Islamic regime and are not politically or religiously very active. Most of them do not interact with other Muslim groups. The only exception is a very small, but rather well organized, group that closely cooperates with the official representatives of the Islamic Republic of Iran in Austria.[23]

The largest Muslim community in Austria still consists of Sunni Muslims, followed by Alevites and Muslims of Kurdish origin from Turkey. Their interaction in terms of discourse as well as alliance building with other organizations has been determined, on the one hand, by the politics of their home country and, on the other, by their attempts to reconstruct identity and mobilize and institutionalize their pluralist identities in Austria.[24]

The Kurdish population in Austria is estimated at around 20,000 to 40,000, the majority of whom still are Turkish citizens.[25] The Kurdish diaspora has resulted from the general phenomenon of labor migration from Turkey since the 1960s and the repression and expulsion of Kurds from Turkey.[26] Within Turkey, the Kurdish movement is not homogeneous, and the leftist PKK is opposed by "Kurdish right-wing nationalists" and the Islamist Hizbullah.[27] However, for the PKK, which has the most extended political, social, and recruitment structures in Western Europe, Islam has never figured prominently either in its ideology of resistance or in its political vision, which ranges from political-territorial autonomy to cultural self-determination within the borders of Turkey.[28] The main Kurdish religious group is a rather small association, the Kürdistan Aleviler Birligi (Union of the Alevites of Kurdistan).[29] This organization is very cautious in dealing with other Alevite organizations from Turkey. Their main criticism of other Alevite organizations is their hesitation to affirm a national (i.e., Kurdish) identity. They accuse other Alevites of cooperating with "the Turkish government"[30] by reducing identity to religious and cultural elements.

The major organization of Turkish Alevites is the Federation of the Unions of Alevites in Austria (Avusturya Alevi Birlikleri Federasyonu; AABF) founded in 1991. According to the AABF's estimates, there are about 10,000 to 17,000 Alevites in Vienna, of whom 2,000 to 3,000 are said to be in contact with the organization. Until 1995, the AABF was called Association of the Members of the Alevi, Ehlibeyt and Bektasi.[31] The AABF strives to "provide the Alevites in Vienna with a social homeland and to serve their interests."[32] It also attempts to "preserve the cultural identity and religious and cultural values of the Alevites in Austria and to promote their development."³³ The representative of the AABF noticed an improvement in relations between Sunnis and Alevites in Vienna. Though Kurds are said to be among the visitors of the AABF, they tend to distance themselves from the "Kurdish nationalists" because "Alevism has nothing to do with nationalism," and therefore the AABF finds it easier to communicate with Turkish Sunni or Turkish leftist organizations than with Kurdish nationalists.³⁴

Muslims from Arab countries constitute a minority within the Muslim community. Moreover, because of the variety of their countries of origin, caution is required when talking about "the Arab Muslims." There are a number of cultural organizations or Austrian-Arab organizations—such as the Austrian-Egyptian Association and the Austrian-Arab Society—that make no particular reference to religion. They either promote diplomatic relations and other cooperation between Austria and their countries or want to inform Austrian society about the Arab world.

Arab Muslims, however, hold important positions within the IRCA. They opened the first Islamic Academy for Religious Education in Vienna, which has been operating since 1998 to 1999 and intends to promote and carry out an Islamic educational program in Austria. The objective is to educate Austrian Muslims or the second- and third-generation Muslim immigrants and to enable them to take over those functions foreseen in the constitution of the IRCA, for example, pastoral workers, imams, Islamic teachers, etc. While the IRCA's first president was originally from Afghanistan, the second and current one is of Syrian origin. Turkish Muslims, though statistically the largest group and very active in organization building, so far have not held leadership positions within the IRCA. This situation results from two facts: (1) Because of the diversity of Arab communities in Austria, for them the IRCA functions as a central representative body for religious affairs, and (2) the patterns of immigration of Turkish Muslims since the 1970s and Bosnian Muslims since the 1990s are not reflected in the leadership structure of the IRCA but rather in the conflicts and quarrels about representation within the IRCA and within "Turkish Islam" in Austria. It is empirically impossible to answer the question of whether or to what extent Arab-Muslim organizations such as the Muslim brotherhood, the FIS, HAMAS, and others are represented or supported by Muslims in Austria. One mosque in Vienna is said to be close to the Muslim brotherhood and has a publication in German called *Die Wahrheit* (*The Truth*). What is clear is that a very small minority of Austria's Muslims supports radical organizations.

The Turkish Muslim community is the largest one in Austria and Vienna, and it is a highly diversified one in terms of ethnic, political, brotherhood, and organizational affiliations. In recent years, these organizations have not been trying to get more "members" but rather have tried to develop services and institutions for special target groups within the Muslim community, especially the youth and women. The development of Turkish Muslim organizations in Austria is similar to those in Germany. These organizations were founded in the mid-1970s, and their consolidation began in the early 1980s, when immigration from Turkey was actually stagnating. Imams for these organizations were sometimes recruited among migrant workers but were soon imported directly from Turkey. In line with an increasing influx of Turkish immigrants in the early 1990s, the former private meeting rooms turned into registered associations and were then organized into unions. The most important organizations of Turkish Muslims are the Islamic Federation (Milli Görüs, MG), the Union of Islamic Cultural Centers (ICC), and the Turkish Islamic Union for Cultural and Social Cooperation in Austria (ATIB), the representative organization of the Turkish Directorate for Religious Affairs (Diyanet).

Milli Görüs—Austria

This organization was established in Austria in the early 1980s. Those mosques and Muslim infrastructures affiliated with the political ideology and Islamic politics of MG are coordinated by the "Islamic Federation," which was founded in 1988. Though founded by Turkish Muslims in Austria in response to their religious and social needs, the Islamic Federation has consolidated its structures and strengthened its institutional links with its partner organizations in other European countries, in particular Germany. Twenty-six mosques in Austria (of which eight are in Vienna) are coordinated by the Islamic Federation. Members of the cadre and activists of MG stress the fact that each of the mosque associations is organizationally independent, which is correct in the legal sense. Each mosque also has to fund itself via fees or contributions by its own local Muslim communities. From these financial contributions, the mosque associations have to pay their rents, electricity, and staff such as imam(s) and others working in the teahouses or the grocery shops attached to the mosques.

MG is one of the most active associations and has expanded its infrastructure and activities. Its clientele in Vienna is (self-)estimated at about 2,000 to 3,000 people. The MG established the first private Islamic High School in Vienna as well as a women's branch and a youth branch. An academic branch is planned. The youth branch has recently been turned into House of Cultural Activity and Tolerance (Haus der kulturellen Aktivität und Toleranz). MG strives for the "Islamization" of all areas of life.[35] In the political arena, although the MG does not challenge the secular democratic state, it believes that it should be changed through the Islamization of society. In the diaspora, however, the democratic secular state is more fiercely defended than in Turkey because it leaves the religious realm entirely to the associations themselves. This attempt to "Islamize modernity" is also an attempt to "modernize and democratize the Islamist movement." The concept of "parallel society" applies particularly to the sociopolitical project of MG. MG tries to establish institutions that mirror the Austrian ones, thus providing its followers with opportunities for upward social mobility in the Austrian society but with an Islamic way of life. MG has a very professional staff that facilitates its contacts with the IRCA and the district-level institutions in Vienna. Contacts with other Turkish Muslim organizations are characterized as good but are not institutionalized.[36]

Union of Islamic Cultural Centers

The UICC (Islam Kültür Merkezleri) was founded in Austria in 1980. It is a coordinating body for legally independent mosque associations. One factor that accelerated the formation of the ICC in Austria was the attempt of some Turkish Muslims to distance themselves from the MSS and the IRCA. The number of its followers is not as large as that of MG, but it claims to appeal to about 40 to 50 percent of the Austrian Muslim population, a claim that is unrealistic. Naqshbendi Sufi brotherhood is an important organizational and religious element of the ICC. It has always been a matter of importance for the organization to recruit imams who represent their particular Islamic school of thought, that is, that of the Süleymanli. Initially, therefore, the ICC kept their distance from the IRCA, and there were often tensions between the ICC and the IRCA on organizational grounds and because of disagreement on matters related to imams' recruitment and Islamic religious affiliation. This situation seems to have changed, and relations have improved considerably. If the MG might be called a modern Islamist group that focuses on Muslim integration in Austria and in Europe, the ICC is a neotraditionalist organization focusing on issues of religious education and skills deemed necessary in this context, especially for the younger generations.

Turkish Islamic Union for Cultural and Social Cooperation in Austria

The ATIB was formally established in Austria in 1990 to 1991. ATIB's foundation was a reaction to the limited and sporadic activities of the Turkish Diyanet in Austria since the 1970s. The Viennese center of ATIB represents fifty-two independently registered associations spread throughout Austria and founded according to the Austrian Law of Association. The individual ATIB associations in Austria, although each has its own statutes, are in principle tied to the constitution of the ATIB Center in Vienna. Functionaries (civil servants) of the Turkish Diyanet work on long-term contracts (maximum four years) in thirty-one of the ATIB associations, with the other nineteen serving on the basis of short-term contracts. Unlike other Turkish organizations, ATIB's relations with IRCA are rather tense. The question of formal recognition of teachers of Islamic religion and imams has been the principal source of disagreement between the two organizations.

In short, the degree of interaction among Muslim organizations is limited at official, formal, and institutional levels of cooperation and alliance building. The IRCA functions as an important umbrella organization in administrative issues (recognition of imams, Islamic teachers, etc.) and certainly as a symbolic body in relation with Austrian society and organizations. It is, however, also evident from the interviews with various leaders, imams, and members of Turkish Muslim organizations, plus the Alavite and Bosnian organizations, that the specific versions and forms of Islam are upheld in the diaspora in order to serve various Muslim communities and to maintain their cultural, ethnic, and religious peculiarities and beliefs. The Advisory Council of the IRCA in which the leaders of the most important Islamic organizations in Austria are represented certainly reflects this reality. From the point of view of Muslim organizations, their own community and mosque associations are of greater importance than the IRCA.

INVOLVEMENT IN AUSTRIA'S POLITICAL LIFE

None of the Muslim organizations mentioned advocates a particular political strategy for its members in Austria. However, in individual conversations, leaders of different associations will tell which Austrian party they would recommend to their members who are Austrian citizens and therefore can vote. Owing to the fact that in Austria, foreign citizens are not entitled to vote even at the local level, Austrian political parties—with rare exceptions—have only recently discovered foreigners and Muslims as a potential source of votes. Turkish Muslim organizations such as MG and ICC take political positions only when directly asked. All of them would support the establishment of Councils of Foreigners similar to those that have already been set up in many European countries since the 1970s and 1980s. These Councils of Foreigners or Councils of Migrants may be established at the level of local governments, but so far only two councils have been set up in Graz/Styria and Linz/Upper Austria. This lack of electoral rights is not limited to the political sphere. Austria is the only member state of the EU where workers and employees with foreign citizenship are not entitled to vote in elections to various factory or job-related committees.

Not only these "hard institutions" needed for political integration are lacking in Austria and Vienna, there are no "soft institutions" such as public forums and platforms or advisory councils that could enable immigrant organizations to become visible and to be heard on all aspects of communal, political, and social life. Existing local institutions, which are concerned mainly with general migration policies and politics, have, for many reasons, not taken up the issue of Islam and migration.

The degree of communalism among Muslims is rather high, and the Muslims' level of social and political integration is far from satisfying, because of the paucity of opportunities offered by the Austrian legal system and Austrian society. Nevertheless, the efforts and readiness of Muslim organizations to institutionally, socially, and politically integrate into Austrian society must be stressed. Turkish Muslim organizations not only initiate and participate in activities serving the interreligious or intercommunal dialogue, they also aim at what they call "filling up the social and organizational vacuum of the Austrian state and society."[37] Though this "vacuum" is certainly filled with Islamic elements, the effort for "empowerment" and for generating upward social mobility for their members and other Muslims is an important contribution to the integration of Muslim community within the society.

CONCLUSION

Austrian Islam essentially reflects the peculiarities and dynamics of the Turkish community and Turkish Islam in all its variants. This is not surprising because the majority of Austria's Muslims are of Turkish origin. However, as other Muslim immigrants, notably Bosnians, have come to Austria in the last decade, Austrian Islam has become ethnically and culturally more diverse and the sociopolitical dynamics of the community have become more complex.

Since the recognition of the IRCA in 1979, Muslim communities in Austria have developed an increasingly well established and successful institution whose efficiency and legitimacy have never been seriously questioned. The IRCA has proved to be a viable partner for Austrian organizations.

The overall trend has also been toward the professionalization and consolidation of Muslim, especially Turkish, organizations. Although over time, these organizations have increasingly accommodated their strategies to those of the IRCA, differences exist between the two in respect to organizational issues and the question of political "independence" plus the promotion of "Turkish Islam." A third force in this framework has been ATIB. Whereas most Turkish Muslim sociopolitical networks have proved very critical of the relationship between the state and religion in Turkey, ATIB is eager to show and promote a nationalist image of Islam. This is meant to facilitate Turkey's goal of becoming a member of the EU.

Austria's Muslims have made considerable adjustments—intellectually, socially, and otherwise—to their new environments. In doing so, they have contributed to the development of a European Islam. Nevertheless, the community's patterns of behavior and the dynamics of relations within the community are still shaped more by their history of migration and the peculiarities of their communities than by any vision of what "European Muslims" can be like in the future.

NOTES

1. Statistics are not very precise, and current figures refer to the last national census in 1991 and to figures according to the amendment to the Law of Registration in 1993, which also foresees the announcement of one's religion (Österreichischer Bundespressedienst, 1998).

2. Mustafa Tavukcuoglu, *Avrupa'da türk ailesi ve din egitimi: Avusturya örnegi)* [The Turkish family and religious education in Europe: the case of Austria] (Konya: Mehir Vakfi Yayinlari, 2000), 33.

3. See Anna Strobl, *Islam in Österreich: Eine religionssoziologische Untersuchung* [Islam in Austria: a study in religious sociology] (Frankfurt am Main: Peter Lang, 1997), 64–68.

4. See Smail Balic, "Zur Geschichte der Muslime in Österreich," in *Islam zwischen Selbstbild und Klischee: Eine Religion im österreichischen Schulbuch* [Islam between self-portrait and cliché: a religion in Austrian schoolbooks], ed. Susanna Heine (Kön und Wien: Böhlau-Verlag, 1995), 24–25.

5. Ibid. Also Zitta Rainer and Christine Wessely (eds.), *The Turks and What They Left to Us* (Vienna: Aus Österreichs Wissenschaft), 1978.

6. Balic, "Zur Geschichte der Muslime," 71.

7. Legal recognition depends on the fulfillment of certain conditions by the church or religious community. The ultimate criterion for recognition is that these churches or religious communities must be regarded by the state as being "in the public interest." Official recognition is granted by the "Kultusamt," a special unit linked to the Ministry of Education, Science, and Culture. In 1998, the criteria for recognition changed significantly; for example, numerical criteria were introduced into the list of conditions.

8. Strobl, *Islam in Österreich*, 21–24; also, Balic, "Zur Geschichte der Muslime," 27.

9. The founders were Smail Balic, Teufik Velagic, and Husein Gradascevic. See Balic, "Zur Geschichte der Muslime," 28.

10. The Vienna Islamic Center mosque is used especially for large gatherings and religious holidays.

11. The IRCA has started to build a third mosque in Vienna close to its main building. Other Muslim associations have their own mosques, or rather, praying rooms.

12. Islamische Glaubensgemeinschaft in Österreich, http://www.iggioe.at. In 1979, the IRCA was recognized according to the Hanafi rite on the basis of the Law of Recognition of Islam in 1912. The IRCA saw itself as the representative

body of all four Islamic schools of law. Also all Shi'a rites, Twelver, Zaidi, and Ibadi, etc., were acknowledged as equal to all Sunni rites.

13. The four Islamic communities cover the nine Austrian federal provinces.

14. See Strobl, *Islam in Österreich*, 38.

15. See Constitution of the IRCA, http://www.iggioe.at.

16. The IRCA estimates that "school-age Muslim youth" number about 70,000 in Austria but notes that only 35,000 to 40,000 Muslim children are registered with the IRCA. Moreover, only 28,000 children are "taken care of" by the IRCA's services and religious education. According to the IRCA, there are 232 active instructors for Islamic religion (see IRCA, http://www.iggioe.at).

17. Since Alavites are not recognized as a religious community in Austria, there is no possibility of providing exact figures. Even rough estimates may vary widely. Strobl suggests that about 20 percent of the immigrant population originating from Turkey may be Alavites (*Islam in Österreich*, 59).

18. Though figures often can be given for all of Austria, the infrastructure of Muslim organizations has been mainly developed in Vienna. Therefore, references and conclusions regarding Vienna are also valid for all of Austria.

19. On these issues, see the volume edited by Günther Seufert and Jaques Waardenburg, *Turkish Islam and Europe—Europe and Christianity as Reflected in Turkish Muslim Discourse and Turkish Muslim Life in the Diaspora* (Istanbul: Orient-Institut der Deutschen Morgenländischen Gesellschaft, 1999).

20. The idea of Islamic modernity and the "modernization of Islam" in the context of migration cannot be discussed here. We have to acknowledge, however, that in the context of Western host societies, Islam—as "traditionalist" as it often might seem from the outside—has adopted many modern features in terms of discourse, politics, internal structures, institutions, organizational patterns, and daily life that do not exist in the countries of origin. See Patrick Ireland, *The Policy Challenge of Ethnic Diversity: Immigrant Politics in France and Switzerland* (Cambridge: Harvard University Press, 1994); also Nilüfer Göle, *Republik und Schleier: Die muslimische Frau in der modernen Türkei* [Republic and veil: the Muslim woman in modern Turkey] (Berlin: Babel Verlag, 1995).

21. Sabine Kroissenbrunner, *Soziopolitische Netzwerke türkischer Migrantinnen in Wien* [Sociopolitical networks of Turkish immigrants in Vienna] (Vienna: (Institut für Konfliktforschung, 1997), 70.

22. Ibid.

23. Strobl, *Islam in Österreich*, 57–58.

24. Ireland, *Policy Challenge of Ethnic Diversity*.

25. These figures are based on estimates by Kurdish organizations in Austria such as ERNK/Feykom (National Liberation Front of Kurdistan). One estimate claims that about 20 to 30 percent of immigrants from Turkey to Western Europe are of Kurdish origin. Strobl, *Islam in Österreich*, 68–69; Karl Michael Reiser, "Identitäts und Interessenspolitik 'türkischer' Migranten organisationen in Wien" [Identities and politics of interests. Turkish immigration organizations in Vienna], Ph.D. thesis, Vienna, 2000, p. 237.

26. See Jochen Blaschke, "Die Diaspora der Kurden in der Bundesrepublik Deut," *Österreichische Zeitschrift für Soziologie* 3 (1991): 8–93; also, Martin van Bruinessen Agha, *Sheikh and State: On the Social and Political Organisation of Kurdistan* (Rijswick: Europrint, 1978).

27. Henri Barkey and Graham E. Fuller, *Turkey's Kurdish Question. Carnegie Commission on Preventing Deadly Conflict* (New York: Rowman and Littlefield, 1998), 73.

28. Ibid. Also, Oktay Pirim and Süha Örtülu, *PKK nin 20 Yillik Öykusü* (Istanbul: Boyut Kitaplari, 1999), 340.

29. Reiser, "Indentäts und Interessenspolitik," 231.

30. Ibid., 147.

31. Ibid., 148.

32. Ibid.

33. Ibid.

34. Ibid.

35. See Ertekin Özcan, *Türkische Immigrantenorganisationen in der Bundesrepublik* [Turkish immigration organizations in the Federal Republic] (Berlin: Hitit, 1992).

36. Ibid.

37. Based on personal interviews.

8

Islam in Spain

Bernabé López García and Ana I. Planet Contreras

INTRODUCTION

Attention is frequently called to the important role that Islam has played in the development of modern Spain. No doubt, Islam and Spain have a long, varied, and turbulent history of interaction. Yet, the present Muslim community in Spain comprises only a few thousand faithful of Spanish ancestry, and most of the country's Muslim population is made up of immigrants from Muslim countries, whose numbers have been growing in recent years.

Spain's situation in regard to Islam is also different from that of other European countries. The most important difference lies in the fact that despite a past marked by many centuries of Islamic rule, at present Muslims are not numerically significant in Spain, and the Muslim community in Spain, both naturalized and immigrant, totals just 350,000. Two reasons explain this situation: Only in the last fifteen years has Spain become a receiver of immigrants, and unlike other European countries, Spain has had no lasting colonies in Muslim countries. Spain's colonial experience in Morocco was short-lived and of limited geographical scope; it had colonized in northern Morocco and the western Sahara, an area that is barely 20,000 square kilometers, with 200,000 inhabitants. Nevertheless, the Spanish presence in the North African cities of Melilla and Ceuta, considered part of Spain, has led to the development of a Spanish Islam of Moroccan origin, with its unique characteristics.

NUMBERS AND ETHNIC COMPOSITION OF SPANISH MUSLIMS

The number of Muslims who hold Spanish citizenship and therefore can be identified as "nationalized [naturalized] Muslims" is very limited. Most Spanish Muslims are former citizens of Islamic states who have acquired Spanish citizenship or Spaniards who have converted to Islam. This is due to the fact that Islam has lacked a significant base in Spain ever since the expulsion of the Moors in 1609 and the subsequent prohibition of the practice of Islam. In the twentieth century, the Catholic state, which reached its peak during the rule of General Francisco Franco, delayed the appearance of a Spanish Islam. However, it did not impede the formation of a religious minority in Spain, through the naturalization of citizens from those Arab and Islamic countries with which Spain had established cordial relations by the end of the 1940s. This minority, which enjoyed no special legal protection and had little organizational capacity, mainly consisted of Muslim students studying in Spanish universities. Many of these students later settled in Spain and acquired Spanish citizenship.

The number of naturalized foreigners increased significantly between 1960 and 1997, reaching a total of 125,247 people. Of this number, 24,730 are from Africa and 13,998 from Asia, a total of 38,728 or 30.9 percent of all naturalizations. The great majority (80.7 percent) of Afro-Asian naturalizations were carried out within the context of the first Law on Foreigners, which was passed in 1985.

As shown in Table 8.1, most nationalized Muslims are former Moroccan citizens, followed by Palestinians, Syrians, and Lebanese, although a fair portion of naturalized Lebanese are Christians. Moroccan citizens include a portion of the Muslim Moroccan residents of the border cities of Ceuta and Melilla. From a legal standpoint, this group must be considered as part of nationalized Islam because while some of this population has lived in those cities since the beginning of the century, until recently, with few exceptions, they did not hold Spanish citizenship. Their legal tie to the cities was reduced to a "statistics card" certifying their residence in the country. After the publication of the Law on Foreigners in 1985, a process was initiated to grant citizenship to this group.

The Aliens' Act was published in July 1985 as part of a process to make Spanish laws compatible with those of the European Community, following Spain's admission to it. This law, which was modified in 1999 and in 2001, focused on the stabilization and regularization of the position of Latin American citizens living in Spain and others "with an identity and cultural affinity with Spain, such as Portuguese, Filipinos, natives of Equatorial Guinea, Andorrans, Sephardi Jews, and inhabitants of Gibraltar." But this law did not consider the case of Muslims of

Table 8.1
Nationality of Citizens of Primarily Islamic Countries, 1980–1997

AFRICA		ASIA	
Algeria	303	Afghanistan	21
Egypt	333	Bangladesh	17
Gambia	86	Indonesia	24
Libya	30	Iran	889
Mali	14	Iraq	221
Mauritania	26	Jordan	925
Morocco	19,817	Kuwait	1
Nigeria	39	Lebanon	856
Sahara	39	Malaysia	19
Senegal	98	Pakistan	402
Sudan	57	Saudi Arabia	3
Tunisia	97	Syria	1,666
Total	**20,939**	**Total**	**5,044**

Source: 1997 Immigration Report.

Moroccan origin living in Melilla and in Ceuta. What this omission meant was that following the passage of this law, they could be expelled from these cities because of their illegal situation. Therefore, quite understandably, this law was unpopular in those cities, and its passage led to protests and demonstrations by a number of small Muslim political associations. In the course of these protests, the protestors' demands underwent a change; initially, they were asking for recognition of their status as foreign residents, but later they demanded Spanish citizenship.

The combination of the introduction of this law and the protest it generated ultimately resulted in the naturalization of 13,000 Muslims of Moroccan origin between 1986 and 1990 (see Table 8.2).

SPANISH CONVERTS

The second and smaller component of Spain's Muslim community consists of Spanish converts. According to some accounts, their number stands at around 5,000, but other authors and analysts estimate their number to be as low as 1,000.[1] A realistic estimate is perhaps around 3,000. Spanish converts to Islam live mainly in the southern provinces of Cordoba, Granada, and Seville—historic centers of Islam in Spain—

Table 8.2
Citizenship Granted to Moroccan Nationals in Ceuta and Melilla, 1986–1994

Origin	1970–1975	1976–1980	1981–1985	1986	1987	1988	1989	1990	1991	1992	1993	1994	Total
Morocco	190*	337*	861*	3	175	144	40	262	427*	597*	987*	897*	2,012
Ceuta				762	1,674	1,231	1,432	1,243					6,342
Melilla				836	3,090	1,890	560	170					6,546
Total	190	337	861	1,601	4,939	3,265	2,032	1,675	427	597	987	897	14,900

*Data include nationalizations from Ceuta and Melilla.

Source: Ministry of Justice.

and have very active religious organizations, a fact that gives them a high profile in these cities.

Most of the converts are Sunnis, but some are Shi'as. They are grouped within a large number of associations, mostly located in the Province of Andalucia. One of these associations is the Yama'a islámica al-Andalus (Islamic Society of Andalucia), which currently has a university in Cordoba, the Universidad Islámica Internacional Averroes de Al-Andalus (Averroes Islamic International University of Andalucia). Similar groups include the Comunidad Islamica de Sevilla-Umma (Islamic Community of Seville-Umma), the Asociación Musulmana de Córdoba (Muslim Association of Cordoba), and the Movimiento de Musulmanes Europeos al-Murabitun (European Muslim Movement—Murabitun).

Initially, most of these associations were formed by Spanish political activists belonging to various nationalist and leftist splinter groups. At first, their goal was to promote a separate "Andalusian identity" and use it to obtain political autonomy for the region as other regions, such as the Basque country or Catalonia, had done. In doing so, they used the historic experience of Al-Andalus as a center of Islamic civilization, and in the process, they became influenced by Islam and the Islamic dimension of the whole concept of Al-Andalus. In other words, the transition from a specific Andalusian identity to an Islamic faith and identity was achieved without much difficulty.

IMMIGRANT ISLAM

As shown in Table 8.3, according to the census of 31 December 1999, there existed 211,033 residents in Spain from Islamic countries. This number should be increased by the 118,000 individuals affected by the extraordinary regularization (legalization) process underway until June 2000.[2] Because of the nature of Spain's legal system, every year foreign residents must renew their identity cards and legal resident permits. It is not easy to obtain a residency permit, and this is why the number of illegal foreign citizens living in Spain has been increasing. Once every four or five years, an "extraordinary regularization process" is organized by the authorities in order to give residency permits to these people. It is a much simpler process and provides permits for the number of newly arrived immigrants and those immigrants who used to have permits but had "lost" them.

SECTARIAN DIFFERENCES

The overwhelming majority of Spain's Muslims are Sunnis. But there is also a small Shi'a community, which includes a number of Spanish converts. The Shi'as live mostly in Barcelona, Madrid, and Valencia.

Table 8.3
Residents in Spain from Primarily Muslim Countries

Country	Legal residents December 1999	Newly legalized immigrants
AFRICA		
Algeria	8,495	9,551
Chad	9	12
Djibouti	9	0
Egypt	972	465
Ethiopia	105	18
Gambia	8,524	1,411
Libya	185	28
Mali	2,281	842
Mauritania	1,651	3,742
Morocco	161,870	78,759
Niger	62	34
Nigeria	4,214	4,277
Senegal	7,744	8,303
Somalia	99	24
Sudan	116	56
Tunisia	590	201
ASIA		
Afghanistan	22	14
Bahrain	3	1
Bangladesh	850	1,086
Brunei	3	0
Indonesia	201	41
Iran	1,959	245
Iraq	702	110
Jordan	646	92
Kuwait	24	3

Table 8.3 (continued)

Country	Legal residents December 1999	Newly legalized immigrants
Lebanon	1,093	137
Malaysia	127	38
Mongolia	2	4
Oman	8	0
Pakistan	5,126	7,698
Palestine	201	52
Qatar	2	1
Saudi Arabia	240	3
Sri Lanka	195	22
Syria	1,010	264
Turkey	498	105
United Arab Emirates	5	1
Yemen	14	3
OTHERS		
Albania	204	60
Bosnia	929	129
Kazakhstan	28	41
Uzbekistan	15	14
Total	**211,033**	**117,887**

Source: Immigration Office, Madrid.

SOCIAL AND ECONOMIC PROFILE

Spain's Muslim community is also marked by sharp differences along gender, age, and employment lines. These divergences are the result of the time and conditions of their settlement in Spain and their differing socioeconomic status. Data on these differences are available only regarding the large communities, namely, Moroccans, Algerians, Iranians, Pakistanis, and Egyptians. Similarities in the profiles of various groups relate mainly to the members' employment situation. In terms of gender distribution, Algerians and Pakistanis have the least number of women (between 4 and 2 percent of total population, respectively), while the figure is higher for Iranians and Moroccans (between 20 and 15 percent, respectively). These differences are explained by the recent arrival of the Algerian immigrants and the strictly economic character of Pakistani immigration. The larger number of women within the Iranian and Moroccan communities is due respectively to the political nature of Iranian immigration following the Islamic revolution of 1979, and the geographical proximity and process of family regrouping of the Moroccans. Because of social and economic changes in Spain in the 1980s and 1990s, notably the increasing number of working women, there has been a rising demand for domestic help and childcare help (nannies). Many Moroccan women have filled these jobs. Today, Moroccan women can find a job and get a work permit faster than can Moroccan men.

The Algerian and Moroccan communities have the highest number of young people twenty-five and older—almost 30 percent in the case of the Algerian community and 20 percent in the case of the Moroccans. The Iranian community is the most evenly distributed in terms of age groups, with a family structure that has a lower proportion of youths (5.4 percent) and a larger group of over fifty-five year olds (almost 5 percent). This indicates the high number of asylum seekers among Iranian immigrants.

In terms of employment, most Algerians are engaged in agriculture (47 percent), especially in fruit picking. They are concentrated in eastern Spain. Pakistanis are involved mainly in mining (44 percent, especially in Jaen and Leon) as well as in the textile industry throughout Spain. Iranians are mostly (32 percent) engaged in commercial activities. Moroccans are mostly employed in construction and other industry, followed by agriculture (28 percent). The service sector provides employment to a quarter of each of these communities, except the Algerians.

There are no statistics for Muslims from other Middle Eastern countries that provide a similar breakdown along gender, sex, and employment lines. Nevertheless, the employment profile of the Egyptian community shown in Table 8.4, which indicates that approximately 18 percent of them are professionals, technicians, or employed in management positions, allows the inference that Syrians, Palestinians, and Jordanians also have a similar profile because they all represent groups consisting of former students at Spanish universities.

MUSLIM INTEGRATION IN SPANISH SOCIETY

The disparity of their ethnic origins, circumstances, and timing of their settlement in Spain coupled with the fact of the presence of a well-established Muslim community in Spain—notably in Melilla and Ceuta—have affected the way in which each Muslim community has lived its religious life. These factors have also shaped attitudes toward the formation of associations as a tool for resolving practical religious needs.

The Muslim groups referred to previously present varying degrees of

Table 8.4
Profiles of Muslim Immigrants in Spain by Sex, Age, and Profession, 1992 (in percent)

Professions	Morocco	Algeria	Egypt	Iran	Pakistan
Professionals/ Technicians	1.90	3.8	13.5	18.2	3.6
Management	0.07	0.3	4.3	4.2	0.9
Administration	0.90	1.8	6.5	31.7	0.9
Trade	10.40	3.8	17.4	25.4	23.4
Services	24.00	16.3	23.9	0.6	23.7
Agriculture	28.00	47.0	9.0	11.5	2.3
Ind./Constr./Min.	34.20	26.0	23.9	0.4	43.6
Unclassified	0.40	0.9	1.3	—	1.6

Age Groups	Morocco	Algeria	Egypt	Iran	Pakistan
< = 20 years	2.8	2.2	0.2	0.4	3.04
20–24 years	20.2	29.2	11.5	5.0	29.20
25–54 years	74.4	68.2	86.0	89.6	68.20
> 55 years	2.3	0.4	2.2	4.9	0.40

Sex	Morocco	Algeria	Egypt	Iran	Pakistan
Males	84.6	95.8	88.5	80.1	98.1
Females	15.4	4.2	11.5	19.8	4.1

Source: Spanish Immigration Office.

integration into the Spanish community. The level of integration is very high in the case of naturalized Muslims and Spanish converts. However, the majority of the Muslim community in Spain consists of immigrants who have settled in Spain only for economic reasons and who have achieved a more limited level of integration.

Although the number of immigrant Muslims is much higher than those of "nationalized Muslims," Spanish legislation relating to religion has been developed only in light of the needs of the Spanish Muslim community and does not extend to Muslim immigrants. Similarly, the pattern and character of Muslim religious associations do not reflect the presence of immigrant Muslims and focus mainly on Spanish Muslims— indigenous or naturalized.

MUSLIM ASSOCIATIONS IN SPAIN: BACKGROUND AND PRESENT SITUATION

The first Muslim association in Spain was created in 1971 as a cultural association, Associación Musulmana de España (Muslim Association of Spain) and within the framework of the new legislation regarding associations passed at the end of Franco's regime. This legislation allowed other religious beliefs to assert their presence, provided that they respected Catholicism and the church. Because the Muslim community in Ceuta and Melilla represents about a third of these cities' total population, it was natural that the first Islamic association in Spain was established in Melilla, Asociación Musulmana de Melilla (Muslim Association of Melilla), registered on 23 November 1968. Ceuta followed suit two years later, on 9 October 1971, by establishing an association called Zaouia Musulmana de Mohammadia (Muslim Muhamadia Azouia).

In Spain itself, the first Muslim association to be included in the Register of Religious Entities of the Ministry of Justice was the aforementioned Asociación Musulmana en España. It was headed by a Syrian-born, naturalized Spanish doctor, Riay Tatary Bakry. This association built the first mosque in Madrid, which has since become a major meeting place for Muslims.

Other institutions, such as the Comunidad Musulmana de España (1979), directed by the Spaniard Alvaro Machordom Comins, appeared only at the end of the 1970s. During the period of political transition from Franco's regime to democracy in Spain, groups of Spanish converts to Islam appeared in the country, especially in Andalucia. Between 1979 and 1983, these converts established organizations such as the Comunidad Islámica de España (Muslim Community of Spain) (Granada), the Asociación Musulmana Autónoma de Córdoba y Provincia (Autonomous Muslim Association of Cordoba) (1980), the Comunidad Musulmana de Al-Andalus (Muslim Community of Al-Andalus) (Granada, 1981), as well as other groups in Malaga, Seville, Almeria, and Jaen. At that time, other groups, consisting mainly of immigrant Muslims, also appeared in Andalucia. For example, in 1983, an association with a strong ethnic base was formed in Linares in order to unite Pakistani immigrants residing in the province of Jaen.

From the mid-1980s, the existing religious associations have been trying to attract the new immigrants settling in Spain and to incorporate them within their organizations. Meanwhile, the embassies of some Arab and Muslim countries have become interested and engaged in the activities of various Muslim communities and have tried to influence them by creating new organizations. As a result of these developments, the Comunidad Musulmana Marroquí de Madrid-Al-Umma (Moroccan Muslim Community of Madrid-Al-Umma) was created on 20 March

1986. The organization's president is Muhammad Bulaix Baeza and its secretary is the journalist Muhammad Chakor. It has close links with the Moroccan Embassy. Another organization is the Consejo Continental Europeo de Mezquitas (European Council of Mosques), established on 18 July 1989. It is led by Muhammad Bahige Mulla, and Muhammad Chakor is its treasurer. Saudi and Kuwaiti authorities, in collaboration with the Moroccan Embassy, have supported and promoted the council.

One of the most common problems encountered by these associations is the availability of financial resources, which enable them to continue their operations and carry out their activities. It is difficult to ascertain the main sources of funding of these organizations. Their directors and other officials claim that membership fees are the main source of financing, supplemented by occasional assistance from international Islamic organizations and the embassies of some Muslim states. In fact, except for Saudi funds, which have financed the construction of the largest mosque in Spain—the Madrid Islamic Cultural Center—it is difficult to identify the sources of financing.

The most important Shi'a organizations in Spain include the following:

1. The Islamic Community of Granada (Communidad Islámica de Granada).
2. The Society of Ahl-ul-Bait (AUB refers to the family of the Prophet). The society has a Center for Islamic Studies called Centro de Estudios e Investigaciones Islámicas, which is closely linked to the Islamic University in the city of Qom in Iran.
3. The Islamic School of Imam Riza (La Madrosah Islamica Imam Ar-Rida). In addition to religious courses, the school offers courses in Arabic and Persian. The society publishes a review called *Kanzar*. It appears, however, that there is not much interaction between the Shi'as and their organizations, largely supported by Iran, and the Sunni groups.[3]

LEGAL RECOGNITION OF ISLAM IN SPAIN

In April 1989, the Asociación Musulmana en España requested the official recognition of Islam's presence in Spain as a basic requirement for negotiating an agreement for cooperation with the Spanish state, as stipulated in the Constitution of 1978. Reaching such an agreement is very important for the Muslim community because it regulates important issues such as the status of Muslim religious leaders and their specific conditions and rights, which derive from the exercise of their religious role (ministry); legal protection of mosques and Muslim cemeteries; provision of tax benefits for these and other nonprofit organizations; religious marriages and the commemoration of Muslim religious holidays; the rights of Muslim workers during religious holidays; and Muslim religious instruction. In order to prepare such an agreement, it was necessary that various associations join forces and form a single interlocutor with whom the state could negotiate. Such unification was necessary to prove the significant presence of Islam in Spain.[4]

As a result of these efforts, in July 1989 the Advisory Board for Religious Freedom of the Ministry of Justice approved the recognition of Islam as a religion with a "considerable presence" in Spain, in the following terms:

> The Islamic religion has been present in Spain since the 8th century, with significant diffusion in the earlier centuries, and a greater or lesser presence thereafter depending on the period and historical circumstances, and has remained so uninterruptedly to present times. The Islamic communities cover a great part of the Spanish territory. Their presence is especially significant in the lower third of the Iberian Peninsula and in the Spanish territories in North Africa. There is, in our opinion, a clear awareness among Spanish citizens that the Islamic religion is one of the spiritual beliefs that historically has had a presence in Spain, a presence which continues until present times.[5]

After receiving a favorable ruling from the Ministry of Justice, the most difficult task of the Muslim community in its drive to negotiate with the state remained the creation of a sole interlocutor to interact with governmental authorities. The diverse character of Muslim associations in Spain, reflecting the heterogeneous composition of the community, meant that they were forced to reorganize. Thus, two months later, on 17 September 1989, the Federación Española de Entidades Religiosas Islámicas (Spanish Federation of Muslim Religious Entities) (FEERI) was created in Madrid.[6] The federation began talks with the Spanish state to negotiate the Agreement for Co-Operation of the State with Muslim Communities Established in Spain. Initially, rather than uniting Islamic associations, this process tended to fragment them. For example, eight Muslim groups emerged from the Asociación Musulmana en España, which were spread throughout Spain.[7] Eventually, on 10 April 1991, these communities joined together to form the Unión de Comunidades Islámicas de España (Union of Muslim Communities of Spain) (UCIDE).

Continued divisions within the community impeded progress on completing the negotiations on the Agreement for Co-Operation. Finally, in April 1992, the federation and the union were joined into a single entity named the Comisión Islámica de España (Islamic Commission of Spain), which signed the Agreement for Co-Operation with the state on 28 April

1992.[8] The agreement, in line with those signed with evangelical religious entities and the Jewish community, establishes general rules regarding a number of issues, notably: (1) the structure of the Islamic Commission, (2) management of places of worship and religious personnel, (3) related economic matters, and (4) Islamic religious education in Spanish schools.

The agreement concerns matters of great importance for Spain's Muslim citizens, including rules regarding the status of Islamic leaders, legal protection of mosques and cemeteries, and tax benefits to certain goods belonging to Muslim associations. There are different articles related to religious marriages, the commemoration of Muslim holidays, and the rights of Muslim workers during these festivities. The agreement, however, does not address the question of the financial and economic situation of Muslim associations, which creates many problems for the practice of Islam in Spain. This neglect is due to the fact that the Spanish government does not provide financial assistance to religious institutions besides those connected with the Catholic Church.

The implementation of the agreement's provisions, after almost eight years since its publication, has been fairly limited. Perhaps the most important cause of this failure has been the internal divisions within the Islamic Commission of Spain, caused by diverging objectives of the two federations that make up the commission. The existence of ideological differences and personal rivalries has made it nearly impossible for the commission to develop coherent policies and positions and submit them to the government. Consequently, even today, conditions for the practice of Islam in Spain are not as good as they could be. Because the agreement is a framework or reference text, its content has been modified within a long and complex process in order to reach consensus between the two factions in the Comisión Islámica de España and representatives of the Religious Issues Authority of the Ministry of Justice.

The area receiving most constant attention has been the teaching of Islam in Spanish public schools. This is due partly to the fact that traditionally, the teaching of the principles of the Catholic religion has been a common practice in Spanish schools. This practice has served as a model for religious instruction that, in recent years, has been revised in order to incorporate other religions.

DEVELOPMENT OF A LEGAL FRAMEWORK FOR ISLAMIC EDUCATION

Article 10 of the agreement, dealing with education, left pending two fundamental matters: (1) the establishment of a curriculum for teaching Islam and (2) questions related to teachers' qualifications, their salaries, and their relationship with various educational centers.

During the negotiation of the agreement, representatives of the Islamic

Commission requested that the instruction of Islam be considered as any other subject and that the instructors teaching Islamic principles form part of the faculty. The state at first rejected both these proposals. But it finally agreed that instructors teaching Islamic principles should enjoy the same treatment, at least in theory, as teachers of other religions. Other remaining issues were resolved four years after the signing of the agreement. As a result, the Curriculum for the Teaching of Islam in Public State-Run Educational Centers was published in January 1996, and in March 1996, the Ministry of Education and Sciences and representatives of the Spanish Islamic Commission signed the Agreement of the Designation and Remuneration of Persons Responsible for the Teaching of the Islamic Religion in Primary and Secondary Educational Centers. There were, however, disagreements regarding the contents of an Islamic curriculum. These derived from differences of view between the two main federations of Islamic associations that formed the Comisión Islámica de España. The curriculum proposed by the FEERI had two clear objectives: (1) to be open, accessible, and attractive to non-Muslim students and (2) to ensure that the teaching of Islam did not remain limited to an explanation of rites and religious principles but included philosophical and historical dimensions of Islam. UCIDE leaders, however, maintained that Islamic teaching should not treat Islam in historical terms but principally as a religious belief system.

The curriculum that finally emerged is broad, includes religious, historical, and philosophical subjects, and can be adapted to the needs of students at different educational centers and levels. The lack of teaching materials, however, has delayed the implementation of this curriculum.

According to the March 1996 agreement, the designation of teaching staff will be handled by the Spanish Islamic Commission, and their salaries will be paid by the state, provided that there are at least ten Muslim children in each school.

Representatives of both Islamic association federations agree on the qualifications required for teaching staffs. Teachers must be Muslim, with an adequate knowledge of Spanish and a good understanding of Arabic. Standards are higher for instructors in secondary schools. Nevertheless, agreeing on a list of teachers has not been easy. This factor, coupled with difficulties in obtaining funds, has hampered the progress of Islamic teaching in Spanish schools, and therefore the scope and level of Islamic education remain limited.

PARTICIPATION IN SOCIAL AND POLITICAL SPHERES

The largest group of Muslims in Spain consists of immigrants who do not have Spanish citizenship. This makes the political expression of their needs extremely difficult and even discourages them from forming associations. Political parties and trade unions do not pay any special attention to this community.

Certain groups, consisting of Spanish converts to Islam, have emerged in Andalucia, such as the Yama'a Islámica al-Andalus (Islamic Community of Andalus) and the Liberación Andalusa (Andalusian Liberation), the Comunidad Islámica de Sevilla-Umma, and the Asociación Musulmana de Córdoba; all have a political orientation, albeit on a purely local scale. Their main goal is to bring together the growing community of Muslim immigrants, for two reasons: to help them live in Spain and to use them as an instrument to force the government to negotiate. There is also a rising political consciousness among Spanish Muslims in Melilla and Ceuta. Initially, the government favored this trend. But today this heightened consciousness has been transformed into a desire to establish more independent religious and political organizations.

Meanwhile, as a result of the naturalization process in Melilla between 1980 and 1990, these "new Spaniards" have become very attractive for competing political parties. Consequently, some Spanish political parties have encouraged the formation of Muslim parties in order to gain the Muslim vote and influence the outcome of elections. For example, in 1987, the Spanish Socialist party unsuccessfully supported the creation of the Independent Hispano-Berber party. However, the party did not participate in the elections.[9] In Melilla, during the preparation for the municipal regional elections of 1995, a similar policy was pursued. It was based on the strategy of creating "hinge parties," which could collaborate with the main party and enhance its chances of success. Thus, the Socialist Party of Melilla supported the creation of a "pseudo-religious" or "ethnic" party in order to obtain the votes of the significant number of Muslims in the city. The Coalition for Melilla Party was created only a few months prior to the elections, with the support of a group of local businesspeople. It obtained four seats in the Municipal Assembly.

In 1999, another entity, the Social Democratic Party of Melilla, was created in order to attract Muslim voters. The intention in this case was to undermine the influence of the coalition among the Muslims. This party, however, was an offshoot of the Terra Omnium association, which had led the movement against the application of the Law on Foreigners of 1986. The results of this division of forces were not good for the new party, which received only 498 votes, 1.8 percent of the total. The Coalition for Melilla obtained the second largest number of votes in the city, and its candidate, Mustafa Aberchán, was elected mayor amid a media frenzy that surrounded the election of the city's first Muslim mayor. This development is closely related to the fact that the region's population has become disenchanted with the two major national parties: the Socialists (Partido Socialista Obrero Español) and the Popular party (Partido Popular). This situation has led to the political fragmentation of the region and the emergence of a number of small parties, some of which are Muslim.

During the period 1995 to 1999, the local government linked to the Partido Popular, which currently controls the national government, helped consolidate the Coalition for Melilla party. Its main focus has been problems of social integration, employment, and education of Muslim communities. These efforts seem to have helped improve the living conditions of a community that is still discriminated against. During the four years that this government was in power, the Coalition for Melilla party was consolidated as a political force. Because of the party's influence, there has been considerable social progress in the city, and the living conditions of a population long subjected to discrimination have improved.

Taking a lead from the inhabitants of Melilla, Muslims of Ceuta have also begun to organize, and they actively participated in the 1999 elections. That year, Muslims managed to elect three representatives to the local government. However, Muslims in these two cities do not constitute a single and unified voting bloc. Moreover, their voting pattern is determined by how various local and national governments deal with their needs and grievances rather than by religious issues.

The Muslim vote carries considerable weight in these cities. However, voters do not always vote on the basis of party allegiance but also in reaction to how various governments have dealt with their economic and social grievances, especially the question of discrimination.

CONCLUSIONS: BEING MUSLIM IN SPAIN

The presence of Islam in Spain has less to do with the historical past than it does with Spain's becoming a recipient country of immigrants. Although still a relatively small community, because of continuous migration, Islam is becoming more visible in the public sphere and is attracting the attention of the public and the political elites, including governmental authorities. Yet, Spain's small and diverse Islamic community has found it difficult to make progress in various fields, and it has faced many problems. These are made worse by the need for Muslims to present themselves as a single interlocutor vis-à-vis the state. The current legal framework is quite advanced, but in reality Spanish Muslims consist of small communities, which are trying to improve the conditions under which they can practice their religion as "neo-Muslims" or to pass their beliefs to a second generation. Other problems result from the fact that old structures of the community are no longer sufficient for the needs of its members. Therefore, there is a need for new structures, including at the neighborhood level, in order to ensure positive and peaceful interaction between Muslims and non-Muslims.

Local authorities continue to have problems in identifying viable partners among different Muslim associations and federations. The Islamic Commission in Spain is perceived as a very intricate association, with too many diverging tendencies and internal differences. Moreover, local authorities fear that they may be manipulated by these associations or used by foreign governments.

Bonds with Islamic countries—countries of origin and others—are being strengthened because of the need for funds to build places of worship. But these links cause fear among Spanish authorities that foreign forces may try to manipulate them through the intermediary of various Islamic associations. This adds to the difficulties involved in communicating with the Muslim community, in order to address various issues and problems and to solve them. In sum, the Muslim community, with its growing numbers and varying degrees of integration in Spanish society, is characterized by dispersion and lack of cohesion. This, coupled with other problems discussed here, is gradually turning the question of Islam and how to deal with it into a very sensitive issue in Spain, at the national and local levels.

NOTES

1. Emilio Galindo belongs to the second category in his study, "El Islam en la España actual," in *Al servicio de la unidad. Homenaje a D. Julián García Hernando* [In the service of unity. Homage to Julian García Hernando] (Madrid: Editorial Atenas, 1993), 531–551.

2. It should also be mentioned that not all residents in Spain from primarily Muslim countries are Muslims themselves. In the case of countries like Lebanon, it is more likely that a considerable number of its citizens living in Spain are Christian. In the case of Ghana, we have not included the 1,925 people regularized in 2000 because only 20 percent of the population is Muslim.

3. For more information, see www.Islam-Shia.org.

4. All information on the legal texts dealing with Islam in Spain can be found on the Ministry of Justice web page (www.mju.es/mreligiosos) as well as a listing of Islamic religious entities legally inscribed.

5. The ruling was issued by the Advisory Board for Religious Freedom on 23 July 1989 and was drawn up by A. Fernández González and D. Llamazares Fernández.

6. Interesting information on the FEERI can be found at www.verdeislamica.com and www.webislam.com.

7. The communities are distributed throughout Spain in Valencia, Granada, Madrid, Zaragoza, Galicia, Asturias, Terrassa, and Alicante.

8. Law 26 of 10 November 1992 (Official State Gazette of 12 November 1992) will formalize this agreement.

9. See Ana I. Planet, *Melilla y Ceuta, ciudades-frontera hispano-Moroccans* [Melilla and Ceuta, Spanish-Moroccan border cities] (Melilla: Universidad Nacional de Educación a Distancia-Ciudad Autónoma de Melilla-Ciudad Autónoma de Cauta, 1998).

9

Islam in Greece

Thanos P. Dokos and Dimitris A. Antoniou

INTRODUCTION

Muslim presence in Greece must be placed in the larger context of Greece's political borders and the broader issue of immigration from Europe's southern—and overwhelmingly Muslim—periphery prompted by the economic difficulties and youthful population of the countries located there. There are serious concerns in many European circles about the disruptive impact of such large immigration on their social, political, and cultural structures, including the growth of racist reflexes and groups, especially during periods of economic hardship. Greece is no exception.

In fact, various studies and opinion polls show that a majority of Greeks view illegal immigrants as a major problem for Greek society. This phenomenon is perceived as a burden, not so much for the Greek national economy, but rather to the country's social welfare and educational systems and its public order.

Today, there are between 500,000 and 1 million economic immigrants in Greece from Eastern and Southeastern Europe and from Africa and Asia, including the Middle East. But nearly two thirds of illegal immigrants in Greece are Albanians.

The facts that Greece borders two Muslim countries (Turkey and Albania) and two other states with important Muslim communities, notably FYROM (Former Yugoslav Republic of Macedonia) and Bulgaria, and that it also has a small, but strategically important, Muslim community in its own soil make the question of Muslim presence in Greece of great importance both domestically and in terms of its external relations. Indeed, with the collapse of the Soviet Union and the opening up of new, and partly Muslim-inhabited, areas of Southeastern Europe, the Islamic factor has become even more important in shaping Greece's view of its security environment and hence its security and diplomatic strategy. The new conditions have also enhanced the importance of Greece's Muslim population in this broader context.

GREECE AND THE ISLAMIC WORLD: A BRIEF HISTORY

The connections between Hellenic and Muslim worlds go back to early centuries of Islam.[1] In the ninth century AD, the Abbasid caliph Al-Mamûn established *Bait al-hikma* (House of Wisdom) and gathered Greek and Muslim scholars. His goal was to translate Hellenic scientific and philosophical works into Arabic and to create a synthesis between Islam and Hellenic civilization. In this way, hundreds of Greek manuscripts were saved, thus making possible the later rediscovery of classical Greece by Europe, a fact that contributed to the Renaissance.[2] Trade links established in medieval times also led to increased cultural exchanges between Greece and the Muslim world. However, Greco-Muslim relations were not always marked by peaceful and constructive intellectual and commercial exchanges. The conquest of Constantinople in 1453 by the Ottoman Sultan Muhammad the Conqueror (*Fatih*) and the later expansion of Ottoman rule to Southeastern Europe, including Greece, marked a long period of tension and animosity between the two worlds, the legacy of which is still felt. This past experience has had the greatest impact in shaping the character of Greek-Turkish relations, which have been marked by long periods of tensions. In the last two years, there has been a significant improvement in Greek-Turkish relations, which, if continued and deepened, would be beneficial to Greece's overall relations with the Islamic world. In the last fifty years, Greece has succeeded in establishing cordial ties with Arab and other Muslim countries. The absence of a colonial past has facilitated the forging of such relations.

ETHNIC AND ECONOMIC PROFILE OF GREECE'S MUSLIM COMMUNITY

The question of whether Greece's Muslim population should be defined in terms of "community" is very controversial. Some Greek scholars have argued that it is desirable that Greek Muslims be identified as a community, comparable with other communities with a recognized leadership. They maintain that this would increase their lobbying power and their ability to bid for funds from the government and other sources.

Table 9.1
Demographic Composition of Western Thrace

Prefecture	Total population	Christians	Muslims	Muslims %
Evros	144,000	135,000	9,000	6.25
Xanthi	91,000	51,000	40,000	43.90
Rhodopi	103,000	40,000	63,000	61.16
Total	**338,000**	**226,000**	**112,000**	**33.14**

Source: Thanasis Vakalios, ed., *To provlima tis diapolitismikis ekpaideysis sti Ditiki Thraki* [The problem of a multicultural education in Western Thrace] (Athens: Gutenberg Editions, 1997), 23.

Others, however, suggest that moves in this direction might inhibit personal freedoms and threaten ethnic or religious minorities within the Muslim population as one or two larger groups may dominate the others.

Greece's Muslims do not constitute an ethnically or culturally homogeneous group. Islam in Greece consists of the Muslim minority in Western Thrace and of Muslim immigrants, whose growing presence has become noticeable only during the 1990s. According to Thanasis Vakalios, the Muslim minority in Western Thrace numbers approximately 112,000.[3] Other sources put the number at 120,000.[4] This minority consists of three different ethnic groups. The largest group is of Turkish origin and numbers about 60,000; the second group is the Pomaks, who number approximately 30,000; there are also 20,000 Athigani (Roma Gypsies).

Among Muslims of Turkish origin, two groups can be distinguished: (1) old Muslims, who make up the largest part of the community, and (2) the reformist Kemalist group.

The Pomaks' origins are a subject of disagreement. The Greeks consider them as people indigenous to the region with no ethnic connections to Bulgarian Muslims, who are also called Pomaks. They lost their native tongue and espoused Islam during the Ottoman rule. They speak a dialect akin to Bulgarian mixed with Turkish words and reside in villages in the Southern Rodopi. Many Pomaks also live in Komotini and Xanthi, and some live in Didimotikhon (Evros Prefecture) (see Tables 9.1 and 9.2).

Gypsies have lived in Thrace since the middle of the eleventh century. Features of their language and their religious customs suggest that after they settled in Thrace, they embraced Christianity and came under the influence of Greek language and culture.

After Thrace came under the Ottoman rule in the mid-fourteenth century, many Christian Gypsies converted to Islam, while others remained

Table 9.2
Demographic Composition of the Muslim Population in Western Thrace

Ethnic Background	Population	Percent
Roma	18,000	16
Pomaks	38,000	34
Turkish origin	56,000	50
Total	**112,000**	**100**

Source: Thanasis Vakalios, ed., *To provlima tis diapolitismikis ekpaideysis sti Ditiki Thraki* [The problem of a multicultural education in Western Thrace] (Athens: Gutenberg Editions, 1997), 24.

faithful to Christianity. When the Treaty of Lausanne was signed in 1923, Muslim Gypsies living in Thrace were excluded from the exchange of populations and henceforth, together with other Muslims (those of Turkish origin and Pomaks), formed part of the Muslim minority of Western Thrace. Like other Muslims, the Muslim Gypsies are divided into two religious branches: (1) Sunni Muslims, and (2) those who share the doctrines and mystic teachings of Thrace's Bektashis and Qizilbashis. By and large, the religious faith of Muslim Gypsies is not profound. Those of them who follow the mystic teachings of the Bektashis and the Qizilbashis also include certain Christian principles. These relate mainly to the church calendar and the veneration of saints. They have a closer relationship with the religious tradition and life of Thrace's Orthodox Greeks.[5]

Sizable (Muslim) immigration in Greece began almost twenty years after similar waves of immigration to Western Europe, at a time when the Greek economy began to prosper and Greece changed from a labor-exporting to a labor-importing country. It was at the beginning of the 1970s that African and Asian laborers (mainly Pakistanis) began to arrive in Greece. But it was in the late 1980s that Greece saw a massive influx of foreign immigrants, most of whom are working illegally. Some of them arrived with tourist visas, whereas the great majority entered the country without any legal documents. In the 1990s, Albanians were the largest group among the immigrants. But there are also sizable communities of Middle Eastern Arabs, Bangladeshis, Pakistanis, and Iranians. There are no official statistics regarding the number of Muslim immigrants living in Greece because the Greek census does not include questions on religious affiliations. When the fact that many immigrants try to hide their religion and nationality in hope of getting better employment opportunities is taken into account,[6] it quickly becomes clear that it is very difficult to find hard data about immigrants in general and

Table 9.3
Number of Muslims in Greece That Have Applied for a "White Card"

Country of origin	Number	% of total	Male	% of total male	Female	% of total female	% of male in total of both sexes
Albania	240,150	65.0	194,062	72.5	40,880	43.7	82.6
Pakistan	10,866	2.9	10,371	3.9	51	0.1	99.5
Egypt	6,225	1.7	5,698	2.1	347	0.4	94.3
Iraq	2,832	0.8	2,364	0.9	416	0.4	85.0
Morocco	408	0.1	263	0.1	138	0.1	65.6
Lebanon	246	0.1	192	0.1	45	0.0	81.0
Algeria	229	0.1	210	0.1	14	0.0	93.8
Sudan	210	0.1	182	0.1	25	0.0	87.9
Turkey	149	0.0	126	0.0	19	0.0	86.9
Jordan	146	0.0	132	0.0	9	0.0	93.6
Iran	137	0.0	113	0.0	24	0.0	82.5
Palestine	85	0.0	77	0.0	5	0.0	93.9

Source: Labor Employment Organization; processing of data: National Employment Institute.

Muslim immigrants in particular. The Labor Employment Organization, however, does provide a rough unofficial estimate by supplying the number of Muslims in Greece that have applied for a "white card" (work permit), as shown in Table 9.3.

In contrast to the Muslim inhabitants of Western Thrace[7] who are employed in agriculture (their primary product being tobacco) and in livestock farming (see Table 9.4), Muslim immigrants are, in most cases, underpaid and are generally considered by the public as cheap, tax-free labor. Those living in the Greek countryside are employed mainly in seasonal harvesting of various crops and fruits. Those living in the larger provincial cities and in the greater metropolitan Athens are employed as unskilled manual workers.

GREEK SECURITY CONCERNS AND MUSLIM GRIEVANCES

Latent Turkish aspirations vis-à-vis the Muslim minority in Thrace constitute a factor of serious concern for Greek security analysts. Occa-

Table 9.4

Structural Composition of the Economically Active Population of Thrace (in percent)

Sector	1961	1971	1981
Agriculture	80.3	63.5	61.2
Industry	9.5	16.2	16.4
Services	10.2	20.3	22.4

Source: Thanasis Vakalios, ed., To provlima tis diapolitismikis ekpaideysis sti Ditiki Thraki [The problem of a multicultural education in Western Thrace] (Athens: Gutenberg Editions, 1997), 36.

sional threats by certain extremist Turkish elements who call for intervention in Thrace in order "to liberate their oppressed kin" exacerbate these fears. But, so far, these extremist views have not been supported by the Turkish government.

Meanwhile, the Greek government and society are slowly beginning to acknowledge that the Muslim minority of Thrace has for many years been the victim of administrative discrimination. Therefore, in the last five to six years, several measures have been introduced to address this problem and to find ways to improve the living conditions of Muslims. The behavior of the Greek state can be largely explained (although not necessarily justified) by the very active propaganda and other "suspicious" activities of the Turkish consulate in the region and the irredentist sentiments expressed by leading members of the Turkish-speaking group of the minority. For example, the Istanbul-based Solidarity Association of Turks of Western Thrace (Bati Trakya Turkleri Dayanisma Dernegi) is one of the most active secessionist organizations. During an April 1995 conference in Istanbul organized by the Bati Trakya Turkleri Dayanisma Dernegi, the creation of a Western Thrace Parliament-in-Exile was decided. The Istanbul-based International Affairs Agency over the years has been a constant source of secessionist propaganda.[8]

MUSLIMS IN GREEK POLITICS

In assessing the extent of the involvement of Greece's Muslims in the country's political process, distinction must be made between the case of the Muslim minority of Western Thrace and that of Muslim immigrants.

The Case of the Muslim Minority of Western Thrace

Any analysis of the nature and level of the involvement of the Muslim minority of Western Thrace in Greece's political process must keep in mind the following points:

- The Muslims of Western Thrace are Greek citizens and therefore enjoy full civil and political rights since the signing of the Treaty of Lausanne in 1923. The treaty gives them the right to establish associations, unions, and political parties as well as to vote and be elected. Currently, there are seven Muslim associations in Western Thrace.

- The Muslim community of Western Thrace is concentrated in a specific geographic region (the prefectures of Xanthi and Rodopi). This results in a high level of representation at the local/municipal level as well as the national levels. To illustrate, during parliamentary elections, all major political parties regularly include Muslim candidates in their party's electoral lists. In almost all Parliaments since 1927, Muslim deputies (an average of two) were elected and participated actively in parliamentary work.

In the late 1980s, some members of the minority chose to stand for election as independent candidates. They created parties such as *Guven* (Confidence) and *Demokrasi, Esitlik, ve Baris Partisi* (Democracy, Equality, and Peace Party).[9] This split in the minority vote and the multiplication of minority candidates, however, worked against the Muslims and prevented the election of Muslims to Parliament in the 1993 elections. The above combination of factors did not occur in the following parliamentary elections. Consequently, in the current Parliament, which resulted from the elections of April 2000, there are two Muslim deputies, who belong to the governing PASOK (Panhellenic Socialist Movement) party. Despite these advances, Greece's Muslims in Western Thrace are not fully integrated into the Greek society. Two factors have played a role in this regard: (1) the influence of communalist tendencies and (2) the dynamics of the cold war and Greece's desire not to antagonize Turkey because of integrationist policies toward the Muslims of Western Thrace. The latter has been evident in the educational policies of the Greek government, which has encouraged the teaching of post-Ottoman Turkish. Thus, as Professor Irini Lagani has noted:

The result of this approach has been that unlike other minorities, various Greek governments, and Greek society in general, have not insisted on the linguistic and cultural Hellenization of the Muslim community, even though they are Greek citizens. This has had both positive and negative consequences: on the positive side it has contributed to the preservation of the identity and special cultural and religious features of this minority; and on the negative side it has caused the social marginalisation of Muslims, most of whom have not been integrated into Greece's social and community life. . . . It should be noted that the teaching of Turkish extends to the Pomaks as well, thus limiting the use of their native Pomak language exclusively to the immediate family environment. This fact contributes to *the Turkification of the Pomaks, and to the gradual absorption into the Turkish Minority.* . . . Undoubtedly, the greater number of hours devoted to the study of Turkish language compared to the number of hours devoted to the spoken Greek language is the main reason for the non-integration of Muslim pupils into the structures of the Greek national educational system.[10]

The Case of the Muslim Immigrants

In contrast to the case of Muslims of Western Thrace, Muslim immigrants in Greece are not represented in national and local institutions. Nevertheless, it is conceivable that Muslim immigrants in the future could form group(s) that would represent their interests and lobby for the community with local and national authorities. For instance, following the arrest of Abdullah Ocalan by Turkish authorities, a number of Kurdish immigrants and political refugees expressed their deep dissatisfaction with the role of the Greek government. Furthermore, a substantial number of Albanians expressed their concern regarding Greek public opinion's strong rejection of the North Atlantic Treaty Organization campaign in Kosovo. Nevertheless, still the primary concern of the majority of Muslim immigrants in Greece is the politics and future of their countries of origin because, like other early immigrants to other European countries, they hope to return home with enough money to establish a new life for themselves. This attitude in turn means that they have limited interest in establishing any form of institutions or organizations in Greece. For example, such an important issue as the establishment of the Athenian Central Mosque has involved only ambassadors from Muslim countries and the Greek Ministries of Foreign Affairs, Education, Culture, and Environment, and there have been very limited interest and participation on the part of the Muslim community.

In addition to the above factors, the following attributes of Greece's Muslims contribute to their limited interest in establishing religious and other organizations:

- The majority of immigrants are Sunnis, who believe that there is no established clergy in Islam. Thus, the creation and maintenance of religious institutions in Greece might be a new experience for them.
- Most Muslim immigrants in Greece originate from states in which governments organize, subsidize, and administer religious institutions. In most of these states, civic organizations, especially private Islamic institutions, are considered suspect and a potential source of threat to the government's legitimacy.

However, as has happened in the case of other immigrant communities in Europe, if Greece's immigrants gradually abandon the myth of return, there will inevitably be a tendency to create religious, cultural, and educational infrastructures.

ISSUES OF INTEGRATION: THE CASE OF THE MUSLIM IMMIGRANTS

In contrast to the case of the Muslim minority of Western Thrace, the degree of integration of Muslim immigrants into Greece's social and political landscape depends largely on whether they have visas and work permits. This is due mainly to the fact that the Greek constitution guarantees a number of rights to foreigners who enter the country legally but virtually no rights to those who enter the country without official permits. From the hundreds of thousands of immigrants that have crossed the Greek frontiers, relatively few have had visas, and even a smaller percentage have had work permits. In 1999, new legislation was introduced to facilitate the acquisition of work permits, but the new system has not yet produced the expected results mainly because of bureaucratic delays.

The fact that the majority of immigrants are illegal has, according to recent studies on immigrants, the following consequences:

- The majority of immigrants do not have access to public services. Public and municipal services are legally bound not to take into consideration any requests made by persons without legal documentation.
- Legally, they do not have the right to any form of hospitalization. However, illegal immigrants are generally accepted by the Greek hospitals.
- Since the overwhelming majority of Muslim immigrants in Greece are not legally registered, they cannot study at any educational institution, including programs for learning the Greek language.

- Owing to their numerous social problems, some immigrants—mainly Albanians—have become involved in criminal activity.

- Following a pattern familiar to almost every Western European capital, a sizable minority of Muslim immigrants become isolated and form ghettos.

THE CASE OF THE ATHENIAN CENTRAL MOSQUE AND THE ISLAMIC CULTURAL CENTER

On 30 June 2000, the Greek Socialist government, according to Article 7 of the Law on Issues of Preparation of the Olympic Games 2004 and Other Arrangements, approved the building of the first large-scale Islamic Cultural Center and Mosque in Athens.[11] The opinion, however, was polarized: Fifty-five deputies voted in favor and forty against the construction of the mosque. The building of this complex would be a major breakthrough in legitimizing Muslim presence in Greece, since until now Muslims living in Athens have been practicing their religion in converted houses, work houses, and stores.

The new mosque is to be constructed in Peania in an area comprising 35,000 square meters, about twenty kilometers east of the center of Athens. The center will be a "legal person of private law" and it will be under state supervision.[12] The Greek Ministry of Foreign Affairs has been drafting a law in cooperation with the Ministry of Culture and the ambassadors of Morocco, Jordan, and Palestine. Meanwhile, there have been discussions concerning the financing of the project with the governments of Kuwait and Saudi Arabia. The law calls for the establishment of a place of worship, study, and information.[13]

Before the bill had even reached the floor of the Parliament, a heated debate had already begun and controversial opinions were expressed by politicians, religious figures, and the public at large. Even though the Greek government and the hierarchy of the Greek Orthodox Church agreed on the creation of the Athenian Central Mosque and the Islamic Cultural Center, there were many others who strongly opposed this decision. This opposition was neither limited to a specific political party nor reflected a common ideology. In fact, these reactions can be divided into three categories: (1) reactions from members of Parliament and political parties, (2) reactions from the clergy of the Orthodox Church of Greece, and (3) reactions from local authorities and citizens.

Reactions from Members of Parliament and Political Parties

The opposition expressed, virtually in unison, serious objections to the project. But the objections were not so much directed at the issue itself as to the way the government was handling it. The main opposition party, New Democracy, disagreed with the choice of the locale. It argued that there had been no prior study on the suitability of the area and the needs of the Muslims living in Athens. New Democracy also disapproved of the way the government had tried to include the draft law on the mosque and the Islamic Cultural Center in legislation involving the 2004 Olympic Games in Athens. George Kalos, New Democracy deputy in charge of religious affairs, stated, "The governmental reasoning is absurd. The Olympic village is to be built fifteen km north of the capital and the planned mosque would be too far from the village for the athletes to use it." This claim appears justified. Indeed, the establishment of the Athenian Central Mosque has more to do with Greece's foreign policy interests in the Middle East and its will to maintain good relations with the Arab world than with Athens 2004 Olympic games.[14]

On the other hand, a deputy belonging to the Greek Communist party stated that the Arab League has been asking for a place of worship in the Greek capital since 1971 and that the party has always regarded the establishment of the Athenian Central Mosque as a necessity. She suggested, however, another place for the construction, which is closer to the historical center of the capital (Gazi district). The Coalition for the Left and Progress (SYNASPISMOS) deputy Maria Damanaki also spoke about the necessity of the establishment of a mosque in Athens and referred to respective decisions of the municipal council of Athens, which had suggested the Gazi district as the most suitable area for the establishment of the central mosque.[15]

Over and above these objections, there were independent deputies, as well as deputies of the ruling party, who were against the building of the Athenian Central Mosque and the Islamic Cultural Center for ideological reasons. A characteristic example is the case of a former minister and member of the ruling party who argued that there should be a *quid pro quo* from Turkey: "There should be reciprocity. To open a mosque, they 'should give us the keys' of Aghia Sophia."[16] Another deputy of the ruling party has also expressed his objections on the basis that "Athenian Central Mosque and the Islamic Cultural Centre . . . could become a center of international terrorism." These opinions reflect both the dynamics of Greek-Turkish relations and the identification of Islam in general with extremism, a view that is widespread in many European countries.

Reactions of the Orthodox Church of Greece

Despite the decision of the hierarchy of the Greek Orthodox Church to accept the construction of the mosque, several members of the clergy, from the very beginning, declared their strong disagreement with the idea of the construction of a mosque in the district of Peania. Both the local bishop (Metropolitan Agathonikos) and the majority of local priests tried several times to inform local citizens of the oncoming "danger." Metropolitan Agathonicos, in his annual report on the metropolis for the year 1999, referred to the issue of the Athenian Central Mosque and Islamic Cultural Center in the following manner:

> I owe to you, my beloved flock, to include in my annual report an issue of great importance and interest. I would like to inform you of an issue which will result in numerous problems and realignments. I am referring to the Athenian Central Mosque and Islamic Cultural Centre, which is to be built on a top of a hill in Peania. Our holy Metropolis in cooperation with the local authorities and the local population will strongly react to the effort to adulterate the religious, cultural, social and traditional structure and life of the citizens of Mesogeia. I call everyone to struggle in order to prevent the establishment of foreign, dangerous and heretic elements in our region.[17]

Reactions from Citizens Living in the Area and Local Authorities

With the exception of the mayor of Peania, all other local authorities, including the municipal opposition and the prefectural council of Eastern Attika,[18] strongly opposed the building of the Athenian Central Mosque in Peania by running resolutions of protest and organizing public protests. The most common objections against the mosque and the cultural center were the following:

- The establishment of the Athenian Central Mosque and the Islamic Cultural Center would encourage large numbers of Muslim immigrants to settle in Peania, thus downgrading the quality of daily life. It would also result in the erosion of property values.
- There were no significant numbers of Muslims living in the area in which the mosque was to be constructed.
- The establishment of a mosque in Peania district was not only culturally but also stylistically inappropriate.

Only few supported the view that the establishment of the Athenian Central Mosque and the Islamic Cultural Center would not affect the region or the local inhabitants. They gave as an example a Hindu ashram, which has existed in the area without causing any problems.

THE MUSLIM CHALLENGE IN GREECE

Muslim communities are now an established part of Greek society, and owing to Greece's geographical location, their number is expected to rise steadily. Thus, the principal challenge the Muslims pose to the Greek society—as indeed to other European societies—is whether it is capable of accepting the fact of increasing ethnic and cultural diversity and is prepared to integrate its emerging Muslim communities.

So far, Greece, one of the most ethnically and religiously homogeneous countries in Europe and one with a more recent history of Muslim immigration, has not been able to find adequate answers to these questions. Indeed, when the issue of the establishment of the Athenian Central Mosque and the Islamic Cultural Center surfaced, the inability of the Greek state and society to deal with issues of multiculturalism became clearly noticeable. It was only in 1999, when the debate on the Islamic center became public, that many people realized that immigrants who lived in the country were Muslims and needed a place of worship.

Regrettably, the Greek society has not yet understood that Islam is now a "domestic" religion and not some foreign phenomenon. Furthermore, the case of the Athenian Central Mosque is only one of the many issues that the country will face within the next few years. The movement toward a multicultural society is undoubtedly a difficult process. Nevertheless, Greece could benefit by taking into account not only the many social problems that arise from Muslim presence but also many important opportunities such as the revitalization of the long-existing cultural and trading links between Greece and the Islamic world, either on a bilateral basis or in the framework of the Euro-Mediterranean Partnership that this presence may create.

CONCLUSIONS AND RECOMMENDATIONS

The foregoing leads to the following conclusions:

- The presence of Islam in Greece is not a new phenomenon, as it dates back to the Ottoman conquest of the Byzantine Empire and the Balkan peninsula.
- Islam in Greece is not institutionalized.
- There has been very limited integration of Muslims into the Greek society.
- The Greek society, like other Western societies, has its share of prejudices against Islam. One of the more common mistakes among decision makers and ordinary people is the interpretation

of Islam as a monolithic, rather than a complex and diverse, phenomenon.

• So far, Greece has been spared the worst aspects of racism and xenophobia, such as the emergence of political parties based on one-dimensional, racist, and xenophobic platforms and frequent incidents of racist violence. But one can identify signs of undercurrent xenophobia, mainly because of concerns about increased criminality.

Greece's integration policies must be based on the conviction that integration needs to be a mutual, creative, and stimulating process of change that embraces the whole community and not just a one-sided adjustment on the part of the immigrants. The policy objective should be the achievement of equality of opportunity for everyone, irrespective of ethnic or cultural background, as well as the creation of a social security safety net. A new authority must be set up to implement these policies and apply new legislative measures to monitor and evaluate social development aimed at safeguarding cultural diversity. Such policies should include the following:

• Creation and implementation of local development programs in urban areas with the cooperation of local and central authorities.

• The promotion of ethnic and cultural diversity in the workplace with the state administration having particular responsibility for setting a good example.

• Official encouragement of the representation of Muslim citizens in various social and economic bodies and forums and the provision of financial support to a Muslim religious body.

• Following the example of Sweden (autumn 1999), the government, in order to counteract "Islamophobia," should initiate a national dialogue with Muslim communities and promote dialogue at the local level between religious communities.

NOTES

1. For a comprehensive analysis of the relations between Islam and Hellenism, see Anastasios Giannoulatos, *Istoria triskevmaton* [History of religions] (Athens: University of Athens, 1995).

2. Among Islam's philosophers and scholars, Al-Farabi and Ibn-Sina (Avicenna) best represent Greco-Islamic synthesis.

3. Thanasis Vakalios (ed.), *To provlima tis diapolitismikis ekpaideysis sti Ditiki Traki* [The problem of a multicultural education in Western Thrace] (Athens: Gutenberg Editions, 1997), 24.

4. See www.mfa.gr

5. Efstratios Zeginis, *Oi Mousoulmanoi Athiganoi tis Trakis* [The Muslim Athiganoi of Thrace] (Thessaloniki: Institute of Balkan Studies, 1994).

6. Many Albanian immigrants pretend to be Greeks from North Epirus.

7. Thrace remains among the least developed areas in the European Union. However, in 1991, the Greek government put forth a plan for its economic revitalization.

8. See Yannis Valinakis, *Greece's Security in the Post–Cold War Era* (Ebenhausen: Stiftung Wissenschaft und Politik, 1992), 39–40.

9. For more information, see Dimosthenis X. Dodos, *Eklogiki geografia ton meionotiton* [Electoral geography of the minorities] (Athens: Eksadas Editions, 1994).

10. Irini Lagani, "Greece's Muslim Minority in Western Thrace," in *Briefing Notes on Islam, Society, and Politics*, vol. 3, No. 1, ed. Shireen Hunter (Washington DC: Center for Strategic and International Studies, 2000).

11. See *National Gazette* 1 (30 June 2000).

12. See Greek Parliament, Records of Proceedings, fourth sitting, 15 June 2000.

13. See "Apoktima gia tin Athina to Islamico temenos," *Kathimerini* (19 September 2000).

14. Panos Beglitis, spokesperson of the Hellenic Ministry of Foreign Affairs, recently stated that the establishment of the Athenian Central Mosque and the Islamic Cultural Center "has nothing to do with the Olympic games" as well as that Arab embassies in Athens have long asked for a place of worship in the Greek capital and even offered to pay for it, but the idea stumbled on objections by the Greek Orthodox Church.

15. See Greek Parliament, Records of Proceedings, fourth sitting, 15 June 2000.

16. He was referring to the famous Byzantine church in Istanbul, which was first turned into a mosque and then into a museum.

17. Despite reactions at the local level, the Orthodox Church of Greece—which is not separate from the state—was one of the first institutions to provide legal advice and material support to Muslim immigrants and conduct studies on interfaith issues. For more information regarding the constitutional status of the Orthodox Church of Greece, see Panagiotis Christinakis, *Elliniko ekklisiastiko dikaio* [Hellenic ecclesiastical law] (Athens: Symmetria Editions, 1995).

18. Dimitris Markopanagiotis, "*Antidraseis gia tin anegersi temenous stin Peania*," *Attikos Kirikas* (20 June 2000).

10

Islam in Portugal

Fernando Soares Loja

INTRODUCTION

Portugal's Muslim community is very small in number compared with those in other European countries. It is also of a more recent origin. By contrast, the history of Portugal's interaction with Islam and the Islamic world is very long and complex. This long history has left a deep imprint on the Portuguese views of Islam and of Muslims, whose impact can be seen even today. Indeed, certain historical memories and perceptions create the psychological and cultural context for the interaction between Portugal's Muslim community and the broader society and therefore need to be briefly analyzed at the outset.

HISTORICAL BACKGROUND

In the beginning of the twelfth century, Alfonso VI, the ruler of the Iberian Peninsula, was fighting against the Muslim kingdoms with the objective of conquering the southern territories of the peninsula. The task was not easy; thus, he solicited the help of Christian knights, some of whom came from France to assist him. Among those knights were his two future sons-in-law. To the older, Alfonso gave the entire conquered territory of "Spain" to rule over. To the younger, he gave the smaller extent of land and the title of count. In 1143, after a long war of independence between Alfonso's children, the smaller territory became the independent kingdom of Portugal.

In 1143, the king of Spain recognized Portugal as an independent kingdom. However, recognition from Rome came only thirty-five years later. The reason given for such a long delay was that the then-pope was upset to see Christians, who were supposed to be united against the "infidels," fighting among themselves instead.

So, Portugal was "born" amid two sets of wars: one between Christians and Muslims and the other among Christians themselves.

The land that is Portugal today was occupied by Muslims during a period lasting from the beginning of the eighth century AD until 1349 AD, when the last of the Muslim kingdoms fell. Since then, for historical and religious reasons, Muslims have been seen by the Christians first as enemies and later as a threat. Even today, Christians do not understand Muslim beliefs. Similarly, Christian beliefs are difficult for Muslims to accept. One fears the other, without any rational explanation, at least in the Western world.

Even after the elimination of Muslim political power from "Portuguese territory" and after more than six centuries since the conquest of the last Muslim kingdoms in the south (1349), Portuguese people still fear Muslims and consider them totally alien to their culture, their way, and view of life.

Yet, it is a historic fact that Muslims have left an important imprint on the Portuguese language and culture and a rich inheritance in mathematics, medicine, agriculture, architecture, and other areas. Nevertheless, people feel that this inheritance is the inevitable result of 700 years of occupation and thus has no contemporary relevance. It is therefore in this historical and psychological context that the contemporary situation of Islam in Portugal should be analyzed.

THE EMERGENCE OF THE PORTUGUESE MUSLIM COMMUNITY: AN ETHNIC AND SECTARIAN PROFILE

The first Muslims arrived in Portugal in the early 1950s from Mozambique and consisted of single students of Indian origin. Until 1974, when the process of decolonization began in Portugal's overseas possessions, the number of Muslims in Portugal remained limited. For example, in 1968, when the Islamic community of Lisbon (*Communidade Islamica de Lisboa*) was founded, it had only twenty-five or thirty members.[1]

However, there were many Muslims in Portugal's colonies in Africa who, by law, were considered Portuguese citizens. After 1974, with the end of the anticolonial struggle and the achievement of independence by all former Portuguese colonies, Portugal received hundreds of thousands of refugees from its ex-colonies. Many of these refugees were Muslims. Today, Portugal has between 35,000 and 38,000 Muslims living in its territory.

Most Portuguese Muslims come from Mozambique; among this group, most are of Indian origin, who came to Portugal because of the Africanization policies of the new government and later the civil war. The other group is from Guinea. Ethnically, this group is divided between those whose origins are in the Indian subcontinent and those who are natives of Guinea. It is difficult to determine which ethnic group is larger. In the 1980s and 1990s, smaller groups of Muslims from North Africa, the Middle East, and Asia came to Portugal, thus giving Islam in Portugal a more ethnically diverse aspect.

The largest Muslim community consists of Sunnis, followed by the Sevener Shi'a Ismailis. There are also a limited number of followers of the Ahmadiyya sect. The Ismaili community is estimated to number between 5,000 and 7,000.

PATTERNS OF SETTLEMENT AND SOCIOECONOMIC PROFILE

Most of the Muslim community in Portugal lives in the capital, Lisbon, and its surrounding areas in a pattern similar to that of other European countries. Other Muslim communities can be found in Loures, Vila Franca, Coimbra, Almada, Porto, and Faro.

The present economic conditions of Portugal's Muslims, to some degree, reflect their position before immigrating to Portugal. For example, most of the Muslims of Indian origin who came to Portugal from Mozambique had a middle-class background judged on the basis of their skills and qualifications. Many of them and their descendants work in commercial and banking fields. Others were traders. Consequently, their ability to become integrated in many professional fields was fairly high.

Similarly, many of the Muslim immigrants from Guinea-Bissau were students, a condition that also facilitated professional integration.[2] Therefore, relatively speaking, Portuguese Muslims' economic conditions are satisfactory. However, still, a significant portion of the community (one third), consisting mostly of the black African minority and recent immigrants from the Middle East and South Asia, live in poverty. The members of this group are mostly engaged in manual labor, especially in the construction sector. The Ismaili community is the most economically well off, and many of its members are successful businessmen.

MUSLIM INSTITUTIONS

The most important Muslim institution in Portugal is the Islamic Center of Portugal (*Centro Islamico de Portugal*), which also houses the central mosque. It was founded in 1976 and built with the financial assistance of Muslim countries, notably Saudi Arabia, Kuwait, and the United Arab

Emirates.[3] It is interesting to note that, while the request for building the mosque was submitted in 1966, permission to construct the center was granted only in 1978, after the oil revolution of 1973 and the increasing economic and political importance of Arab countries. In fact, the Portuguese government thought agreeing to the construction of the center would benefit Portugal's relations with the Arab countries.

The Central Mosque of Lisbon was finally opened in 1985. Today, there are four Sunni mosques and fifteen informal prayer houses. Other important Sunni Muslim institutions include the Portuguese Center for Islamic Studies and the Association for Islamic Education. In addition, the community publishes a newspaper, *Al-Furqan*, also called *The Islamic Voice in Portage*. It additionally publishes monographs and leaflets on Islamic subjects.

The Central Mosque of Lisbon also has a committee whose principal goal is to provide financial and other assistance to the needy members of the community. The principal institutions of the Ismaili community are the Aga Khan Foundation of Portugal and the Focus Foundation.

In addition to the institutions that they have created in Portugal, the Portuguese Muslim communities—both Sunni and Ismaili, and especially the latter—have close links with Muslim communities in other European countries, especially the United Kingdom.

INVOLVEMENT IN SOCIAL AND POLITICAL LIFE

The level of social integration and political participation of all immigrants in the Portuguese system is still limited. But this is not due to religious reasons.

According to its constitution, Portugal is a secular state, and Portuguese culture has been becoming more and more secular. Many politicians are agnostics or followers of other religions. For instance, one member of the Parliament is a well known Buddhist. There are many examples of people who are very involved in politics despite their religion. If Muslims are not openly involved in politics, it is not because of active discrimination but the result of their personal choice. In the last decade, however, Portugal's Muslims have become more visible, including in the media. Some Portuguese newspapers publish articles on the occasion of the beginning or end of Ramadan and provide information about the country's Muslim community. As the Muslim community establishes deeper roots in Portugal, their level of involvement in the country's social and political life should also increase. Furthermore, the passage and enactment of the new Law on Religious Freedom should have a positive impact in this regard.

THE CURRENT LEGAL STATUS OF RELIGIOUS COMMUNITIES

In order better to understand the advantages of the Law on Religious Freedom that was passed by the Parliament on 26 April 2001, it is important to examine the current Portuguese legal system as it affects the status and position of various religious communities.

From its birth until 1911, Portugal was a Roman Catholic country. It was illegal for a Portuguese subject to be anything other than Roman Catholic. Only after the enactment of the Constitution of 1911 (the first Republican Constitution) did Portuguese citizens begin to enjoy religious freedom, that is, the right to choose their own faith. Legal persecution was over, but legal and social discrimination continued.

In 1940, Salazar, the dictator who ruled Portugal for four decades, signed a concordat with the Vatican by which the Portuguese state accorded to the Roman Catholic Church a privileged position, and in August 1971, the Parliament enacted a religious freedom law (under which no religious denominations were registered) that confirmed the privileged position of the Roman Catholic Church. That law was still in effect as of this writing (spring 2001). Therefore, as of 2001, in Portugal, a country that is a full-fledged member of the European Union, a law enacted in the final years of the Salazar dictatorship ruled such an important matter in personal and social life as freedom of religion. This situation is regrettable. It seems that, as Carlo Arturo Jemolo once commented: "When a country loses its freedom, the first right to be banned is religious freedom, and when freedom is recovered, religious freedom is the last to be achieved."

The best way to describe the legal status of non-Roman Catholic Portuguese is to provide some examples illustrating the differences between the status of Roman Catholics and that of other Christians and Muslims. The Constitution of Portugal, adopted 2 April 1976, in its Article 13, provided: "None shall be privileged, benefited, damaged, persecuted, deprived of any right or exempted from any duty because of one's . . . religion." Moreover, Articles 41 to 44 provide that "churches and other religious communities shall be separated from the State and free in organising themselves and in the exercise of their functions and worship."

Despite these constitutional provisions, the Roman Catholic Church has preserved its privileged position. By contrast, other religious communities, in order to achieve legal personality, have had to follow a certain pattern of organization.

The following illustrates the position of the Roman Catholic Church and those of other religious communities, most notably Muslims.

Privileges of the Roman Catholic Church

First, the Roman Catholic Church is the only religious community recognized as a church and a corporate body of international law. By contrast, other religious groups, in order to create a corporate body, must do this by obtaining a deed from a public notary and registering with the Ministry of Justice. At least seven people must be engaged in this process. The process through which religious communities can become a corporate body is similar to those of sport or cultural associations.

Second, important events and activities concerning the Roman Catholic Church, such as Sunday mass or the festivities of Fatima on May 13 each year, are reported on public TV channels. By contrast, with few exceptions, and then only for one or two minutes, important events and activities related to other religious groups are not reported on public TV channels.

Third, Roman Catholics can be civilly or legally married in their churches. The priest who conducts the ceremony has the power to declare that the marriage is legally performed. In the eyes of the law, this is the only recognized religious marriage. Only Roman Catholics are entitled to have religious and civil ceremonies at the same time. But in order to be married according to law, Muslims and other non-Catholics must apply to a public officer and make their vows in his presence and in the framework of a "civil marriage." After the completion of the ceremony, they are considered legally married. If they want to sanctify the event through a religious ceremony, it is no concern of the law. In short, marriage according to non-Roman Catholic religious rites has no legal status.

Fourth, Roman Catholic priests can enter any hospital or prison, at any time, to visit any inmate. Muslim clergy—imams—can make such visits only during allotted visiting times. Furthermore, Roman Catholic patients, inmates, and soldiers can be spiritually assisted by Catholic chaplains whenever they need. Muslim patients, inmates, and soldiers must wait until normal visiting hours to receive such help.

Fifth, all chaplains in hospitals, jails, or the army are Roman Catholic priests. So far, to the knowledge of the author, no Muslim imam or non-Catholic clergy have been appointed as chaplains.

Sixth, Roman Catholic priests do not declare their fees as priests, and they do not pay taxes on them. They are not considered as ordinary workers, and therefore they are not subject to the labor tax laws. This is a correct practice, because the legal notion of worker is not applicable to a spiritual leader. Meanwhile, imams and other spiritual leaders who assist their communities are expected to declare their income and pay taxes as if they were ordinary workers. Roman Catholic priests or nuns are not considered as workers. But foreign imams are required to register as foreign workers and provide the authorities with a written contract with the communities they are going to serve.

Seventh, the Roman Catholic Church is exempt from paying value-added tax, inheritance tax, and taxes on property donations, on bank interest paid on capital deposited, on buildings or land it owns, whether or not it is used for religious activities. Other religious communities, schools, and institutes all must pay value-added tax, even if the goods acquired are used exclusively for religious or social assistance. Nor are they exempt from any taxes, with one exception: If a community acquires a building to be used exclusively for religious activities, this transaction is exempted from taxes.

Furthermore, financial records of the Roman Catholic Church have never been examined by tax agents, whereas those of several other religious communities have been subjected to such examination.

Eighth, the Roman Catholic Church owns many adequate places for worship and social activities. This situation is as it should be. However, other communities have difficulties in finding a suitable place for worship or social activities. Often, even when a community buys a flat or a commercial building for its activities, the building administration or a single flat owner in the building can file a lawsuit to remove the community. Often the courts decide in favor of the plaintiff. This has occurred several times.

The New Law

Twenty-seven years after the revolution that restored freedom of conscience and speech in Portugal (Article 37 of the Portuguese Constitution), the government is finally ready to change the law on religious freedom in order to grant equal rights to followers of all religions. In April 1996, the government appointed a committee to draft a new bill on religious freedom. However, its approval was delayed for several years. As noted, the bill was passed by the Parliament on 26 April 2001, but, as of this writing, it still needs the signatures of the president and the prime minister in order to be published in the official gazette, after which the new bill will become effective. This process could take a few more months.

Benefits of the New Bill

The proposed bill will introduce many changes in the legal status of non–Roman Catholics, namely, Evangelical Christians, Muslims, Jews, Hindus, and others, and it will address the rights of all Portuguese citizens. The legal status of Portuguese Muslims will change for the better in the following areas.

Religious Marriage Ceremony

Muslim couples will be entitled to be married according to the rites of their religion,[4] by the imam,[5] within their community. The state will recognize the marriage before the imam as a legal marriage whenever a Muslim decides to combine civil and religious ceremonies.

However, this right (civil benefits) is granted only to those Muslims whose religious communities are registered with the Ministry of Justice and are recognized as settled in the country. To be recognized as settled in the country, a religious community needs to prove that it has existed as a social organization for more than thirty years or that it is a branch of an international church or religious community that has existed for more than sixty years. Although the imam can perform a civil marriage on behalf of the state, he is still a religious minister and is never considered a public officer.

Religious Assistance to Soldiers and Inmates

The Constitution states: "None shall be . . . deprived of any right . . . because of one's . . . religion." After the passage of the bill, Muslim soldiers, patients, and inmates will have the right to receive spiritual assistance or guidance by an imam any time they need it and to practice acts of worship, to the extent that this is included in their right to religious freedom, and its exercise would constitute the visible expression of such right.[6]

Working and Studying on Religious Holidays

For Muslims and members of other religious communities, working and studying on religious holidays or days of rest has been a point of contention for many years. The new bill will be beneficial primarily for students; the workers' rights will continue to be conditioned by whether they work a flexible schedule, which is not very common in Portugal except in the case of professionals. Thus, in order to be off on their respective holidays, they need to work a flexible schedule. In addition, both students and workers are required to be members of a religious community that has sent to the Minister of Justice during the previous year the list of religious holidays and periods of rest.[7] This is just a matter of notification, and the "list" does not need to be acknowledged or receive "official approval."

Names of Children according to the Religion of the Parents

Until now, in Portugal people were not free to choose the names of their children and had to select names from a government-approved list. The new bill will allow parents to choose any name they want for their children, according to their beliefs and traditions. This will be a new right in the Portuguese legal system.[8]

Proselytizing

In some countries (France and Israel), attempts are made to ban proselytizing. In Portugal, the new bill expressly states that religious freedom includes the right "to look for new believers." The committee that drafted the bill clearly understood that this is a natural expression of one's faith: to share what one believes with others. As Tariq Ramadan recently expressed, "The best thing I can offer a friend is my belief." This is what many people feel about their faith, and the bill clearly recognizes this reality.[9]

Protection of Temples and Places of Worship

One of the major difficulties for religious communities is to find suitable places for worship without facing hostility from neighbors. According to civil law, for example, if part of a condominium is used for a purpose different from what it was intended for, one owner of a unit in the condominium is able to file a lawsuit and prohibit the person or corporate body from using the premises. This is true, even if the person is the owner of the flat or the store. Inasmuch as buildings never contain spaces reserved for religious purposes, it is extremely difficult to find places to meet for worship. This will change under the proposed new law, as it will not be so easy to prevent religious communities from gathering and worshipping in places that were not originally intended for that purpose.[10]

Town Planning

Along with the last-mentioned right, the bill grants to registered religious communities (which will be the case of Muslim communities in Portugal) the right to be heard by town halls and government authorities on issues regarding urban planning in areas in which they have an organized social presence.[11]

Tax Exemptions and Deductions

All religious communities will have basically the same tax privileges that today are granted only to the Roman Catholic Church. Rights referred to in Article 30 apply to all religious communities.[12] However, exemptions listed in Point 1 of Article 31 will apply only to religious communities registered with the Ministry of Justice, which means that the extent of rights on this matter would depend on the legal status of the religious community.[13]

Every citizen, believer or not, will be able to claim a charitable deduction of up to 15 percent of his or her income, which is given to any registered religious community. This means that a donation to a religious community that is not registered with the Ministry of Justice cannot be deducted from the income of the donor.[14] Beyond this deduction, each citizen will be able to benefit a religious community with 0.5 percent of the tax on income for religious or social activities, provided the religious community is settled and has requested the tax benefit.[15]

Religious Teaching in Public Schools

Thirty years ago, religious education (i.e., Roman Catholic instruction) in public schools was optional, provided that the parents applied for a dispensation. In other words, such teaching was not mandatory, but parents were required to take the courageous initiative of asking for a dispensation for their children from religious instruction. If parents remained silent, the teaching was mandatory.

Today, parents must declare that they want their children to have religious instruction in school. If there are at least ten children to constitute a class[16] they can apply for religious instruction, be it evangelical or Muslim or Jewish or any other religion. Religious education is completely dependent on the will of parents, and it will remain so.[17]

Furthermore, parents can promote religious teaching in the schools attended by their children in cooperation with their religious communities. The teachers will be chosen by the state in cooperation with the communities or their representative organizations.[18]

Broadcasting

Public television service already broadcasts weekly programs produced by several religious communities. It is always a problem to find a balance and give equal time to different religious communities, because the number of adherents is the criterion used to determine the amount of broadcasting time allotted to religious communities each week. According to the new bill, registered religious communities are guaranteed broadcasting time.[19]

LEGAL STATUTES OF MUSLIM COMMUNITIES

The best achievement from this bill for Muslim communities in Portugal, as well as for evangelicals, Jews, and Hindus, will be their recognition as "settled" in the country.[20] This is the greatest step forward, for it means equal status, equal rights, equal opportunities, and equal obligations before the state. Nevertheless, it is not yet clear that the passage of the bill will mean the end of religious discrimination.

Some constitutional experts have a particular view on the principle of equality: They accept negative discrimination between two religious denominations on the grounds of the number of their adherents. In other words, Roman Catholics are entitled to a status of privilege because they are historically "the church" in Portugal and about 90 percent of population declare themselves to be Roman Catholic. On this basis, some scholars argue that there is no discrimination involved in giving some privilege to those who are not equal. To discriminate, they say, is to deal in a different way with that which is equal. According to these "experts," the principle of equality only forces the state to treat equally what is equal and to treat differently what is different. This is a formal definition of the principle contained in Article 13 of the Constitution mentioned above. On the other hand, a few constitutional law "experts" defend the opposite idea, namely: One single evangelical, Muslim, or Jew is entitled to the same treatment as a Roman Catholic because, in the past, they had been subjected to discrimination. Therefore, as a compensation for the time their ideas and beliefs were banned and were not allowed to be shared freely, they should be the recipient of positive discrimination. In other words, they should achieve privileged treatment in order to help them achieve the same status as the Roman Catholics and thus establish a balance among various religions. In all likelihood, this issue will be brought before the constitutional court to be settled.

CONCLUSION

The foregoing has illustrated that Portugal's small Muslim community is relatively well integrated in the society. From a socioeconomic perspective, its conditions are tolerable, although a segment of the community suffers from economic deprivation.

From a legal standpoint, the new bill should benefit the Muslims. However, the extent to which this will be the case will depend on how far the principle of the separation of church and state will be observed in practice.

Article 41.4 of the Portuguese Constitution states that churches (plural) and other religious communities are separate from the state, a provision that has been retained in the new bill.[21] Yet, in practice, so far, this has not been completely the case. For example, in many public ceremonies, only Roman Catholic priests or bishops are invited by the authorities to bless a new bridge, a new road, or a new monument. If there were total separation, Roman Catholic priests would not be invited—or, at least, would not be the only ones invited. The second example concerns the structure of religious corporate bodies. In order to acquire legal personality and to become a corporate body, each religious community (except for the Roman Catholic Church) must be established as a civil legal entity with a specific organization. This requirement fails to respect the purpose of religious community. Every new civil association, which is the legal format given to each religious community, must have a general assembly, a board, and an accountant board to check the board's administration. This is something quite inadequate for the majority of religious communities. For example, the Ismaili community in Portugal to this day has no legal personality because they refuse to accept these rules. They look forward to seeing the new bill enacted in order to acquire a new flexibility in running their own organization. This will be a very practical way to experience the separation of religion from the state.[22]

However, separation will not be as complete as many people would like it to be. The language of the new bill reveals that the Portuguese government wishes to keep at least some control over the religious phenomena in the country. The state will grant several rights to religious communities. However, this will depend on a previous registration according to four categories. These categories ultimately will be determined not by the courts but by an advisory committee to the minister of justice, named Committee for the Religious Freedom, and by the minister.[23]

In short, the new bill will go a long way to establish religious equality and to consolidate the principle of the separation of religion and state. Nevertheless, some inequalities and some overlap between religion and state will remain.

NOTES

1. See Nina Clara Tiesler, "No Bad News from the European Margin: The New Islamic Presence in Portugal," *Islam and Christian-Muslim Relations* 1 (2001).

2. For more details, see Fernando Luis Lopes Machado, "*Da Guine-Bissou a Portugal: luso-guinean imigrantes*" [From Guinea-Bissau to Portugal: Luso-Guinean immigrants], *Sociologica, Problemas e Practicas* 26 (1998).

3. See Tiesler, "No Bad News from the European Margin."

4. "Article 9 (Right to Religious Participation). Freedom of religion and worship includes the right, in accordance with the respective ministers of religion and according to the norms of the church or religious community chosen, to: . . . b. Celebrate marriage and be interred according to the rites of one's own religion." Project of Law on Religious Freedom, 24 April 1999, http://www.uni-trier.de/~ievr/konferenz/papers/sousabri.pdf.

5. Portuguese Religious Freedom Act, Article 18 (Religious Marriage Ceremony).

6. Ibid., Article 12.

7. Ibid., Article 13 (Exemption from Work, Lessons and Examinations for Religious Reasons).

8. Ibid., Article 7.

9. Ibid.

10. Ibid., Article 28.

11. Ibid., Article 27.

12. Ibid., Article 30 (Tax-Free Contributions).

13. Ibid., Article 31 (Tax Benefits).

14. Ibid.

15. Ibid.

16. Decree 329/98, 2 November 1998.

17. Portuguese Religious Freedom Act, Article 10 (Religious Education of Minors).

18. Ibid., Article 23 (Religious Education in Public Schools).

19. Ibid., Article 24 (Times of Religious Broadcasts).

20. Ibid., Article 36 (Churches and Religious Communities Settled in the Country).

21. Ibid., Article 3 (Principle of Separation).

22. Ibid., Article 21 (Freedom to Organize Churches and Religious Communities).

23. Ibid., Article 51 (Committee of Religious Freedom). The Committee of Religious Freedom is set up as an independent advisory body of the Ministry of Justice.

PART II

CROSS-NATIONAL ISSUES

11

Europeanization of Islam or Islamization of Europe?

Tariq Ramadan

INTRODUCTION

Today, it is clear that Islam is part of Europe's demographic and cultural landscape. Europe's Muslims are no longer guests that one day will return home, but rather Europeans of Muslim faith, who will remain a permanent part of Europe's social and political fabric. This state of permanency coupled with gradual emergence of Muslims—especially second and third generations—from their voluntary or imposed isolation has given rise to questions on the part of both Europeans and Muslims about the implications of this permanent implantation of Islam in Europe.[1] Unfortunately, so far, most questions have to do with mutual fears rather than benefits that both parties can derive from this situation.

From the indigenous European perspective, the main question reflecting a sense of fear is: What do you (Muslims) want exactly? Do you want to Islamize Europe, to convert our people? As a European Muslim, I face this kind of suspicion all the time. From the Muslims' perspective, the main fear is the potential loss of their religion, culture, and distinct identity. They fear that they will be culturally colonized or, worse, totally assimilated. These are principal facts of European Islam today and must be addressed. Before doing so, however, the following points need to be emphasized because they are fundamental to a discussion of Islam in Europe.

The central point is that Islam is, first and foremost, a divinely revealed religion, with belief in its universal validity, a way of life, a concept of life and death, and not merely the cultural characteristic of a specific population coming from countries outside Europe. Indeed, without taking into account this religious dimension, all discussions about other aspects of Islam in Europe—social and political integration, economic progress, or other matters—would be, if not futile, highly inadequate.

A further point is that analysis of Islam and Muslims in Europe must be centered on how they—the Muslims—define themselves and how they understand Islam, and not how they are viewed and classified by the Europeans. Yet, this is a dimension that is missing in current scholarship on Islam and Muslims in Europe. Therefore, the main goal of this study is to remedy, to some extent, these shortcomings.

ISLAM AS RELIGION

If one accepts the centrality of the religious dimension in any definition of Islam in Europe, one must also speak about God, revelation, worship, and religious practice. One must also ask the question: What is the place of revelation in a Muslim's state of mind; what is his or her concept of life? When someone characterizes me as an Egyptian born in Geneva and representing a prototype of a second-generation Muslim, he or she is talking about the way I deal with the society in which I live. But to understand the current and future dynamics of Islam in Europe, one has to look at how Muslims, like myself, define themselves and how they see their presence in Europe and their own and their children's future. This type of definition is also about values, limits, and ethical behavior.

The second point regards the definition of "who is a Muslim." Many analysts make a distinction between practicing and nonpracticing Muslims. But this is an inappropriate and even false dichotomy. A Muslim is someone who "feels Muslim" irrespective of the extent to which he or she adheres to the principles of faith and how strictly observant he or she is.

The third point is the universality of Islam and its revelation. The recognition of this fact is important, because Muslims are often asked to relativize and to put into context—social, geographic, cultural—their sense of their faith's divinity and universality. What I believe in and what I feel are universal in my view, even if I do not want to impose my view on others: I will not accept the proposition that my faith should be considered as "a relative creed or aspiration." The key question is how my sense of universality will be able to deal with diversity; how my link to God, the revelation, will force me to understand and to respect the diversity of humanity and its civilizations. Muslims do not want to relativize their universal values, but from their universal values they can, and have to, deal with diversity. One should not expect Muslims to forget or remove from their heart what for them is universal and timeless.

This means that if there is to be a true and equal dialogue between Muslims and Europeans, Europe's universal values should enter into a dialogue with Islam's universal values. Yet, presently, relativity is considered to be an absolute value, which in itself is a paradoxical statement. Nevertheless, if one does not subscribe to the principle of relativity, he is considered a dogmatic. Again, this attitude itself is a form of dogmatism in the sense that it considers relativism as an absolute value.

In short, Europeans must accept the fact that Muslims believe in having universal values. It does not mean that they cannot understand concepts of relativity or diversity. But, in order to manage a sense of diversity within society, one has to promote a dialogue from within the respective senses of European and Islamic universality. This is an important point, and it is not easy even for Muslims to perceive it in this manner. In his or her daily life, a Muslim refers to a link to God and a particular concept of life, and yet it is possible for him or her to speak with the "other," to understand him and, in turn, to be understood by him. Thus, a sense of universal transcendence can coexist with a sense of human relativity. It is at this level that the dialogue of tomorrow should be structured and conducted.

RELIGIOUS AND POLITICAL DIMENSIONS OF ISLAM

In order to understand Islam properly and enter into a constructive dialogue, a widespread idea, which is viewed as obvious even by many Muslims, must be reexamined. In discussing Islam, no difference is made between political and religious fields. Indeed, it is assumed that in Islam, religion and politics are one and the same. Yet, this statement is not valid. On the contrary, from the early beginnings of Islam, in the theoretical categorization of the various fields in *Fiqh*, the *'ulama* drew important distinctions, not with regard to the main sources, which are the Qur'an and the Sunna, but in respect to the methodologies of their interpretation. This is obvious, for example, when one speaks about *'ibadât* (worship) and *mu'âmalât* (social affairs). This distinction is too important in order to allow one to state that there is no difference between political and religious fields in Islam. By making such a statement, one gives the impression that it is not possible for a Muslim to become open and to integrate into a secular society, which is a completely wrong view. This differentiation is attested to by the philosophical works of Muslims in the Middle Ages. Even within the *Fiqh*, one can find elements of this distinction.

Regarding *'ibadât*, Muslims have to do what is strictly prescribed. If one wants to pray, for example, one needs to have a text specifying how to perform it. But in social affairs, the situation is completely different. One can do whatever one wants as long as it does not contradict a prescribed principle. To be prevented from doing something, somebody must come up with a reliable text that says that such action is not permissible. In other words, in the first case ('*ibadât*), in order to do something, one needs a text, whereas in the second case, a text is required in order not to do something. Indeed, from the very beginning, this was the way Muslims organized themselves in new environments. They took from the Arabs and other peoples those aspects of their culture and customs that did not contradict their fundamental and global principles. This was how Islam, from its early days, integrated a great diversity of cultures and, as such, was influenced by, and became integrated into, large numbers of societies. In other words, there is one Islam in the sense of a divinely revealed religion, and in terms of their commitment to Islam's spiritual and divine essence, Muslims form a unique community. However, within this unique Islamic community, there are various customs and schools of *Fiqh*. All along their history, Muslims have taken from other countries and cultures everything that is good and does not contradict their universal principles. This is why Islam peacefully penetrated Africa and Asia, among other places, established roots, and felt at ease in these places. They will feel so in Europe as well. But the Europeans need to be patient. Muslims are going to do it the same way as they did it in the past. Today, they are trying to face the new realities by adopting what is good in Europe and yet does not contradict their essential texts. This applies to the field of social affairs, but Muslims are not going to change the way they pray because they are in Europe; they will pray as they pray in Egypt, Pakistan, Malaysia, or other parts of the Islamic world.

If Europeans want to understand the way Muslims are coping with their new environment, they must be aware of this dual dimension of Islam. Because the religious dimension is ignored, they cannot understand the Muslims' speeches or discourse. As a result, they suspect Muslims of using a double language and believe that the Muslims' ultimate goal is simply to Islamize Europe. But this is not the case. Muslims are adapting themselves to Europe in the same way that other Muslims did before throughout history in other geographical and cultural contexts.

A very important principle regarding the field of social affairs is *al-ibâha al-asliyya* (principle of original permission), which allows Muslims to take what is good from other cultures. When I wrote my book *To Be a European Muslim*,[2] a Muslim came to me and said that I should rather title it *To Be a Muslim in Europe*. I said, "No. It is *To Be a European Muslim*"—because this will be my future, the future of my children, and the future of many other Muslims. I am a European Muslim, and there is no contradiction in this situation. If one can think of African Islam or Asian Islam, then why not also think of European Islam? The reason why this has not yet happened is because of fear and ignorance of some basic tenets of Islam. Today, most Muslims are not speaking out of confidence, because they do not know their own principles, which means they do not know themselves well. And because they do not know themselves, they are afraid of their environment. The same applies to some Europeans. They, too, at times, do not know who they are and therefore are afraid of those Muslims who have religious convictions and a better sense of who they are and what they want from the future.

The dynamics unleashed by the process of European integration, on the one hand, which is putting cultural strains on many European countries, and the forces of globalization, on the other, are creating identity-related tensions for many Europeans. These difficulties in turn make them afraid of the impact that the Muslims may have on their societies and their collective identity.

If this analysis is accepted, then three issues need to be examined: (1) What will be the Muslims' future? (2) What are their intentions in Europe, and what is the role of Muslim organizations in Europe? and (3) What will the Muslims' new situation lead them to do in the near future?

THE MUSLIMS' FUTURE IN EUROPE

The Muslims' new situation in Europe will allow them to get back to the essentials of their religion and reread its principal sources. In the new European context, some sources must be reread and reinterpreted, and this is what is meant by *tajdid* (renewal). It does not mean changing the text, but reading it with a new perspective. This reexamination is important for many Islamic concepts, and this is what is happening now in the United States and in Europe—in order to have a new look at Muslims' religious sources and to develop a new vision.

Indeed, since the 1990s, Muslim *ulema*—both from Islamic countries and from Europe—have been engaged in dialogue with the purpose of providing guidelines for Europe's Muslims on how to practice their faith while being good citizens.[3]

In this context, four examples stand out: The first and the most important one is the concept of *shari'a*. Many Muslims in Europe think that this is a complex concept and that it has to be removed from Muslim vocabulary. I do not agree. I use *shari'a* every day, but in a new definition, which goes back to the original definition of the term. In its original sense, *shari'a* meant "the way to the source," and not only "a legal system" or Islamic law that the *Fuqaha* have tried to define within their field of specialization.

Shari'a is the Muslims' way to remain faithful to their universal principles anywhere in the world. Thus, Muslims need to return to a more authentic definition of *shari'a*, without making this common differentiation between, for example, Orthodox and Sufi attitudes. All Muslims—

Orthodox, Sunni, Sufi, or Shi'a—are part of the same understanding of the *shari'a*.[4]

Shari'a is not only a "penal code" that Muslims want to implement. Rather, it is a global perception of how to remain faithful to God and to his commands. It is a general and global concept of creation, of existence, of death, and a way of life derived from a normative reading of Muslim scriptural sources. It is a reading that is normative but one that still enables Muslims to extract a global meaning. This particular understanding of the *shari'a* is very important, because it will change Muslims' vision of Europe.

Closely related to this issue is the question of Muslim integration into European societies. There are, of course, different levels of integration such as social and political integration. It is clear that integration on a social level and to some extent political levels is working everywhere in Europe. For instance, half of the Muslims in France now are French citizens. But there is another kind of integration, namely, a religious and philosophical integration. To illustrate, if Muslims define the *shari'a* as a global vision, then they have to integrate, within their perception of how to remain faithful to their faith, everything that is good in European societies and to accept that these aspects are part of their *shari'a*. What this means is that Muslims are integrating and are not only being integrated. For instance, when I read the French or any other European constitutions, there are numerous articles that I find in accordance with my vision of justice. I do not have to respect them only because they are part of a constitution with which I have a "moral contract" of allegiance as a function of my European citizenship. It is more than that. I respect them because they meet a deep requirement of my religious conscience and thus become part of my intimate values. In this way, I am integrated at the social level, but I am also integrating at a philosophical/religious level. This is a two-way process, and for Muslims to think in this manner and reach this level of understanding is a new experience. In particular, many of them cannot yet fully understand that many of the European values are indeed also part and parcel of Islamic values. To illustrate, principles of justice and equality are integral to Islam as well as to ideals proclaimed by the Europeans. Thus, Muslims ask, "How can you say that what we, until now, have had as the cultural and legal background in Europe, is already Islamic?" But it is so. Everything that is in Europe also belongs to Muslims, and this is not a completely new reality.

ESSENTIAL AND SECONDARY MATTERS

The second point is that Muslims must differentiate between essential and secondary issues. For example, to pray is more important than to eat *halal* or *haram* food. When dealing with principles, it is necessary to know what is *sâbit* (immutable) and what is *mutaghayr* (subject to change), what is essential (*asl*) and what is secondary (*far'*). This process is intrinsic to Islam. Things are changing and moving, and Muslims have to deal with this process. Moreover, their new environment forces them to make this distinction. The *ulema* must take the lead in this regard. Such a process will also help Muslims develop rational attitudes toward their environment. Islamic rationality means dealing with your environment, and this is what we are witnessing today in Muslim communities in the United States and in Europe. This is part of the process of globalization. Muslims are trying to remain faithful to their principles while facing these new realities and coping with the intellectual and practical challenges that they pose.

DAWA (THE CALL)

The third issue is to redefine what is *dawa*. Why exactly are you, a Muslim, here in (Europe)? Are you here to convert me? Europeans have to understand an important point, and sometimes Muslims must be told so as well: Muslims do have a universal message ("We have sent you but as mercy for the world," Qur'an), but their real role is to "bear witness." *Dawa* means that, wherever a Muslim is, he or she is a witness of Islam's message, through his or her speech, behavior, and manner of dealing with people. To bear witness is the Muslims' principal role, not to convert others.

Last, Europe's Muslims must promote an Islamic European culture. By this I mean that Muslims must take from the European culture what is in accordance with their principles and in turn contribute to the European culture as Muslims while respecting the Europeans' values. This is necessary for the creation of a true European Muslim. I am not asked to be a Moroccan or Pakistani Muslim in Europe; I am asked, and want, to be a European Muslim respectful of the Islamic principles. This means that I have to promote a new culture that fits my new environment while respecting my religious values. This is what is meant by Europeanization of Islam.

Regarding Islamization of Europe, one needs to bear in mind the following points: (1) It is important to remind Europe of its own history. All indigenous Europeans forget that Muslims are part of European history. They speak as if Muslims "have come late." There is a selective memory in Europe. Yet, Islam's legacy in Europe is very substantial. Muslims have been part of the building of the European conscience and of the European mind. This is not a process of Islamization but a reminder to Europeans of their own past. (2) Take a fresh look at the place of spirituality and religion in society. I want the European countries to be realistic and respect my spirituality. Nowadays, to be from an Arab background, to be a Muslim, and to come from the suburbs are three major handicaps in Europe. And when one says that one is a practicing Muslim, one is very close to being branded as a fundamentalist. The question is: Is it possible both to be open-minded and tolerant of others and to practice one's own religion?

CONCLUSION: COMMON CHALLENGES

What matters today is no longer to know what the *place* of Muslims in Europe is or will be. The question that must be addressed now is to know how they will *contribute* to the social, economic, cultural, and spiritual development of their respective societies. Muslims are not the only people who are asking themselves fundamental questions about spirituality, education, social participation, etc. Women and men of faith or conscience, humanists in the broad sense of the word, are all preoccupied with the future of our societies, which seems increasingly oriented toward production, economic performance, and more consumption. Indeed, despite prosperity, many Europeans feel something lacking—a spiritual void. This is perhaps why a few years ago the European Commission's forward studies unit conducted a study on how various religions and humanist values could contribute to the building of a new European identity with a spiritual dimension that can be emulated by different faiths and communities in Europe. Indeed, in presenting this initiative to the European Parliament on 14 September 1999, President Romano Prodi called it a "search for a common identity—a new European soul."[5] Certainly, Muslims can and should contribute to the development of this spiritual dimension of European integration, a spirituality that would be based on what is best in all religious and nonreligious ethical systems.

1. *Relearning subtlety and complexity.* Listening to a woman or a man, being attentive to their expectations, to their emotional wounds, to their doubts, is acceding to complexity. Our conception of the world may be simple, our principles may be crystal clear, but life is complicated, as are the hearts and intelligence of every human being irrespective of race or creed. Anyone who is attentive and respectful of him- or herself and of others knows this fact. It is strange indeed that what we know almost instinctively in our daily and emotional relationships suddenly vanishes into thin air as soon as we consider others who belong to another religion, another culture, another history. Here, our relations are built on concise, quick, clear-cut, almost definitive information. We want to understand our friends deeply but find it sufficient to gather superficial information about other people's historical, cultural, and spiritual realities. We give some people, out of friendship and love, what we refuse

to others because of indifference and prejudice. Yet, all the time we advocate dialogue.

We must absolutely learn again the meaning of study, of in-depth understanding, and accede together to a deeper perception of the complexity upon which other people's references and lives are organized. Listening, learning to understand again, admitting, at times, that one does not understand, are all paths leading to deep, subtle thought, often silent and without judgment. Our common enemies, today, are caricature and prejudice: lack of information used to keep us ignorant of some cultures, some realities, or some events. Today, sketchy, superficial information, if not misinformation, give us the illusion of knowledge. Yet, this illusion of knowledge is far more dangerous than yesterday's ignorance: It breeds complacency and definitive and crude judgments and fosters intellectual dictatorships. The movement goes both ways: One should, on the one hand, be careful to avoid simplification and, on the other, grant others access to the complexity of one's being and references. Such seems to be the challenge of a real and constructive dialogue in a culturally plural society.

2. *Spirituality.* The essence of the Qur'an's message is the heart, spirituality, and love. Living one's relationship with God under the impulse of the energy and inspiration of reminder and proximity is the finality of all human life according to Islam's teachings. Such is the enlightening spirituality for which moral norms are but milestones and landmarks. All the religions and spiritualities in the world are concerned with protecting this intimate energy, which makes for balance, harmony, "humanizing" distance—in short, which makes for mankind's humanity and dignity. Even agnostics are always speaking of their desire to live and give meaning to a spirituality, a vital inspiration, the consciousness of a meaning that must be preserved. We all speak about this, and we all realize how terribly difficult it is to live a coherent spirituality in the midst of the modern life styles that engulf us. Living and protecting one's spirituality in an overmodernized society are difficult. It is a real challenge that we must take up together. Spirituality, meaning, and values are all areas that must preoccupy us—or else tomorrow, because we neglected or avoided debates on fundamental issues, we may have to admit that we have left a clear field to all sorts of sectarian and exclusion-fostering deviations. We are faced with real questions that must again occupy the sphere of reflection and thought of humans in rich and industrialized societies. To be concerned with spirituality and the heart is to ask oneself: What role does faith play in my daily life? How does my conscience influence my choices and neglects? What value and meanings do things have beyond their financial worth? How can we be with God today? How can we live with humans? These are unsettling

questions—an earthquake, sometimes, for those who accompany their children along the road and suddenly start to ponder.

3. *Education.* All educational systems in the modern world are being questioned daily, and they are severely criticized as if they alone were responsible for all the failings of society. Teachers at the same time become scapegoats for every frustration: School is no longer what it used to be and "everything is wrong." Muslims, like all other citizens, are interested in this issue: The school system as a whole, teaching curricula, and life at school are social issues and must involve all the actors in society. Whether in Muslim families or in any other family, the old clearcut divisions (family providing education and school providing learning) are dead and gone: Such spaces of ideal complementarity have now left their place to a sort of haze in which respective duties and responsibilities are hard to define and discussions often lead to transferring responsibility onto others. Education is one of the most important stakes of modern times. Discussing it requires that all the actors in our European societies, whatever their faith, their spirituality, their humanist beliefs, work in concert to determine the objectives of school education and its place in our society. A community, a nation of responsible beings, can be assessed through its readiness to invest in the education and training of tomorrow's adults. Our aim cannot be only to transmit abstract learning and skills, leading to an almost total mastery of the environment and enabling individuals to obtain social recognition with a good salary. What exactly do we want? It is high time we asked ourselves this question together. What is it we want? To train worthy and responsible beings? To live together in the respect of others and of plurality? To defend right and justice? Pupils, students, and academics more or less guess where they are being led, but they no longer really know *who* they are as they acquire such training. An often curtailed memory as to their history and the particularly blurred horizons of their cultural identity blend with a most widespread religious illiteracy. All those elements contribute to multiplying fears and misgivings: How can one serenely and respectfully recognize others without having a clear notion of one's own identity? A multicultural society demands exacting and adequate education, or else it may produce the worst possible racist and xenophobic deviations. The role of school education, today even more than in the past, is to train individuals who are capable of questioning meaning, of discussing values, and do not remain confined to a mere selective management of technical abilities and performances. This issue concerns all responsible European citizens, irrespective of their faith.

4. *Social rifts.* European societies are going through deep social and economic crises. The question of unemployment is haunting many people and more and more pockets of economic marginalization, social exclusion, and hence delinquency are developing. Violence and insecurity

are the daily lot of many towns, cities, and suburbs throughout Europe. We know but too well that all these factors are liable to increase racism and xenophobia, because the populations who are most deeply struck by such scourges are often those of immigrant descent. It is urgent that we develop partnerships at local levels in order to fight all types of social deviations. Short-term work is an indispensable first step, but it must be accompanied with more long-term strategies for social and urban development. All citizens, whatever their beliefs, must take part in this effort toward social reform and greater justice that must be distinguished from purely voluntary and cooperative action. The latter is, indeed, necessary, but it should be considered as an additional contribution rather than as a substitute for a firmer political commitment to these goals. Fighting unemployment, opposing discrimination in employment (when names, colors, or clothes seem to come from elsewhere), promoting social welfare, intervening against suburb violence, and looking after marginalized persons (the poor and the elderly) are some of the many challenges that we must take up together, as partners and fellow citizens.

The need is therefore great today to promote better mutual knowledge between Muslims and the society in which they live. To fight historical liabilities as well as the heavy weight of existing prejudices will not be possible through mere speeches or sincere testimonies of "good will." The conflict seems so deep, and so tense, that the process leading to establishing mutual trust between Muslims and natives will take a very long time; it will, above all, have to rely on better understanding stemming from genuine dialogue, joint activities, especially in the field of education, and necessarily dynamic coexistence. From Muslims' point of view, this means they should acquire the confident feeling that they are *at home* and that they must be more involved within European societies. These European societies are henceforth their own, at all levels, from strictly religious affairs to social concerns in the broadest sense, as discussed earlier. The *re*active posture expressed by Muslims either through total dilution and assimilation in the environment or through violent opposition to it is incompatible with the idea of building a future forged of mutual trust, respect, and collaboration.

Islam is primarily the fundamental expression of the essential links of the heart's life to God. The widespread negative image of Islam today has completely concealed this aspect of its teachings. Sadly, Muslims, because of their often purely emotional reaction, are themselves far from living and expressing this dimension of their religion. Islam is a conception of life that directs believers toward spirituality and meditation over life's meaning. It is both a simple and a very demanding way of life, which requires from Muslims to do their utmost to be better tomorrow than they are today and to choose, at any price, the way of generosity, honesty, and justice. Muslims in Europe, instead of relying only on the principles of their religion in its Asian or North African versions, should come back to these fundamentals of their faith and play their part within industrialized societies. Together with the members of other religious communities and with all men and women of good will, they must participate in the necessary debate about the place of faith, spirituality, and values in the modern and postmodern societies. Their new presence could, as such, be a positive mirror that should be considered as a revelator rather than as an aggressor: Muslims will henceforth have to ask questions, not alone, not *against* the whole society, but *with* their fellow citizens through a sincere and genuine shared preoccupation. This means that a wide involvement in favor of dialogue on ethical as well as religious issues should be promoted from the grass roots up to leading and specialized institutions in all Western countries.

NOTES

1. See Tariq Ramadan, "L'islam d'Europe sort de l'isolement," *Le Monde Diplomatique*, April 1998.

2. Tariq Ramadan, *To Be a European Muslim* (Leicester: Islamic Foundation, 1999).

3. About these contacts and their results, see ibid., p. 3. A large number of *ulema* and European Muslims have already agreed on the following principles:

1. A Muslim—resident or citizen—should consider him/herself bound by a moral and social contract to reflect the laws of the country in which he/she resides;
2. European law (and thus its secular framework) allows Muslims to practice their faith;
3. The old definition of *dar al-harb* (the area of war and disbelief) no longer applies to the case of Muslims in Europe;
4. The Muslims should fully participate in the social, economic, and political life of the country in which they reside while respecting their own values;
5. In the context of European legislation, nothing prevents the Muslims from making choices in accordance with the requirements of their faith;
6. In 1997, Muslim associations in France and Great Britain presented demands that were accepted to protect "une ame pour l'Europe."

Ramadan, "L'islam d'Europe," 5.

4. For an elaboration of these concepts, see Ramadan, *To Be a European Muslim*.

5. See Win Burton and Thomas Jansen, *Citoyenneté droits et devoir. Sociétiés civile. Reflexions et contributions des religions et des humanines et une ame pour l'Europe ethique et spirituel* [Citizenship rights and duty. Civil societies. Reflections and contributions of religions and an ethical and spiritual soul for Europe] (Brussels: European Commission, 2000).

12

Muslim Youth in Europe

Peter P. Mandaville

INTRODUCTION

Muslim youth constitute an increasingly important social milieu in Western Europe. As the second- and third-generation Muslims take their place in society, they develop a diverse range of responses to the sociocultural, economic, and political climates they inhabit.

A considerable part of this group whose ethnocultural background qualifies them as Muslim, even if not strictly observant, feel fully "at home" in Europe and thoroughly comfortable with Western norms. For them, France, Germany, or Britain is a primary source of identification, and Islam, if it figures at all, is of secondary importance in their own self-image. This is the image of the secularized Muslim, the fully "integrated" British Asian or Franco-Arab. For others, however, Islam remains a core component of their self-identity and a key source of their world view. Under certain conditions, a "return" to Islam—sometimes of a particularly radical brand—is prompted by perceived disenfranchisement and socioeconomic discrimination. These two extreme poles— the integrating, secularizing Muslim, on the one hand, and the "traditional," or radical adherent, on the other—are often held up as representative of two major trends among contemporary Muslim youth in Europe. Such easy dichotomies, however, inevitably mask a far more complex reality. To frame the situation in this way is to ignore the far

Portions of this chapter are reprinted from Peter P. Mandaville, *Transnational Muslim Politics: Reimaging the Umma* (New York: Routledge, 2001), courtesy of Routledge Press.

more fluid and nuanced forms of youth identity that are to be found today. This chapter's goal is to highlight the complicated and creative richness of the contemporary Muslim youth culture in Europe and to explain how—when these dualisms do appear—the seemingly incompatible dynamics of integration and alienation can be understood.

In this context, the primary focus is those young Muslims who have made Islam a major part of their identities and way of life. They tend to be more religiously "observant" and strive, to the extent possible, to integrate the practice of Islam into their daily lives. They are often active in youth movements and organizations and seek to establish a space for Islam within the European public sphere. However, these are not set and confined categories; rather, Muslim youth culture is notable for its ability to defy easy categorizations such as "secular" versus "religious." There are circumstances under which those young Muslims who would usually be more inclined toward the secularism turn to Islam as a language of social protest or as a means of distinguishing themselves from the culture of the majority. By contrast, there are observant Muslims who view Western norms, popular culture, and life styles as mostly compatible with Islam. They do not see inherent conflict in their dual identities as Muslims and Europeans. Thus, they represent the continued cross-fertilization and closer integration of these two cultural worlds and the possibility of creating a distinctively "European Islam."

DISCRIMINATION AND IDENTITY

For many young Muslims, the experience of life in Europe has been profoundly disenchanting. Young Muslims find themselves caught between the culture of their parents and that of Western society, which either refuses to accept them as bona fide members of society or—often—actively discriminates against them on the basis of their "otherness." Images of marginalized and unoccupied young Arabs in Marseilles or the depressed suburbs of Paris spring to mind here, as does the disenfranchised generation of young South Asians who grew up in Thatcher's Britain in the 1980s.

Yet, in terms of their relation to Islam, attitudes of Muslim youth are varied and complicated. For some, the rejection of Islam ("the old-fashioned ways of my parents") serves as a form of rebellion. For those who attend public schools in Western Europe, there is the added pressure to conform with the norms of majority youth culture. This leads the young Muslim to de-emphasize those aspects of their identity that seem as obstacles to their "fitting in." More official forms of intolerance also discouraged public displays of Muslim identity in Western Europe into the 1990s. The headscarves affair in France, where girls were prevented from wearing the *hijab*, highlighted the extent to which signs of difference, and particularly those perceived as threatening the French secular tradition (*laicité*), would not be tolerated. The demands of wider national societies for the integration or "assimilation" of Muslims implied the complete abandonment of their culture.

This intolerance of cultural difference and demand for total assimilation led to a converse reaction: the embrace of Islam, partly as a form of rebellion against an inhospitable social environment. This reaction demonstrated that there is a point beyond which discrimination and rejection by the majority society result not in Muslims' denial of their religion, but rather in its reaffirmation. Rejected and unwanted, they turn to that which sets them apart as a form of cultural self-assertion and a basis of identity. Islam also becomes a form of self-defense and a source of solidarity against a hostile dominant culture. This response is observable even among those Muslims for whom religion had never been particularly important. This dynamic was evident during the riots and demonstrations that took place in Bradford, in 1989, against Salman Rushdie's *The Satanic Verses*. The outcry among Muslims at the Rushdie affair was caused by and reflected this dissatisfaction with their general socioeconomic conditions. Young Muslims, particularly South Asians, joined the protests against the book not only because they saw it as an insult to their religion, which for many had never been a large part of their lives, but also because it represented the extent to which they felt alienated from, and rejected by, British society. These examples show that, in most cases, the crude dualistic categories of secularism versus religion are not valid.

Anti-Muslim prejudice is still pervasive in Europe, although at times "Islamophobia," which reached its height in the late 1980s and early 1990s, may appear to be in abeyance. However, as the antiimmigrant, especially Muslim, riots in northern England in the spring and summer of 2001 demonstrated, the risk of reappearance is always present. Yet, young Muslims seem determined to claim a place for their religion in mainstream society, and the numbers certainly bode well for this undertaking. Britons of Pakistani and Bangladeshi descent almost doubled between 1981 and 1991, and nearly half of them were born in the United Kingdom. The age dispersion compared with that of white Britons is also striking, with twice as many under-sixteen year olds among the South Asian population as among the white Britons. Only 2 percent of this community is over the age of sixty-five compared with 17 percent among Britain's white population.[1] This pattern repeats itself across Muslim populations in most parts of Western Europe.

In the lives of the vast majority of Europe's young Muslims, their minority status looms large. For those only recently arrived, it means coming to terms with an unfamiliar set of circumstances, a requirement to engage with new cultures and an ability to adjust to inevitable changes in one's own tradition. However, as Barbara Metcalf has put it, one cannot assume "that the old and new cultures are fixed, and that change results from pieces being added and subtracted."[2] The issue is hence not one of loss and gain or of Islam's simply "disappearing" through cultural assimilation in Europe. The reality is a much more complex condition, one in which Islam has space to shift and change. Much of this process involves bringing Islam into the forums of popular culture and public space. Television, videos, and the Internet have all become spaces of religious discourse.[3] Above all, religion has to be seen to offer something to those young Muslims who find themselves unemployed, alienated, or lost in the majority society. Some argue that this can be accomplished by attempting to relate aspects of wider popular culture in various European countries to a Muslim identity. In order to appreciate the implications of this shift in the delivery of knowledge, however, one needs to reorient one's analysis of Islam and focus on flux and disjunction rather than on stability and continuity. The spaces of European Islam can provide fertile venues for the rethinking and reformulation of tradition and the construction of an Islam for the coming generations.

Young Muslims are also embroiled in complex debates about the very nature and boundaries of their religion. What does Islam mean to Muslims living in the West? From whom can reliable knowledge about Islam be gained? How can one differentiate reliably between "good" and "bad" interpretations of Islam? Such conversations are intensified in Western contexts owing to the sheer volume of human traffic that flows through them. Muslims in Europe come face to face with the myriad shapes and colors of global Islam—Turks meeting Egyptians in Vienna or Bangladeshis studying alongside Indonesians in London. These encounters often play an important role in processes of identity formation, prompting young Muslims to compare their self-understandings of Islam with those of Muslims from other backgrounds. Consequently, the new generation has a greater tendency to communicate and interact across sectarian and ethnic divisions and in general has a distaste for such differences.

THE INTERGENERATIONAL DIMENSIONS

Intergenerational issues also affect and shape the various identities and modes of action of Muslim youth. Indeed, differences between parents and their children over the role of Islam and how it is to be understood feature prominently in Muslim youth discourse. As Jørgen Nielsen points out, many mosque organizations are "firmly in the control of the immigrant generation, their parents, and only the most perceptive of these [are] beginning to co-opt their children into the power structures."[4] It is not just a matter of parents keeping children out of mosques, however. Young Muslims are largely dissatisfied with the Islam of their parents. They are aware that in many cases, their parents, as recently arrived immigrants, learned Islam in a very different sociocultural setting. The older generation received both direct and indirect socialization into their religion at home, school, and in societies where Islam was the religion of the majority and its principal ethical frame of reference.[5] Youth today complain that the older generation tries to live as if it were still in the homeland, as if Muslims were still in the majority: "They would talk Pakistani politics constantly," complains one writer, "but never neighbourhood politics. . . . They didn't want to engage with non-Muslims."[6] The sectarian conflicts and divisions between religious schools of thought are also seen by the younger generation as a negative aspect of their parents' Islam. Many young Muslims view these ethnotheological debates as pointless time wasting that only generates dissent.

Because the youth have to practice Islam as a minority religion, there arises the question of the relevance of traditional Islam to the new social setting. Faced with these dilemmas, some young "Muslims" turn away from Islam as an unwanted and irrelevant vestige of the past that emphasizes their otherness. This leads them to embrace secularism, eliminate Islam from their lives, and try to integrate and even "assimilate" culturally and to become as British, German, Dutch, or French as the host society's ethos and prejudice will permit. But they still face racial and ethnic obstacles. Nor can they escape their "Muslim background" because for many Westerners, when it comes to Islam, ethnicity and religion reinforce each other.[7]

Other young Muslims choose to reaffirm their Muslimness. Elizabeth Scantlebury notes that a "significant number of young Muslims are rejecting a religio-ethnic identity in favor of a search for 'True Islam.' "[8] This dual process of search for true Islam and assertion of Muslimness as opposed to other forms of self-identification leads them to question their parents' life styles and Islamic credentials. They see their Islam as tainted or mere "cultural" practice. This rejection thus "takes the form of trying to strip away the varying cultural traditions that first generation migrants have, rightly or wrongly, assumed to be Islamic, from the 'essential core' of the religion."[9] Hanif Kureishi's short story and subsequent film, *My Son the Fanatic*, depicts this process from the perspective of a father whose son has "returned" to Islam. This search has led some young Muslims to join radical organizations such as *Hizb ut-Tahrir*, whose declared goal is the establishment of an Islamic state in Britain. Many of these activists attempt to gain control of the mosques and use them as pulpits for propaganda. Most mosque administrators are tolerant of such behavior because they feel that these youth "have nowhere else to go to let off steam." They "tolerate them because they are lonely in London and angry at the wrongs in their own countries. . . . [But] there is no discipline. Every boy is a leader."[10]

The last few years have seen some positive trends as regards inter-generational issues. The establishment of various youth organizations offers resources for those Muslims seeking to make Islam relevant to the particular conditions of modern life in Europe. In the words of one young Muslim, who became involved with one of the leading youth organizations in Britain, Young Muslims UK:

> I began to feel more comfortable with Islam because it was being articulated in a language I could understand by my own peer group; in English rather than Urdu or Arabic. Everyone was in Western dress. I began to think that maybe I'd misunderstood Islam. . . . So I began to read widely about the religion, entering into a period of inquiry. I didn't just accept Islam. I had a lot of questions that I wanted answered first, about the treatment of women for example. After I had received satisfactory answers I then felt ready to make a commitment to Islam. I got my answers from the leadership of the Young Muslims rather than from the mosque; the imams there are quite fixed in their views and don't like it when people ask too many questions.[11]

What is crucial here is the translation of Islam into a vocabulary comprehensible to those Muslims who have grown up in Western society and who possess certain Western norms in addition to Islam. Indeed, this process is in many ways about emphasizing the areas in which these value systems are compatible or at least highly similar. Religion has to be seen to offer something to those young Muslims who find themselves unemployed, alienated, or lost in the majority society. Aurangzeb Iqbal, a Bradford solicitor, has suggested that sport might be one route by which this could be done.[12] To this end, he has organized a number of football matches for young Muslims in the United Kingdom. Iqbal emphasizes the need for Muslim role models and the importance of prominent Muslims showing the younger generation that Islam can be compatible with success in the West. In this regard, he outlines his own version of "upwardly-mobile Islam":

> Islam tells you to dress smartly, to spend upon yourself, you are not supposed to hoard money. It's wrong to have a big bank balance or build a massive house in Pakistan that no one lives in. That's wrong. Spend that money on your kids, on private education, don't hoard it. Have a nice house, invite your neighbours in regularly. Set yourself high standards, so that other people think, "I like that, I would like to be like that."[13]

Others emphasize the importance of language, which, as we have seen, is one of the issues dividing the generations. There is a need to make

Islam widely available to young Muslims whose first (and sometimes only) language is English. Much of this involves bringing Islam into popular culture and making it available via a wide variety of media.[14] Hence, the importance of popular Muslim youth magazines such as *Q-News* and *The Muslim News*. *Q-News* "appeals to young, educated Muslims, frustrated with sectarianism, and is able through an international language, English, to access innovative and relevant Islamic scholarship."[15] This publication has also contributed enormously toward the availability of sound religious advice through a column by the late Dr. Syed Mutawalli ad-Darsh, a prominent religious scholar in the United Kingdom. Every fortnight in *Q-News*, he would dispense *fatwas* on a vast range of issues relevant to Islam in modern society. Many of these were answers to questions sent in by readers on marriage, sexuality, and contraception, topics that young Muslims often find difficult to raise with their parents or with traditional mosque leaders. Today's young European Muslims are trying to build their lives in a highly urbanized and often cosmopolitan environment. They require an Islam to match this setting. The traditional frameworks of their parents and the associated institutions of religious scholarship are perceived as being in desperate need of transformation. In this regard, publications such as *Q-News* have provided important forums for debating intra-Islamic politics and the future of Muslims in Europe.[16]

CHOOSING BETWEEN TENDENCIES WITHIN ISLAM

A second form of internal debate relates to the divisions between various tendencies in youth Islam. Much of this relates to the question of how young Muslims identify their political imperatives and, more specifically, how they should deal with the West.[17] While the vast majority of young Muslims in Europe stress the compatibility of Islam with Western European culture, there do exist more radical tendencies. Most prominent among the latter in the United Kingdom has been the aforementioned organization *Hizb ut-Tahrir*, a movement that garnered significant support in British university campuses in the early 1990s. This group's stated goal is the establishment of an Islamic state in Britain and restoration of the caliphate.[18]

Hizb ut-Tahrir styles itself and its rhetoric specifically to appeal to young disenfranchised Muslims falling through the cracks of society. They protest against the immorality and imperialism of the West and advocate a return to the true Islam of the Qur'an and Sunna. "Islam," for them, "is the solution." *Hizb ut-Tahrir* has undoubtedly forced young Muslims to deal with questions and issues that they might have otherwise avoided, and the group's aggressive tactics effectively allowed it to define the political agenda for the younger generation. "I would be dishonest if I said I hadn't been influenced by them," reported one young Muslim in the English midlands. "The rise of *Hizb ut-Tahrir* also had a strong impact on other movements. Until then many other groups had been politically apathetic. They were forced to react and relate to the issues—such as restoring the caliphate—that *Hizb ut-Tahrir* had put on the agenda."[19] A common strategy of the group is to label those Muslims living in the United Kingdom or elsewhere in Europe who do not agree with their agenda as 'secular' or corrupted by the West. They create a zero-sum game in which one is either with them—the "true" Islam—or against them, hence becoming traitors to Islam or, even worse, apostates.

Paradoxically, the rise of *Hizb ut-Tahrir* has had a unifying effect among young Muslims. A common sense of opposition to the radical tendency has, for example, brought together previously antagonistic South Asian groups such as the Deobandi-influenced *Tablighi Jama'at* and the Barelvis. Even other Islamists seeking to implement an Islamic political order have expressed dissatisfaction with *Hizb ut-Tahrir*'s methods. They are well aware that European public forums are under the gaze of the world's media and that Muslims need to be careful about what they say and the image they project. As one Islamist based in London remarked: "If you have a slogan that makes you look ridiculous, for example, the claim that you're going to restore the caliphate, then you'll never be taken seriously."[20] By unifying these various tendencies in opposition, *Hizb ut-Tahrir* has, in the words of one observer, "played a positive role in a negative way."[21]

CONCLUSION

Despite the presence of radical tendencies in European Islam, the overall trend is in the opposite direction. The majority of Muslim youth understand themselves to be stakeholders in European society. For them, the fate of European Islam is tied to the fate of Europe. Participation, cooperation, and dialogue are the operative terms. An analysis of the shifting definition and connotations associated with two classic categories of Islamic political thought, *dar ul-Islam* (domain of Islam) and *dar ul-Harb* (domain of strife or war), helps one to group this new spirit.

Traditionally, *dar ul-Islam* refers to those regions in which the principles of Islam are upheld under the rule of a Muslim sovereign. *Dar ul-Harb*, on the other hand, "is that which is not [under Muslim rule], but which, actually or potentially, is a seat of war for Muslims until by conquest it is turned into [*dar ul-Islam*]."[22] Hence, there is an essential element of antagonism between these two abodes, for *dar ul-Harb* represents a space in which Muslims, at least in theory, are at conflict with non-Muslims.

The more radical groups, like *Hizb ut-Tahrir*, still use this divisive vocabulary in their rhetoric. But there is evidence that these concepts are currently undergoing certain transformations and reinterpretations. For example, there are Muslims who claim that the only requirement for a country to qualify as *dar ul-Islam* is that Muslims must be allowed to practice their religion with complete freedom. Some writers also emphasize the extent to which Muslims are actually more often able to fulfill the scriptural obligations of their religion in the West than they are in their own countries.[23] This sentiment echoed in the remarks of the young Muslim woman in Austria who looks forward to attending university in that country because, unlike in her parents' homeland of Turkey, where the secular legacy of Ataturk limits the observance of certain Islamic injunctions in the public sector, she is free to wear Islamic dress at school.[24]

A seminar in France in the summer of 1993 brought together a group of European Muslim scholars to discuss the problems likely to be faced by the next generation of Muslims living in Europe. Not surprisingly, questions related to nationality and citizenship figured prominently. The scholars concluded that young Muslims living in Europe should not consider themselves to be living in *dar ul-Harb*. Such a term, in their view, did not reflect the "contemporary realities" of Muslim life in Europe. Instead, young Muslims should regard themselves as participants in *dar ul-Ahd* (the domain of contract or agreement), a third category of political space recognized by some schools of thought. This concept refers to a region in which Muslims and non-Muslims have entered into some form of agreement as regards the conduct of good relations between them, with an emphasis on participation and social responsibility.

This shift in thinking entails serious implications for the ways in which young Muslims in Europe will conduct their politics. Jacques Waardenburg refers to a "New Islamic Discourse" which emphasizes active participation in community life rather than the introversion that characterized the early phase of Muslim immigration and settlement from the 1950s through the 1980s. Muslims will no longer hold themselves apart from the majority society but will distinguish themselves by offering an alternative order, Islam. This alternative is not, however, viewed by its youthful advocates as inherently incompatible with Western norms. [25]

Young Muslims are hence constructing both new identities and new frameworks for the practice of Islamic politics in response to the conditions of life in contemporary Europe. But what do these new processes imply? What do they mean in the context of the transition from Europe as *dar ul-Harb* to Europe as *dar ul-Ahd*? It can be argued that this shift represents a new disposition towards political engagement on the part of young Muslims and the emergence of a hands-on approach to bringing Islam—and Islamic-Western dialogue—firmly into the public sphere.

As Attaullah Siddiqui points out, the difference also affects one's "whole perception of living. *Dar ul-Harb* suggests temporality, otherness, and a sense of compulsion. *Dar ul-Ahd* suggests participation, belonging, and responsibility."[26] Analysts such as Jocelyn Cesari argue that through the new associations formed by young Muslims in France, "a new form of citizenship is emerging, [one that refers] to concrete and local action rather than voting or involvement with political parties. In other words, the *civil* dimension seems to be more relevant than the *civic* one."[27]

So, as Europe looks toward expansion, so do the horizons of Islam in the region. Increasingly confident of their place on the continent, young Muslims of many backgrounds and persuasions are starting about the business of building new identities and constructing bridges between Islam and the West at many levels: intellectual, cultural, and in everyday life. Although the trajectory of this project is as yet unclear, and its success still not guaranteed, the initial signs are encouraging.

NOTES

1. Phillip Lewis, *Islamic Britain: Religion, Politics and Identity among British Muslims* (London: I.B., Tauris, 1994), 15.

2. Barbara Daly Metcalf, "Introduction: Sacred Words, Sanctioned Practice, New Communities," in *Making Muslim Space in North America and Europe*, ed. Barbara Daly Metcalf (Berkeley: University of California Press, 1996), 7.

3. Peter Mandaville, "Information Technology and the Changing Boundaries of European Islam," in *Paroles d'Islam* [Words of Islam] ed. Felice Dassetto (Paris: Maisonneuve et Larose, 2000).

4. Jørgen Nielsen, "A Muslim Agenda for Britain: Some Reflections," *New Community* 17 (April 1996): 467.

5. Lala Yalcin-Heckman, "Are Fireworks Islamic? Towards an Understanding of Turkish Migrants and Islam in Germany," in *Syncretism/Anti-Syncretism: The Politics of Religious Synthesis*, in ed. Charles Steward and Rosalind Shaw (London: Routledge, 1994), 188.

6. Akbar Ahmed, "Mutiny in the Mosque," *The Guardian*, 19 March 1994.

7. Elizabeth Scantlebury, "Muslims in Manchester: The Depiction of a Religious Community," *New Community* 21 (July 1995).

8. Ibid., 430.

9. Ibid.

10. Ahmed, "Mutiny in the Mosque."

11. Interview with Dilwar Hussain, 28 July 1998.

12. Adam Lebor, *A Heart Turned East* (London: Little, Brown, 1997), 153.

13. Ibid., 154.

14. Peter Mandaville, "Islam in Diaspora: The Politics of Mediated Community," *Gazette: Journal of International Communications* 26 (2001): 169–186.

15. Lewis, *Islamic Britain*, 207.

16. See "Open Letter to FOSIS," *Q-News* 2 (23–30 July 1993), for an example

of how young Muslims are critiquing older student/mosque organizations and ideologies.

17. Interview with Attaullah Siddiqui, 29 July 1998.

18. For a useful self-description, see *Hizb ut-Tahrir* (London: Al-Khilafah Publications, n.d.).

19. Interview with Dilwar Hussain, 28 July 1998.

20. Interview with Sa'ad Al-Faqih, 12 May 1998.

21. Ibid.

22. "Residency Regulations in Non-Muslim Countries: A Necessary Explanation of Several Cases," *Shorter Encyclopedia of Islam*, (Leiden: E.J. Brill, 1991), 68–169.

23. See Sayyid Abd al-Aziz b. Muhammad Al-Saddiq, *Hukm al-iqama bi-bilad al-Kuffar wa-bayan wa-wugubuha fi bad al-ahwal* (Tangier: Bughaz, 1985).

24. Roger Cohen, "Austrian School Drama: Crucifix Meets Ramadan," *New York Times*, 20 March 2001.

25. Jacques Waardenburg, "Muslims as Dhimmis: The Emancipation of Muslim Immigrants in Europe: The Case of Switzerland," in *Muslims in the Margin: Political Responses to the Presence of Islam in Western Europe*, ed. W.A.R. Shadid and P.S. van Koningsveld, (Kampen: Kok Pharos, 1996).

26. Attaullah Siddiqui, "Muslims in the Contemporary World: Dialogue in Perspective," *World Faiths Encounter* 20 (July 1998): 27.

27. Jocelyn Cesari, "Islam in France: Social Challenge or Challenge of Secularism?" Paper presented at the Middle East Studies Association Annual Conference, November 1997, p. 8, emphasis added.

13

Islam, the European Union, and the Challenge of Multiculturalism

Sami Zemni and Christopher Parker

INTRODUCTION: EUROPE AS IDEOLOGICAL BACKDROP

Accompanying the accelerated drive toward European Union (EU) integration and expansion has been an effort to construct and promote a concept of common European identity and culture. More specifically, it has been posited that European national cultures share a common essence and a set of values—for example, democracy, tolerance, respect for human rights, etc.—that allow the continent's national communities/polities to collaborate within a coherent European civilizational constellation. The underlying premise has been summed up in the Charter of European Identity:

> Europe is above all a community of values. The aim of unification is to realize, test, develop and safeguard these values. They are rooted in common legal principles acknowledging the freedom of the individual and social responsibility. Fundamental European values are based on tolerance, humanity and fraternity. Building on its historical roots in classical antiquity and Christianity, Europe further developed these values during the course of the Renaissance, the Humanist movement, and the Enlightenment, which led in turn to the development of democracy, the recognition of fundamental and human rights, and the rule of law.[1]

These values are presented as growing organically and inevitably out of a uniquely European history. It is taken for granted that European national cultures have been fundamentally shaped by this history.

Reference to local European cultures within the context of EU integration serves to ease public and political anxiety regarding the pace and uncertain consequences of rapid political and economic union. It ameliorates feelings of loss of control by the European citizen. It creates the link of equivalence between local identities and the grand project; to be Flemish, for example, is to be European and thus to have a culturally grounded link with the above-mentioned values. The European identity is in turn linked to the project of EU integration, thus completing the circle.

At a time when political and economic rules of the game are being changed through, and in support of, the process of EU integration and expansion, references to culture lend the project a mantle of stability and continuity. This construction of a "multicultural Europe" has thus become an ideological cornerstone of European integration. It lends the project its aura of teleological fulfillment, its universal pretensions, and its moral veneer. It sets the ideological framework for inclusion and, significantly, for exclusion. Indeed, inasmuch as other cultures/civilizational projects contain these quintessentially European values, it is seen as largely by virtue of proximity to and interaction with Europe.

Yet, it must be noted at the outset that in spite of its universalist and essentialist claims, the European multiculturalist vision serves specific interests. This in turn limits the range of meanings that can be attached to it. It is a notion that delegitimizes local opposition to the frictionless movement of capital and goods across the continent, it protects European labor and farmers against the proximity of cheap labor/production in Europe's periphery, and it offers capital an ever more efficient political base from which to exploit this proximity. Accordingly, after the collapse of the Soviet Bloc, it was the economically more robust countries (e.g., Hungary, Czech Republic, Poland, Slovenia) that were considered eligible for inclusion in the union. The ideological legitimation of this enterprise was based on the so-called existence of "Central Europe." Detrez has shown how this idea of Central Europe was created during the 1980s by and around well known intellectuals and writers such as Konrad and Kundera.[2] The idea was given a new content in the 1990s. Central Europe became the "natural" extension of the EU because it shared those cherished values of tolerance, democracy, and freedom.

The concealment of the economic logic behind European expansion is not the work of a "conspiracy" of managers, bankers, or industry lobbies. It is the outcome of the free market economic system at work in the context of globalization. In this context, the economy is seen as a value-free field that responds automatically to the wants and needs of the people. As this system is unquestioned (there is no compelling "European" alternative at hand), those who feel uncomfortable with its consequences have been trying to find an outlet in a fight for multiculturalism, the right(s), and protection of cultural differences. These two enterprises are dialogical, because the growing success of cultural discourses (on religion, identity, ethnicity, local community, etc.) covers up and legitimizes the idea of the "neutrality of free market." Indeed, these discourses are positioned next to each other in such a way that the operative assumptions embedded within one of the discourses are held up to justify some of those embedded in the other. The interaction between and across these discursive fields has a profound impact on policy approaches and practices with regard to "Islam and the West" and "Islam and Europe."

The union posited three basic conditions for membership: European identity, democratic status, and respect for human rights.[3] The vagueness and abstract character of these conditions make them very malleable instruments of policy. In any case, European culture is reduced to those histories, myths, ideas, and patterns of expression that justify and promote the economic and political project of European integration. The fact that fascist or military regimes were in power in states such as Greece, Spain, and Portugal as late as the 1970s, which are now members of the EU, is excused by the mythmakers as an aberration rather than recent examples of an essentially European theme. Indeed, bringing these three nations into the EU was seen as an important obligation aimed at nurturing their "truer European essence." This can be viewed in contrast to the EU's stance toward Turkey, which has been excluded despite its intensive campaign for membership. European leaders do have objective and legitimate concerns about practices of the Kemalist state. However, the underlying tone of the European discussion about Turkey's membership is that the Turks are culturally "not up to it." In other words, the repressive and exclusivist practices of the Turkish state are not mere slips on the path toward the fulfillment of the European enlightenment project but reflect a fundamental incomprehension of it. Eastern Europe, on the other hand, became an ideal vantagepoint for the EU to see itself as an idealized, lovable entity.

ISLAM AND THE EUROPEAN PROJECT

Against this backdrop, Islam has been reconstructed in the European discourse as something of an "anti-Europe": a civilizational concept diametrically opposed to and potentially in conflict with that of Europe. The Iranian revolution, the Rushdie affair, the surge of Islamist-inspired antioccupation and antiregime militancy, the authoritarian Arab regimes themselves, the rise of the Taliban: All have been held up as examples of a fundamentally different cultural dynamic and trajectory. That the dynamics underpinning these phenomena are, in fact, strongly interrelated to and share interdependence with the European and global systems is not considered. For example, the thought that Islamist movements are challenging not the free market system per se, but rather the distribution of resources and power within that system, is ideologically difficult to consider, given the current hegemonic notion of free market neutrality. The notion that violence in Europe's periphery is ethnic or cultural conceals the possibility that many current conflicts might represent the instrumentalization of violence in ways that afford new actors relatively efficient access to the global economic system. Add to this the European and U.S. support for authoritarian regimes that protect their economic interests and phenomena like the Cold War-inspired U.S. support for the Afghan Mujahidin, and the intellectual construction of exceptionalism and uniqueness becomes logically very difficult.

The idea that the supposed cultural differences have the potential to express themselves in conflict with Europe—a notion most prominently developed in Samuel Huntington's "Clash of Civilizations"—has taken a strong hold in European political discourse and popular consciousness.[4] For example, in the early 1990s, Willy Claes, the then-North Atlantic Treaty Organization (NATO) secretary general, pinpointed "Islamic fundamentalism" as the new threat to Europe.[5] As the former enemy had disappeared, NATO had to look for a new scapegoat. It is beyond the scope of this chapter to challenge the assumptions of this thesis in detail. Suffice it to say that the notion is based on a large degree of Western self-idealization. It also elevates culture to the status of independent actor in political and social processes (i.e., it supports the notion that the decisions that lead to conflict are not rational considerations of structural opportunities and constraints, but the inevitable outcome of a cultural logic). It grounds itself in a rather superficial reading of the empirical dynamics and interests that motivate actors and drive conflict. But problematic though these assumptions might be, they have profoundly influenced the dominant discourse of European cultural exceptionalism.[6]

The fact that Europe's immediate periphery is populated by Muslims and that this periphery has contributed strongly to the significant increase in migration to Europe over the last decade (reaching a high point in 2000 and early 2001) have allowed this subjective discourse to take shape against events in the real world. Public and political anxieties—justified or not—have been given a palpable focus. Most significantly for the focus of this chapter, there has been a strong tendency to express these anxieties not in terms of the challenges that this migration poses in terms of humanitarian assistance (i.e., finding shelter and jobs) but in terms of a supposed threat that migration poses to local European cultures and to the grand European cultural values in general. The expression of suspicions and/or anxieties in terms that highlight a supposed challenge or threat to parochial identities and norms is legitimate (as long as they are not expressed in violent or overtly racist terms) because the particular local culture is logically seen as the bulwark against the threat to the European idea as a whole.

THE FAILURE OF INTEGRATION?

Another arena in which the concept of multiculturalism has been applied and contested is the perceived failure of migrants/immigrants of non-European origin to integrate into host societies. The social construction of the migrant—and the Muslim migrant in particular—as a problematic participant in European social and political life has occurred against the backdrop of two objective demographic movements during the last half century. The first is the migration of laborers and their families from developing countries to fill low-wage jobs in European economies between the early 1950s, when migration was encouraged, and the 1970s, when economic downturns led most European states to stop immigration. The second trend relates to the dramatic increase in the number of people fleeing conflict and/or political and economic insecurity in their home countries and arriving in Western Europe after the end of the Cold War.

By the mid-1980s, observers looking into the phenomena of migration and settlement began referring to "the realities of a multicultural Europe." This did not refer to the positive interaction of distinct communities in a common project but rather the challenge or threat posed by the apparent inability of immigrant groups to "get ahead" in the European context. In the political discourse that has emerged since the late 1980s, this apparent failure to integrate has been viewed in cultural terms, that is, as a failure to adopt styles and practices of daily life considered compatible with the norms of hegemonic national cultures. Furthermore, while in the 1970s, the "others" were guest workers from Turkey, Morocco, or Algeria, today the "others" are all "Muslims." The shift in this image is synchronic with the advent of Islamist movements in the Arab and Muslim world and the world political scene. Suddenly, Islam was something in movement, something in resurgence or revival. Migrants, whose "problems" had been seen as a consequence of their low socioeconomic status during decades, were perceived as "culturally different." Through this "intellectual operation," the whole debate on "communalism" gained prominence. By delinking the migrant from nationality and linking her/him onto a civilizational/cultural matrix, it became possible to problematize the migrant's presence without appearing prejudiced, but rather to do so under the pretense of defending European values. The individual "other" seemed to disappear, being revamped as a mere component of a community. Foreigners/strangers are repatriated into their group of origin whether they like it or not.

The notion that the migrant is engaged in and is responding to a variety of sociological processes that influence attitudes and choices is generally considered of secondary significance, if it is considered at all. The debate on Islam is couched in cultural terms and not in terms of flows of migration, societal discrimination, or class politics. The assumptions underpinning what is really meant by the notion of integration are rarely questioned or challenged. Indeed, it is tempting to wonder how many autochthons would be "unintegrated" if they were held to the same criteria of judgment as are migrants. That this observation arose against the backdrop of the current European project is probably not coincidental. It seems clear that these two discourses have fused and interacted in ways that reinforce a notion of culture as a primary determinant of political behavior and that take for granted that different cultures represent fundamentally fixed, closed, and opposing visions of social and political life. Culture becomes something more than a range of tastes and expressive styles that can be seen as developing in more or less identifiable contexts of time and space, something less than an extensive register of ideas and narratives that can be used to justify a variety of seemingly contradictory political and social projects. Cultures are seen as fixed in relation to the structures of polity and world order within which they currently express themselves in different parts of the world. Consequently, embedded within this discourse is a suspicion that the migrant—being essentially determined by his or her culture of origin—is inherently incapable of meeting and respecting the demands and responsibilities of citizenship in the "secular" European state.

Thus, to the issue of "Islam *and* Europe" discussed above is added the socially constructed issue of "Islam *in* Europe." The construction of this discourse at both levels profoundly influences the way European publics and policymakers view and interact with Europe's Muslim communities. It also has real consequences for the Muslims, including how Muslim immigrants/migrants perceive the possibility and desirability of broader civic participation. In particular, the way in which the discourse could serve to legitimize certain discriminatory practices puts the migrant in a socially defensive position.

Methodologically, the real risk is that these assumptions can become self-fulfilling. For example, it is never asked whether the Muslim migrant, whose social and political engagement and awareness do not extend far beyond the horizons of neighborhood and family, is, in fact, fundamentally "less integrated" than the Flemish inhabitant of a working-class neighborhood whose horizons, similarly, do not extend too far beyond the local pub. Nor is the question posed in terms of integrated into what and how. Given the hegemonic nature of the discourse of European identity, the European observer is equally disinclined to analyze the tendency of many Flemish to vote for the extreme right "Flemish Bloc" in terms of trends in Catholic thought that had a strong hold in Flanders around the turn of the last century or in terms of post-Enlightenment romanticization of the nation—a uniquely European contribution to the history of ideas and conflict. Similarly, the idea that Islam can actually contribute to the migrant's potential for a constructive and peaceful social and civic life in the host state—although explored and confirmed in some scholarly research—is not even considered in the mainstream social and political discourse. That "Islam in Europe" poses a "problem" for, or "challenge" to, European norms—both as bearer of alternative values and as instigator of Europe's rightist inclinations—is simply taken for granted.

ISLAM AS CULTURAL INSTIGATOR

The concept of Islam as cultural instigator is apparent in everyday life and policy discourse. Immigrants from Sub-Saharan Africa and Latin America are perhaps viewed as refugees from an artifact culture who aspire to embrace European cultural norms. Muslims, by contrast, are often seen as unwilling to adopt dominant European cultural styles and rituals. European policymakers and publics have interpreted these differences in style as a fundamental rejection of European culture. The European worker who takes a five-minute break to smoke a cigarette is exercising a right and is not seen as disrupting the workplace. But a Muslim's request for a five-minute break to pray is interpreted as a major disturbance and thus as posing a problem. Furthermore, European states regulate and interact with non-Muslim immigrants at the level of individuals. But, partly because of the structural circumstances of their migration and partly because of the assumption of policymakers about their communities, European states have tended to interact with Muslims and attempt to regulate them at the level of larger groups, often in cooperation with the authorities of the migrants' country of origin.

Despite the fact that it is very important to try and understand "the problem of integration" with reference to the variety of processes and situations within which Muslims in Europe engage in the politics and decision making of daily life, this is rarely done in practice. Rather, as suggested earlier, the ways in which most Europeans think about what integration means and how it is create problems. Is the 20 percent of the Flemish population that has voted for the right-wing Flemish Bloc party in recent elections unintegrated? The answer could be positive, depending on what criteria are used. The point to be emphasized, however, is that it is too often taken for granted that "integration" is a self-evident and easy-to-grasp concept, when, in fact, it is a very subjectively constructed concept. Because democracies cannot pass racist laws, they are not willing to establish criteria for interpretation that can be enforced by law.[7] One reason is that such criteria could also be used to assess "the Flemishness of a person of Flemish origin" or the "Belgianness of a 'native' Belgian." Fortunately, most of the indigenous population disapproves of setting such criteria. In practice, integration refers first and foremost to the conditions that migrants have to fulfill in order to benefit socially and economically from their presence in European societies. It is a politically constructed, as well as politically contested, concept; there are no "objective" criteria to define and/or enforce it.

Talking about integration also makes it easier for the indigenous population to avoid issues related to structural racism. Defining Europe along the idealized lines discussed above makes it possible to see multiculturalism as a generic part of its identity. Multiculturalism becomes self-validating in the sense that it is not conceptualized as a "societal project to be constructed" but as an element that has always been part of the European identity. Thus, if there are "cultural tensions" within society (whether they take a religious or ethnic form), it is easy to pinpoint the "others" as a cause of these conflicts. If Europe is multicultural and yet cultural conflict continues to exist, it means that the "others" have not adapted themselves to the European culture. The debates are formulated in such a way that it is the Muslim communities that are required to integrate into multicultural reality. If they do not succeed, it is because of the peculiarity of "their culture." In short, it is the "others" that have to "assimilate" things. Moreover, in evaluating the level of "assimilation," stylistic differences are often elevated to crucial ideological distinctions. The consequence is that the "others," and especially the Muslims, can be easily seen—instead of a victim of discrimination—as an offender, as the instigator of Euro-racism. Thus, Remi Hauman, a Belgian Orientalist, has no qualms about writing in a mainstream and largely diffused daily: "With Islam an intolerant worldview has penetrated our societies and is nourishing intolerant groups from within our ranks [the Flemish Bloc]" and "The sometimes nagging mentality [of Muslims] can annoy some people and is the basis on which the extreme-right prospers."[8] Islam is problematic even as a secondary or "subaltern" feature of the "ideal" European landscape.[9]

ISLAM AS ACTOR

Within this framework of analysis, Islam, and not the individual Muslim, is the presumed actor on the social and political stage. The debate is structured around the key concept of Islam rather than Muslims. The agency of Muslims tends to disappear underneath the leaden weight of a "cultural system" that conditions, regulates, and explains all behavior of Muslims. To illustrate, according to Hauman, "When it has the occasion, it [Islam] tends automatically to absolute domination and is therefore undemocratic."[10] Yet, Hauman ignores the fact that the examples of the French Revolution, the Inquisition, excessive nationalism, communism, etc., prove that there is such a tendency in any ideology. It is not Muslims who produce their history, but Islam that conditions the behavior and identity of Muslims. In the end, a Muslim is reduced to the status of a robot that endlessly and thoughtlessly perpetuates Islam's religious prescriptions. The structural weight accorded or ascribed to Islam stands in sharp contrast with the individualism attributed to "European attitudes."

The problem of domestic violence, for example, clearly illustrates this differential approach. When a Belgian man is accused of beating his spouse, he is negatively judged by society. His violence is seen as a personal flaw. People try to understand his behavior by looking for reasons that could account for it—maybe he was himself an abused child, maybe the family had financial problems, and so on. When a person from Muslim background is accused of the same behavior, however, this contextualization disappears. The beating of a wife is explained through Islam, and reference is made to some Qur'anic verse that "proves" the deterministic relation between the Muslim religion and the specific action. The difference in approach is very important for the European self-image. Domestic violence is seen as the outcome of deviant individual behavior and not as the outcome of structural and/or cultural features of European civilization. The same mechanism is at work in the analyses of racism. Racism is understood as a negative form of behavior but not as a structural feature of Europe.[11]

The sense that the growing visibility of Islam in Europe—that is, its entry into the public sphere—somehow poses a threat rather than reflecting a "normal" interest-based mobilization of a group in a pluralist society is clearly related to the increased influence of the European culturalist paradigm. The growing societal demands of Muslims are not seen as evidence that Muslims feel at home in Europe and that they want to find their place within these societies. Instead, the demands for the building of mosques, the possibility of eating *halal* food in schools, or the introduction of certain religious holidays is seen as a threat to European civilization and/or a danger to secular democracy.

TREATMENT OF ISLAM AND MUSLIMS

European states react to and deal with Muslims in different ways. Many "Islamic" organizations are regulated by European states in collusion with relevant ministries in the migrants' countries of origin.[12] This fact should certainly be considered in the evaluation of integration processes and their meanings.[13] The strength of individual organizations, their commitment to lobbying, an organization's specific policies concerning the "integration" of Muslims, the presence of stronger or weaker xenophobic political parties, colonial histories, and the accessibility of citizenship are only some of the contextual factors that influence the relationship between migrants and European states. Today, one can say that the policy decisions surrounding regulation are situated within a "postpolitical" context. Slavoj Zizek has defined postpolitics as the situation in which

> the conflict between the ideological world-visions—as embodied in different parties that are in competition over the exercise of power—is being replaced by the cooperation of enlightened technocrats (economists, opinion polls, etc.) and liberal multiculturalists. This leads to compromises that are attained by way of negotiation and the watching of interests, and that are presented as more or less a universal consensus.[14]

With the erosion of ideological positions, Islam has assumed the role of an issue around which parties can generate political distinctions and mobilize public anxieties in order to get votes. Barry Buzan argues that a "societal Cold War" between Islam and Europe is, in fact, functional for the latter because it serves to strengthen European identity at a crucial time in its ongoing process of unification.[15] Etienne Balibar comes to the same conclusion when he states that the "immigrant" (not only the Muslim) is by definition a "second class citizen" because while the "real" content of European identity is increasingly taken for granted, immigrants are excluded from full inclusion in the union they are helping to build.[16] As Juan Delgado-Moreira argues, the construction of a European identity is neglecting the cultural demands of the minorities within the member states and fails to produce a pluralist reading of identity.[17]

For politicians, politics is ultimately the game of getting elected and getting reelected. When in power, politicians try to hegemonize their analysis and solutions of the situation. Multiculturalism has become a key "empty signifier" that is consistently used to legitimate European democracies. Empty signifier, here, refers to a term or notion that can acquire, or be filled with, various meanings and contents according to the interests of those who invoke it and according to understandings of the structural and discursive contexts within which it is invoked. Culture as political agent and determinant of relevant and legitimate political difference and multiculturalism in particular have become paradigms accepted by most actors in the mainstream political spectrum, even if there are debates over the limits and precise content of the concept. While a monoculturalist notion of polity can traditionally be attributed to conservative and rightist European political movements, the culturalist tendency—in its multiculturalist expression—now predominates at the left and center of the political spectrum as well. Even most mainstream European conservative parties have adopted the multiculturalist discourse (Britain being a notable exception). The far right political parties, by contrast, are very clear in their rejection of multiculturalism and tend to be situated between the monocultural positions of traditional European national conservatism (which accepted that other races could join the polity if they adopted national "norms, beliefs, and practices") and outright racism. They oppose the idea of peaceful coexistence of different "cultural" communities and perceive the stranger as a danger for a romantically understood national community. Alternatively, the "other" is seen as a threat to one's own culture and/or personal economic security. Officially, this rejection of multiculturalism is not a publicly lauded discourse.

However, even those parties that on the surface would seem to have the most inclusive and open understanding of the multicultural idea, in fact, maintain the mechanism of cultural exceptionalism in thought and, it must be said, in practice. While the far right is trying to control Islam by "getting rid of it," the others are trying to control it by pushing forward their "own Islam." Blommaert and Verscheuren, for example, have shown how several Belgian governmental institutions, nongovernment organizations, and intellectuals are pushing forward an agenda that clearly tries to shape Islam and Muslims along lines of their preferred pattern.[18]

Muslims are hardly heard in this debate in spite of the fact that an elite within European Muslim communities is steadily growing and is engaging in intellectual work. The overrated threat of "Islamic fundamentalism" is used as an easy excuse to lessen the influence of these voices as they are not directly reflecting what "we" Europeans want to hear. The project of debunking some of the multicultural discourse might just depend in part on the ability of Muslims in Europe to "rediscover" the politics at the heart of the issue of Islam in Europe.

CONCLUSION

The notion that Islam—in the form of Muslim migrants/immigrants—poses a threat or challenge to European identity and/or culture is largely a product of a discourse that has grown around culture as a defining element of polity and international relations. Ironically, the notion of Islam and Muslims as a threat or challenge to European identity and culture has grown out of the discourse of European multiculturalism.

The discourse that has grown up around the idea of integration into a multicultural Europe ultimately must also be evaluated in its relation to the more mundane issues of polity and society. Ultimately, it is in the context of the latter—buried in the accumulated politics and choices of daily life—that the meanings of the multiculturalist idea and the implications of its hegemony can be explored regarding the understandings of integration and all that the term implies with regard to the rights and obligations of Muslims living in Europe.

"Foreigners" are now a permanent feature of European societies. Their social position and access to civic participation must not be held hostage to the methodological double standards, nor to the stylistic fetishes of prevailing "national" norms, that characterize some applications of culture within scholarly, political, and public discourses.

The problem with the communitarian thinking embodied within the multicultural ideology is that it can never really obtain what it is looking for: the combination of equality and diversity. It has difficulty going beyond a perspective of "separate but equal." By locking the foreigner into a presumed entity of origin (whether in terms of nationality, race, religion, etc.), both the foreigner and the indigenous deny the realities of interdependence that are not always apparent. It assumes that state, society, and the phenomenon of culture in the broadest sense lack mechanisms that allow for communication across stylistic and ritualistic distinctions of particular cultures. It is misleading to see European national communities as unified, single, and homogeneous entities that are trying to secure their rightful place within a seemingly monolithic EU. The sheer diversity of languages, traditions, religions, and life styles within the union are already an acknowledgment of a pluralist Europe. The same argument also applies to Muslim communities. As public discourses overemphasize communal essentialism, particularly as applied to the relationship between the Muslim migrant and Muslim communities, the danger that social and regulatory processes conflate to create a "communitarian cage" into which all Muslims are expected to fit becomes very real.[19]

Similarly, the multicultural ideology engages in the act of creating "otherness" in order to reaffirm the myth of European tolerance. Indeed, extreme tolerance that comes with cultural relativism encompasses the danger of seeing "others" as completely different within their "communitarian cage," and thus obliterates every possible idea of universal humanity. The notion of authenticity as expressed through group identity is presented as the ultimate freedom. This paradoxically means that tolerance can lead to its opposite: that is, the creation of unbridgeable barriers between "us" and "them."[20] In the postpolitical context, this also serves to generate and politicize the political distinctions that drive mobilization—and that win votes—in an adversarial political system. There is a potentially circular and self-fulfilling relationship between the ideology as manifested in the practice and exercise of public policy and the processes that lead to an awareness of cultural distinction as a problematic feature of the European social landscape.

Finally, the myth of a multicultural Europe needs to be reexamined for the double standards that it sets and the discriminatory practices and standards that it establishes beneath the veneer of "the noble project." Insofar as multiculturalism might offer useful perspectives on, and set an agenda within, a complex European reality, it is a concept still awaiting definition.

NOTES

1. See Samuel P. Huntington, "The Clash of Civilizations?," *Foreign Affairs* 72 (summer 1993): 22–28.

2. See Raymond Detrez, *De Zondebokken Van Europa*, May 5, 1999, http://allserv.rug.ac.be/~hdeley/detrez2.htm.

3. See Juan Delgado Moreira, "Cultural Citizenship and the Creation of European Identity," *Electronic Journal of Sociology*, http://www.sociology.org, vol. 002.003, 1997.

4. Adopted by the 41st Congress of Europa-Union Deutschland in Lübeck, 28 October 1995. See http://www.eurplace.org/diba/citta/cartaci.html.

5. We would rather use the term "Islamism" for several methodological reasons. However, because of the currency of the use of the label "Islamic fundamentalism" in discourses, we will use it in order to analyze the usage of the label. See Wolfgang Seyman, "The Abuse of a Concept: Fundamentalism in German-Speaking Social Science Literature," in *Mediterranean Ethnological Summer School*, ed. B. Baskar and B. Brumen, (1998): 159–171; also, Sami Zemni and Peter Van Royssveldt, "Deuxex machina of een duiveltjeuit een doosje? Islamisatie van de modernisering van de Islam: casus tuneseie?" *Noored-Zuidcahies* (1995): 31–46.

6. For refutation of Huntington's thesis, see Shireen T. Hunter, *Clash of Civilizations or Peaceful Coexistence?* (Washington, DC: Center for Strategic and International Studies and Praeger, 1998).

7. In the procedure of becoming Belgian, one of the criteria asked of the applicants is their "will to integrate." Without any enforceable or controllable criteria, the applicants are left "at the mercy" of the judges who can ask whatever they want, such as "Do you still eat with your hands?" etc. See also J. Blommaert and J. Vershueren, *Het Belgische migrantendabat: de pragmatiek van de abnormalisering* [The Belgian migration debate: the pragmatism of abnormalization] (Antwerpen: Ipr A Research Center, 1992), 114–115.

8. See Remi Hauman, "Vlaanderen Heeft Verlichte Islamologen Nodig," *De Standaard Zondag*, 11 July 1999.

9. Secondary is defined here as a logical, but not necessary, element of a whole. Thus, while other subcultures may come and go, Islam is not seen as compatible with the "greater logic" of the European identity and political project.

10. Hauman, "Vlaaderen."

11. See J. Blommaert and J. Verschueren, *Debating Diversity: Analyzing the Discourse of Tolerance* (London: Routledge, 1998).

12. See Tariq Ramadan, "Entre ingerences extrangere et logique securitaires: les Musalmans d'Europe pris en tenaille," *Le Monde Diplomatique*, June 2000, 12–13.

13. For a description of the mechanism of thought, the "individualization of 'negative' values," see Blommaert and Verschueren, *Debating Diversity*.

14. Instead of fundamentalism, one could argue that Muslims are much more influenced by the policies of their states of origin. Western European states would have more interest in stopping this practice as it would emancipate Muslim communities. See Slavoj Zizek, *Pleidooi Voor Intolerantie* [The appeal of intolerance] (Amsterdam: Boom Essay, 1998), 25.

15. Barry Buzan, "New Patterns of Global Security in the Twenty-First Century," *International Affairs* 67, (July 1991): 431–451.

16. Etienne Balibar, "Bestaat de Europese burger? Over Europese identiteit en burgerschap," *Samenleving en Politiek* 7 (2000): 25–33.

17. Juan Delgado-Moreira, "Cultural Citizenship."

18. Blommaert and Verschueren, *Het Belgische migrantendabat*.

19. Alain Touraine's work has dealt with these issues since the 1970s. His aim is to define the subject that is not reducible to the *homo economicus*, not an individual attached to "traditional" communitarian hierarchies, but to establish a balance between economy, identity, and territory. See Alain Touraine, *Pourrons-nous vivers ensemble? Egaux et differend* [Can we live together? Equal and different] (Paris: Artheme Fayard, 1997).

20. See Alain Finkielkraut, *La défaite de la pensée* (Paris: Folio Essais/Gallimard, 1987).

14

The Muslim Diaspora and the Islamic World

John L. Esposito

INTRODUCTION

For centuries, relations between Islam and the West have been critical theological and political issues in international politics. At the dawn of the twenty-first century, it is as important to speak of Islam *in* the West as Islam *and* the West. Islam is not only the second largest religion globally but also the second or third largest religion in Europe and America. This remarkable demographic and religious reality has underscored the importance of accommodating and integrating Islam in Europe and America.[1] Moreover, it has had a transforming effect both upon relations between Muslims and the West and between Muslims in diaspora Muslim communities and Muslim countries. This chapter will explore the dynamics of interaction between Muslims in Europe and America and their Islamic homelands with special emphasis on the flow of ideas.

In contrast to the past when ideas and influence flowed one way from Muslim countries to the West, today information, ideas, financial resources, and influence flow on a superhighway whose roads and traffic travel in both directions. Indeed, given the more open religious, political, and intellectual climate in Europe and America, Muslim intellectuals and activists have increasingly had a significant impact on Islamic thought and activism by training new generations of Muslims at European and American universities and through their writings, which often reflect fresh reinterpretations (*ijtihad*) on critical issues. The result is a process of reformation that addresses issues of faith and practice, religious leadership and authority, religious and political pluralism, tolerance, minority rights (Muslim and non-Muslim), and gender.

Yet, until recently, the Islamic heartland provided the main source of ideas, new philosophies, and schools of Islamic thought. Thus, the flow of Islamic faith and knowledge, whether in the Muslim world or the West, emphasized the writings and interpretations of a range of intellectuals and activists based in the Muslim world. These included Islamic modernists like Jamal al-Din al-Afghani, Muhammad Abduh, Rashid Rida, Sir Sayyid Ahmad Khan, and Muhammad Iqbal, to the early trailblazers of contemporary revivalism, Islamic activists like Hasan al-Banna, Sayyid Qutb, Mawlana Mawdudi, plus other Muslim intellectuals and Sufi leaders.[2] However different in their interpretations, these thinkers might have been the transfer of information, and communication was one way. Muslims in the diaspora, including those in Europe and America, looked to the Muslim world as their main source for Islamic guidance and information. This was true especially for those students and Islamic organizations in the West, such as emerging Muslim student associations and other organizations, as well as for curriculum development at universities and research for publications on Muslim intellectuals and modern Islamic thought. In short, the flow of information and ideas was one way: from the Muslim world to the diaspora.

However, the situation in the early twenty-first century is changing dramatically. Today, the information sources and flow of ideas have broadened just as the Islamic community or *ummah* itself has expanded and has become more global geographically, as reflected in the growing number of Muslims in Europe and America. Only a few decades ago, it was accurate to talk about Islam and the West. But now, one must also speak of Islam in the West, because Islam and Muslims are not simply "over there" in some distant land. They are very much here, part and parcel of the religious and demographic landscape and social fabric of Europe and America. Islam today is the second or third largest religion in the West. Something that was unthinkable, or even unimaginable, only a few short years ago is now a reality. Today, the cities and learning centers of the Muslim world are not only Cairo, Damascus, Islamabad, and Kuala Lumpur but also London, Manchester, Paris, Marseilles, Amsterdam, Antwerp, New York, Detroit, and Los Angeles.

AN INTERNATIONAL SUPERHIGHWAY

In the course of a few short decades, the flow of knowledge and authority has been expanded and transformed from a one-way (Muslim world to West) to a multilane superhighway with two-way traffic (between Muslim countries and the West and vice versa). It is a movement encompassing diverse people, ideologies, institutions, and mass communications. Two-way communication and exchange occur through scholars' and activists' travels, speeches, publications, video and audio tapes, and increasingly in cyberspace. The process is multileveled, involving individuals (scholars, preachers, activists), movements, and countries. Today, a large number of Muslim scholars and activists, based in Europe and America,[3] speak to Muslims overseas through their writings, their training of Muslim students, and their audios/videos. At the same time, diverse voices in the Muslim world, such as Qatar's Yusuf Qardawi, Lebanon's Faysal Mawlawi and Muhammad Fadlallah, Turkey's Necmettin Erbakan and Fetullah Gulen, and the emir of Pakistan's *Jama'at-I Islami* have a strong presence and impact in Europe and America. The digital revolution has accelerated the pace of development of this information superhighway. For instance, European and American Muslim diasporas can have almost instant access to the *fatwa* (legal opinions) of *muftis* (legal experts) throughout the Muslim world and can obtain answers to their own specific questions on internet sites that feature segments like "Ask the *Mufti*."

Yet, the reverse flow of Islamic thought from the West to the Muslim world has often gone unnoticed in scholarly studies. Old patterns of religious authority and centers of guidance only slowly give way to relatively recent developments. This should not be surprising. It is, in fact, perfectly ordinary human behavior, one that accounts for the tendency to still focus disproportionately on the heartland, the Arab world, overlooking the fact that the Arab world today constitutes a minority of the Muslim world and the Islamic experience. Both Muslim history and imagination and Western scholarship have come to presume and expect that the major centers of learning and ideas of the past, such as Egypt's Al-Azhar University, Tunisia's Qairawiyyun, and the major madrasas of Qom and Najaf would remain the primary sources of Islamic learning, generating both conservative and reformist ideas. However, the reality is far more complex. Some of the major voices and training grounds for reform as well as of conservatism and traditionalism are to be found at universities and centers in Europe and America, as they speak not only to their diaspora communities but also to their Muslim homelands and the worldwide Islamic community, the *ummah*.

Muslim intellectuals and activists in Europe and America have had an increasingly significant impact as individuals, through their publications and students who have returned after completing degrees to their Muslim homelands and through the dissemination of ideas and perspectives in the media and cyberspace. The diaspora or periphery has become "a" center and in time may become "the" center in fact, if not in religious sentiment, in terms of the actual development of Islamic thinking on many important issues and areas of reinterpretation (*ijtihad*) and reform in theology, law, and history. As much of the Islamic world (Muslim countries) remains under authoritarian regimes with limited freedoms of assembly, thought, speech, and expression, as well as shrinking financial and institutional resources, the opportunities afforded in the West present conditions for significant growth and development.

INFLUENCE AND EXCHANGE

The influence of the diaspora on the Muslim world has been both passive and active. Passive influence involves those living in the West who maintain overseas connections, either through regular visits, sending money, or acting as informal ambassadors. Active influence comes from scholars, writers, and activists/organizations who have either targeted the Muslim world as part of their conscious efforts or agenda or who have become popularized by Muslim academics and the media in the Muslim world. Examples of these have included individuals who address substantive issues and reforms, as well as organizations that campaign for international Muslim causes, such as Palestine, Kashmir, Algeria, Egypt, Bosnia, Kosovo, and Chechnya. In addition, Islamic activist organizations, some repressed or banned in Muslim countries, such as the Muslim brotherhood, *Jama'at-i Islami*, Hamas (Islamic Resistance Movement), Hizbullah, *Refah/Fazilat*, and *Hizb ut-Tahrir*, as well as major Sufi orders, have established headquarters in the West. Increasingly influential are institutes, think tanks, and political action groups established in cities such as London, Berlin, Paris, Washington, and New York.[4]

The growth of Muslim populations in Europe and America has quite naturally increased interest in studying their presence and impact, as well as foreign sources of funding available to them, and influence that such foreign elements could exercise upon them.

As with many other religious and ethnic groups before them, continued linkages (through family networks, flow of capital and goods) to home countries (countries of origin) between Muslim communities in Europe and America have been the subject of study both by academics and by some governments. By contrast, far too little attention has been given to the flow of intellectual influence through the medium of information and ideas and the influence of Muslim intellectuals upon the Muslim world. Thus, there have been studies of the activities of Muslim countries, such as Saudi Arabia, Libya, Kuwait, the United Arab Emirates, and Iran, that have funded imams, mosques/Islamic centers, visiting Muslim scholars, schools, organizations, and conferences in order to extend their influence and, in some cases, propagate their brand (interpretation) of Islam. One European diplomat has referred to this process as "invasion by proxy." However, the reverse flow has received far less attention, namely, the equally important impact of diaspora Muslim scholars and activists, their ideas, as well as that of their Muslim students who return to Muslim countries, on the development of Islamic thought and politics in their home countries. Religiously and ideologically, they represent a wide spectrum of orientations, ranging from reformist to militant conservatism or fundamentalism. An early Malaysian example of this phenomenon reveals both the modernist and more conservative orientations of the dynamics of this type of exchange from Europe and America to Malaysia.

BRITISH AND AMERICAN INFLUENCE ON MALAYSIAN ISLAM AND MUSLIM POLITICS

The influence of Western experiences on Muslims has been contradictory, in the sense that it has produced modernist as well as more militant conservative effects. Malaysia provides a vivid example of how an American experience influenced the reformist orientation of the Islamic Youth Movement of Malaysia (ABIM), and the British experience had the opposite effect on many members of Malaysia's Pan-Islamic Party (PAS—Parti Islam Semalaysia).[5]

PAS and ABIM shared many similar goals, such as the creation of an Islamic social order and the denunciation of Westernization, secularism, materialism (conspicuous consumption), economic and social disparities, and political authoritarianism. However, in contrast to ABIM's more moderate, modernist image as an urban-based, Islamic reformist pressure group for Islamically rooted socioeconomic change, PAS was often viewed by many as more strident, intransigent, Islamically conservative, and religiously chauvinistic. It was far more sweeping in its denunciation of the West and traditionalist in its inflexible interpretation of Islam, ranging from general matters of Islamic law to specific issues such as the rights of women and non-Muslims. Indeed, PAS was often quicker to label its Muslim opponents as *kafirs* (unbelievers).

PAS tended to advocate the implementation and enforcement of traditional or classic Islamic law rather than acknowledging, as did ABIM, the need for its reform. Moreover, although PAS insisted that non-Muslims had nothing to fear from the creation of an Islamic state, its equation of Islam and Malay nationalism, insistence on special privileges for Malay Muslims, wholesale rejection of Western values, secularism, and "yellow culture," and its tendency to identify Chinese and Indians as a threat to Malay development and interests (the cause of economic disparities), raised serious questions about the future of non-Muslims in a PAS-dominated Islamic state.

In the late 1970s and 1980s, Malaysian students studying in Europe became influenced by the writings of Pakistan's Mawlana Mawdudi and the *Jama'at-I Islami* and by Egypt's Sayyid Qutb and the Muslim brotherhood, as well as the more militant interpretations to which they were introduced at British universities by Muslim faculty members and fellow students from other Muslim countries. In response to these influences, they organized the Jama'at-inspired Saut-ul-Islam (the Voice of Islam) and the Qutb-inspired Islamic Representative Council (IRC). It is not farfetched to suggest that, had they not gone to Europe, they would not have become exposed to such ideas.

Returning from Britain to take up positions in the universities, schools, and government bureaucracy and professions, Islamic activists were attracted to the more militant Islamic political language of PAS under its new leader, Fadzil Noor, rather than to the moderate approach of ABIM. PAS mirrored their own condemnation of an illegitimate "infidel" secular government, anti-Western rhetoric, and their desire to call for a true, all-encompassing Islamic state based upon the Qur'an and Sunna, admiration and support for revolutionary Iran, and strong emphasis on political activism.

Members of the IRC and *Saut-ul-Islam* became part of the younger guard in a PAS that seized the banner of Islamic opposition from ABIM. They also established a new student *dakwah* (*Da'wa*) organization, the Islamic Republic group, which was committed to the establishment of an Iranian-type Islamic government in Malaysia and which replaced ABIM as the dominant Islamic student organization in the 1980s. The Islamic Republic group espoused a radical ideology and political activism with a rigid world view, confrontational politics, and agenda. For them, there were no gray areas. Both the individual and the state were either Muslim or not, Islamically committed or un-Islamic, believer or infidel, saved or damned. Malaysia's man-made constitutional government, they believed, must be replaced by one based upon the Qur'an and Sunna (model example) of the Prophet Muhammad and guided by the *ulema* and Islamic law (the *shari'a*).

ABIM's ideology was crafted more to speak to the realities of a multiethnic, multireligious society. Thus, its vision of an Islamic state emphasized democracy, pluralism, and social justice. It denounced communalism, racism, and sectarianism and spoke of the need for tolerance and mutual respect. Its advocacy of *shari'a* was accompanied by an emphasis on the preservation of non-Muslim rights in a democratic, multiracial society. The thinking of Anwar Ibrahim, ABIM's charismatic leader, and many of its members was strongly influenced by Muslim intellectuals and activists like the British-trained Naquib al-Attas and later Ismail R. al-Faruqi and Taha Jabir Al-Alwani from America and Yusuf Qardawi from Qatar.

Here, too, the exposure to Europe's democratic systems must have exerted a degree of influence. ABIM's influence proved substantial. While it lost ground to PAS on campuses, its members and former members became a pervasive presence in responsible positions in society during the 1980s and 1990s. They held senior positions in government and the bureaucracy, in university administrations and faculties, in the media and corporate sectors. When Anwar Ibrahim, its founder, became a member of the government of Prime Minister Mahathir Mohammed, ABIM's influence reached its peak.

MUSLIM INTELLECTUALS AND ACTIVISTS IN THE WEST

The more open societies of the West have freed Muslim scholars and students to engage in a rigorous process of reinterpretation of Islamic sources and legal reform. Intellectually, the inevitable necessity of adapting one's identity to the requirements of living in new environments has led to serious thinking about the relationship of tradition to reform (*taqlid* and *ijtihad*), faith to national and cultural identity, religion to politics and society. Muslim experiences in the West have also led to new interpretations and formulations of Islam and its relationship to pluralism, political participation, women's status, and the rights of minorities.

The numbers of European and American scholars of Muslim faith who have been influential in these processes are quite substantial, and many of them are prolific writers.[6] Their views have had far-reaching—both geographically and intellectually—influence.

Reformist (some Muslims would say radical revisionist) ideas of Muhammad Arkoun and Abdullahi Naim, as well as the modernist and traditionalist visions of Ismail al-Faruqi, Ziauddin Sardar, and Fathi Osman, influenced Muslim intellectuals and activists in countries extending from South Africa to Malaysia. Women's organizations, like Sisters in Islam in Malaysia, have looked to reformists like Arkoun, Osman, and Naim as inspiration and have adopted their intellectual approaches as a means to reinterpret Islam and Islamic law with regard to gender issues. In short, Muslim scholars based in the West have had significant influence on Islamic thought and reformist movements from South Africa to Southeast Asia and, in some instances, on government leaders.

While many Muslim publications from the West now circulate widely, an early and particularly influential one was the journal *Arabia*, published in Britain and edited by Fathi Osman, with contributions from many Muslims based in Europe and America. This journal became a source of information and fresh thinking, read not only in the West but in Muslim countries as well. Many of its European Muslim contributors were regular visitors to conferences and institutes in the Middle East and South and Southeast Asia. Today, Muslim centers and institutes in Europe and America publish magazines and journals in English, Arabic, and other Western and Muslim languages and distribute their materials abroad. Various schools and institutes in Europe and America, notably the Institute for Islamic Political Thought at Westminster University, UK, the Islamic Foundation in Leicester, England, and the School for Islamic Social Sciences in Herndon, Virginia, USA, offer courses on wide ranges of issues related to Islam, such as Islamic political thought, Islam and democracy, and other important social and political subjects relevant to the Muslim world and grant degrees.

Meanwhile, ideas of Muslim intellectuals and activists based in Europe and America are disseminated through Arab and Muslim publications and journals, such as *al-Mujtama*, in the Arab and broader Muslim world, Europe, and America. Some of them, like Taha Jabir Al-Alwani, who earned his doctorate at Egypt's Al-Azhar University, function as both scholars and as *muftis*, issuing *fatwas* (legal opinions) on topics such as the participation of American Muslims in national political elections or the regulation of capital markets.[7] Many appear at conferences and on television programs in Western and Muslim countries, and some have their web sites on the internet. Publishing houses in the United States, United Kingdom, and Muslim countries, notably Egypt and Indonesia, translate the works of many European- and American-based Muslim intellectuals and activists.[8]

Just as the writings and activities of those Muslim thinkers and leaders, like Sir Sayyid Ahmad Khan, Jamal al-Din al-Afghani, Muhammad Iqbal, and others, who had been influenced by European ideas, had significant influence in the intellectual evolution of the Muslim world during the last part of the nineteenth and the first half of the twentieth centuries and beyond, recent decades have produced a broad range of European- and American-educated Muslim scholars and activists who have exerted great influence on the intellectual and political evolution of their countries.[9] They have become vice chancellors of universities and academics and have produced a president, a former prime minister and deputy prime minister, speakers of Parliament, prominent lawyers, and leaders of major Islamic movements. Their influences have not only been ideological and political but also methodological. The result is a variety of discourses, ranging from various degrees of reformist thinking to more Islamist and Sufi approaches.

Perhaps the most enduring influence of the Muslim diaspora upon the Islamic world will be the networks of European- and American-trained scholars and activists who may be found today in many Muslim countries. Some have studied with specific Muslim scholars or in specific Islamic studies programs of various universities that specialize in this subject. Others have been influenced by their studies or exposure to the writings of individual American and European scholars and activists in universities and at conferences. The pronounced influence of European and American Muslim scholarship and ideas can be found from Egypt and Sudan to Malaysia and Indonesia. Some, for example, speak of the "Temple mafia," referring to the many former students of Ismail al-Faruqi, Sayyid Hussein Nasr, and now Mahmud Ayoub, based at Temple University in Pennsylvania, USA. Others refer to British, Dutch, or German university connections.

A CLIMATE FOR *IJTIHAD*

The free intellectual climate and the open and, in the case of America, multicultural settings of Europe and America have enabled Muslim thinkers to address many critical questions and issues, notably: What is the relationship of faith to issues of identity and assimilation? What is the need to distinguish between faith and culture in matters of dress and behavior? Is there a single form of Islamic dress and behavior, or can there be a variety of cultural expressions of piety and modesty? How can ethnic and racial tensions within Muslim communities as well as between immigrant and indigenous Muslims be resolved? Can Muslims legitimately choose to live permanently and to participate politically and socially in a non-Muslim society? What are the role and limits of Islamic law in the diaspora?[10] Is Islam compatible with religious and political pluralism and tolerance based upon mutual respect between Muslim and non-Muslim, Sunni and Shi'a, Sunni and Sufi? How are gender relations (including gay rights) to be understood and expressed in family relations, mosques, and society? In addition, all diaspora communities face the daunting task of how to preserve their faith and to pass it on to the next generation. Are they to be brought up European or American Muslims or Muslims in Europe and America? Should emphasis be placed on developing Muslim schools and universities? A particularly contentious point in many mosques and centers, in particular those that have second- and third-generation Muslims, is the role of "imported imams" and the impact of new immigrants who bring, and often seek to impose, their "cultural baggage" and practices, believing that these are integral to Islam. Communities in the short term may redefine the role of imams; many already recognize the need to develop training programs for the development of indigenous imams.

The reformist-conservative and reformist-militant tensions within Muslim communities in Europe and America also have a spillover or crossover effect. Progressive and more conservative and militant Muslim discussions and differences are reflected on the often spirited and at times bitter debates in publications and on the internet, based in the West but accessed and participated in by those in overseas Muslim societies. The impact of globalization is evident on recent Internet sites such as Islam-on-line, iviews, Islamic city, Islamic gateway, and ummah.net, with their centers in Qatar, Egypt, the United States, and United Kingdom, as well as information and discussion groups like MSANews, Progressive Muslims, Ijtihad, and Political Islam.

CONCLUSION

The twenty-first century will prove dynamic and challenging for Muslims worldwide. The Islamic community or *ummah* itself reflects the impact of globalization, both in its changing demographics and in its intellectual and political developments. There are more Muslim minority communities and more Muslims living as refugees than at any other time in history. The struggle of diaspora communities in Europe and America to define, or more accurately redefine, identity and empower themselves, to forge European and American Muslim identities, has produced a dynamic period of transformation. A broad range of interpreters and interpretations has emerged. In various ways, Muslim scholars, students, and ideas have emerged as new voices and actors for change, impacting and influencing the development of Islam both in the Muslim world and in the West.

NOTES

1. See, for example, Steven Vertovec and Ceri Peach (eds.), *Islam in Europe: The Politics of Religion and Community* (New York: St. Martin's Press, 1997); Philip Lewis, *Islamic Britain: Religion, Politics and Identity among British Muslims* (London: I.B. Tauris, 1994); Jørgen Nielsen, *Towards a European Islam* (New York: St. Martin's Press, 1999); Yvonne Haddad and Jane Smith (eds.), *Muslim Communities in North America* (Albany: State University of New York Press, 1994); Jane I. Smith, *Islam in America* (New York: Columbia University Press, 1999); and Sulayman Nyang, *Islam in the United States of America* (Chicago: Kazi Publications, 1999).

2. For information on their thought, see John O. Voll, *Islam: Continuity and Change in the Modern World*, 2nd ed. (Syracuse: Syracuse University Press, 1994); and John L. Esposito, *Islam and Politics*, 3rd ed. (Syracuse: Syracuse University Press, 1998).

3. The following scholars and activists are particularly influential: Muhammad Arkoun, Algerian-born Sorbonne professor; Rashid Ghannoushi, leader of Tunisia's Ennahda (Renaissance party), who is in exile in London; Khurshid Ahmad, founder of the Islamic Foundation in Leicester; Yusuf Islam, the former singer Cat Stevens and prominent Muslim spokesman; Tariq Ramadan, a Swiss academic and Egyptian-born grandson of Hasan al-Banna, founder of the Muslim Brotherhood; Seyyed Hossein Nasr, at George Washington University in Washington, DC; Abdulaziz Sachedina, of the University of Virginia, Charlottesville; Mahmud Ayub of Temple University, Philadelphia, Pennsylvania; and Sulayman Nyang of Howard University, Washington, DC, USA.

4. Examples of such institutes include the Oxford Centre for Islamic Studies, the Islamic Foundation of Leicester, the American Muslim Council, Muslim Po-

litical Action Committee, the Council on American–Islamic Relations, and the United Association for Study and Research.

5. For an analysis of this phenomenon, see Zainah Anwar, *Islamic Revivalism in Malaysia: Dawah among the Students* (Selangor Darul Ehsan, Malaysia: Pelanduk Publications, 1987); John L. Esposito and John O. Voll, *Islam and Democracy* (New York: Oxford University Press, 1996), ch. 6.

6. See, for example, Tariq Ramadan, *To Be a European Muslim* (Leicester: Islamic Foundation, 1999), and *L'Islam, le face a face des civilizations, quel projet pour quelle modernite?* [Islam, the encounter of civilizations, what project for what modernity?] (Lyon: Les deux Rives, 1995); Mohammed Arkoun, *Rethinking Islam: Common Questions, Uncommon Answers* (Boulder: Westview Press, 1994); Bassam Tibi, *The Crisis of Modern Islam* (Salt Lake City: University of Utah Press, 1988); Amina Wadud, *Quran and Woman* (New York: Oxford University Press, 1999); Seyyed Hosseon Nasr, *Traditional Islam in the Modern World* (London: KPI, 1987); Ziauddin Sardar, *Postmodernism and the Other* (London: Pluto, 1998); Fazlur Rahman, *Islam and Modernity* (Chicago: University of Chicago Press, 1982); and Sulayman Nyang, *Islam in the United States of America* (Chicago: Kazi, 1999).

7. Taha Jabir Al-Alwani and Waleed Adel El-Ansary, *Linking Ethics and Economics: The Role of Ijtihad in the Regulation and Correction of Capital Markets* (Washington, DC: Center for Muslim–Christian Understanding, Georgetown University, 1999).

8. For instance, Dar al-Sharouk in Egypt and Mizan in Indonesia.

9. These include Iran's Ali Shariati and Abdol Karim Soroush, Turkey's Ecmettin Erbakan, Egypt's Hasan Hanafi, Kamal Aboulmagd, Selim al-Awa, and Heba Raouf Ezzat, Sudan's Hasan Turabi and Sadiq al-Mahdi, Malaysia's M. Kamal Hassan, Osman Bakar, M. Khalijah Salleh, Pakistan's Zafar Ishaq Ansari, Khalid Masud, and Ijaz Gilani, and Indonesia's Nurcholish Madjid and Amien Rais.

10. See, for example, Tariq Ramadan, *To Be a European Muslim*; Abdulaziz Sachedina, *The Islamic Roots of Democratic Pluralism* (New York: Oxford University Press/CSIS, 2000); Khaled Abou El Fadl, *Authoritative and Authoritarian in Islamic Discourses: A Contemporary Case Study* (Taiba Publishing House, 1997).

15

The Islamic Factor in the European Union's Foreign Policy

Fraser Cameron

INTRODUCTION

Europe's history is intertwined with that of the Islamic world. The two civilizations have interacted in social, cultural, political, and economic terms since the early centuries of Islam's emergence. The best examples of this wide-ranging and multidimensional interaction between the world of Islam and Europe are the Muslim kingdoms, which were established in Spain as early as the eighth century AD, and the extensive Muslim presence in other Mediterranean outposts such as Sicily and Malta. The remnants of this presence are still evident today.

The emergence of the Ottoman Empire in the fifteenth century, dramatically illustrated by the conquest of Constantinople, and its efforts to expand into Europe, added new dimensions to Europe's interaction with Islam. An important element was the relatively large-scale introduction of Islam to southeastern parts of Europe as early as the late fourteenth century. This led to the emergence of an indigenous European Islam.

The long history of Europe's interaction with the Islamic world has its considerable share of conflict, whose legacy is still felt. Less well known and appreciated are equally long periods of peaceful coexistence and mutually enriching scientific and cultural interaction. Until the late eighteenth century, Europe's relationship with the Muslim world was more or less that of equal partners. During the nineteenth century, however, there was a significant shift, as scientific and industrial advances enhanced Europe's economic and military power, while the Muslim world was left behind. This emerging disparity accelerated the pace of Europe's colonial expansion into Islamic lands, thus creating new forms of inter-action and new bonds and relations, whose legacies—both positive and negative—even today shape the dynamics of Europe's relations with the Islamic world.

The twentieth century witnessed a new development in these relations: the arrival of substantial numbers of Muslims to Europe. Today, there are approximately 15 million Muslims in the European Union (EU) coun-tries, of a total population of 370 million, or about 4 to 5 percent of the EU's population.

Since the 1980s, Muslim communities of Europe have become fairly well established, and their numbers have been rising. This expansion, coupled with the emergence of second- and third-generation Muslims, has led to the clear emergence of Islam as the second religion of many European nations. These demographic changes have also intensified in-teraction between Europe and various parts of the Islamic world. In par-ticular, the emergence of a growing Muslim population in Europe has had implications extending beyond the societal and cultural domains. Coupled with the fact of Europe's geographical proximity to the Muslim heartland, this rising Muslim presence has forced European governments and the EU to consider developments within the Middle East with greater attention, especially disruptive events, because of their potential impact on European security. Meanwhile, in the last several decades, Europe has grown increasingly dependent on the energy resources of the Persian Gulf and North African states, notably Algeria. In 1999 to 2000, the EU imports from the Persian Gulf and North African countries were $85 billion, while the EU exported goods worth $110 billion to the Mid-dle East and Persian Gulf states. The fundamentally dependent nature of this economic relationship has forged a linkage between Europe and these strategic regions of the Muslim world that requires a long-term, stable, and equitable relationship.

As this relationship has deepened, the Islamic factor has come to play a growing, but still limited, role in the formulation of EU foreign policy. This is significant at three levels: strategic and economic; the role of Mus-lim communities; and the impact that activities of some extremist ele-ments have on EU member-state relations with individual Islamic countries and, at times, even with the United States.

THE PRIMACY OF PEACE AND STABILITY

Economically, the EU relies heavily on some key Muslim states in North Africa and the Middle East as partners in trade and energy supply. Europe's interests in maintaining these economic relations help shape its political and security objectives, because stable governments are the most reliable trading partners. Europeans are also aware that some of the fiercest fighting in recent history has occurred between Europeans and Muslims in Europe itself, in its immediate neighborhood, or in close proximity. Recent examples include the bloody struggle in Chechnya, the conflicts in Bosnia and Kosovo, French actions in Algeria, and the Israeli-Palestinian conflict. Establishing peace and stability in Europe's neighborhood is thus more than a humanitarian interest. It is also an EU economic interest.

The increased number of Muslims within the EU also requires that European governments be more responsive to the concerns of their Muslim citizens, who have a direct stake in the political conditions of their countries of origin, in regions with a large Muslim population, and in areas where Muslims are under military or other threats. Thus, the EU's efforts to end conflicts in the former Yugoslavia were motivated not only by a desire to prevent the spread of disruptive influences to other European countries but also partly by concern over the negative impact that inaction in Bosnia could have on EU relations with the Muslim world as well as on European Muslim communities, which politically were not very active but sympathized with the Bosnian Muslims.

THE MIDDLE EAST: PROMOTING THE ARAB–ISRAELI PEACE

Because the Arab-Israeli conflict remains a main cause of political radicalization in Muslim societies and a threat to regional stability, the EU has tried to encourage Arab-Israeli peacemaking. Over the years, it has dedicated considerable economic and diplomatic resources to achieve this goal. It is the largest donor of non-military assistance to the region, and it has adopted a more balanced approach than has the United States toward the region.

Since the 1991 relaunching of the Middle East peace process, among the international players, the EU has consistently provided the largest amount of economic assistance. Since 1994, annually it has contributed on average 179 million Euros in direct support to the Palestinian Authority, refugees, and regional peace process projects. Together with indirect European support to the peace process—bilateral and regional aid of more than 630 million Euros to Israel's four neighboring countries—the EU's total economic support amounts to more than 810 million Euros in grants and European Investment Bank loans. The EU has also contributed $2.3 billion (through member states and the European Investment Bank) of total assistance of just over $3 billion to the Palestinians and the United Nations Relief and Works Agency. Also, together with Norway, the EU co-chairs meetings of the international donor mechanism, the Ad-Hoc Liaison Committee for Assistance to the Palestinians.

The EU is also a major trading and scientific and research partner of Israel and a principal political and economic partner of Lebanon, Syria, Jordan, and Egypt. The EU currently chairs the Regional Economic Development Working Group within the multilateral framework of the peace process and is co-organizer of the working groups on environment, water, and refugees.

Through its Common Foreign and Security Policy (CFSP), the EU has been able to expand its political role in the peace process. To this end, in 1996, the EU appointed Ambassador Miguel Angel Moratinos as its special envoy. He is responsible for maintaining close contact with all parties to provide assistance wherever possible. Javier Solana, the EU's high representative for CFSP, has also been directly involved in the peace negotiations. Moreover, the EU and the United States have agreed to work together for Middle East peace in the framework of the New Transatlantic Agenda, launched in December 1995.

Europe's Muslims have had some impact in shaping EU policy, by making clear their sympathy for the Palestinian cause—a sentiment widely shared by many non-Muslims. Nevertheless, EU policy has been essentially determined by long-term security considerations rather than its Muslim population's lobbying.

THE BARCELONA PROCESS: STABILIZING THE SOUTHERN PERIPHERY

The EU also underpins the peace process through the Euro-Mediterranean Partnership, a framework independent of but related to the peace process. The Euro-Med or "Barcelona Process" helps establish conditions for long-term stability and economic development in the region. The Euro-Med partnership was launched in 1995 at a ministerial conference in Barcelona attended by the fifteen EU member states, the European Commission, eleven Mediterranean nations (Cyprus, Malta, Morocco, Tunisia, Algeria, Egypt, Israel, Jordan, Lebanon, Syria, and Turkey), and the Palestinian Authority (now known collectively as the Med 12). The Euro-Med partnership aims at a comprehensive form of cooperation between the two regions.[1]

Cooperation has now been agreed upon in a broad range of political, social, and economic fields:

1. *Political and security partnership.* The European and Mediterranean countries have committed themselves to creating a Euro-Med zone of peace and stability. Issues include human rights, democracy, good governance, and security.

2. *Economic and financial partnership.* The main objective is to speed up progress toward lasting economic development, improved

living conditions, greater regional integration, and creation of a free trade zone between the EU and the Med 12 by 2010. This ambitious goal involves the progressive elimination of tariff and nontariff barriers on manufactured products, plus gradual liberalization of trade in agricultural products and services. Bilateral Euro-Med agreements are intended to facilitate private investment. To help transition to the free trade zone, the union committed almost 5 billion Euros in financial cooperation grants for the Mediterranean partners for the period 1995 to 1999.

3. *Social and cultural partnership.* A collaboration between Europe and the Mediterranean states. To achieve this goal, the EU has provided aid for collaborative efforts in the areas of culture, religion, education, the media, trade unions, and public and private companies.

The Barcelona Process is the only forum within which all regional actors can engage in policy dialogue. It also provides an institutional forum for dialogue that can be used as a model for making peace in the Middle East. At the same time, a main objective has been to stem a significant flow of illegal immigrants into the EU. For their part, Muslim states have been interested in securing the legal status of their nationals within the EU. Cultural contact between the two regions is maintained within the framework of forums known as "civilization dialogues." But the EU's main policy goal has been to stabilize its southern neighbors.

TURKEY

The country with the largest Muslim population on Europe's doorstep is Turkey. Its relations with the EU date from 1963, when Ankara was granted associate status. Relations developed steadily until the end of the Cold War, which triggered a new wave of applications to join the EU. As the Central and East European countries began to move up the queue for EU membership, Turkey feared exclusion from the EU for cultural and religious reasons. The decision of the European Council in 1998 to exclude Turkey from the first wave of accession negotiations intensified this fear. But a year later, following a series of domestic reforms, Turkey was accepted as a candidate country, although no date was set to open accession negotiations. In addition, the EU and Turkey agreed on an Accession Partnership, which provides considerable financial and other assistance to help Ankara meet the Copenhagen criteria for EU accession.[2] This preaccession strategy is aimed to stimulate reforms within Turkey, with special emphasis on human rights. Dialogue and cooperation will be enhanced by Turkey's participation in various

EU programs, agencies, and meetings between candidate states and the EU.

Considering that it applied for EU membership as early as 1987, Turkey's gaining formal status as a candidate for EU membership is a significant political and economic achievement. Since 1996, Turkey has had a customs union with the EU, and the EU accounts for more than 50 percent of Turkish trade and is its most important trading partner.

The EU Commission and other organs support an extensive and varied program to promote relations with Turkey. For example, in December 2000, the commission allocated 10 million Euros for scholarships to Turkish students under the MEDA (Mediterranean Development Assistance) Program. The Jean Monnet Scholarship Program aims to provide young Turkish graduates with one-year scholarships for postgraduate study in the EU, in areas relevant to Turkey's preaccession strategy. The goal is to strengthen links between these Turkish students and the EU.

Turkey has been one of the largest recipients of funds under the MEDA Program, a total of 376.2 million Euros for the period 1995 to 1999.

Because Turkey has a Muslim majority, many Europeans question whether it can ever become part of the "European identity." In terms of the role of Europe's Muslim communities in shaping EU policy toward Turkey, it is interesting to note that the Turkish community in Germany has not used its collective influence to pressure the EU to speed up the process of Turkey's membership.

ASSISTING NATION BUILDING IN MUSLIM REPUBLICS OF THE FORMER SOVIET UNION

The Soviet Union's collapse and the emergence of six new Muslim republics—some energy-rich—in the proximity of regions strategically important to Europe, such as the Black Sea and Persian Gulf, created new challenges and opportunities for the EU. To help these countries make a successful transition from communism to open societies and economies and to avoid political destabilization, the EU has provided them with economic and technical assistance and has tried to create links with EU institutions.

ISLAM AND MUSLIM–EUROPEAN RELATIONS

No doubt, questions related to Islam's presence in Europe have moved up the European political agenda. President Romano Prodi referred to the challenge of Islam in his inaugural speech to the European Parliament in October 1999, and there have been two recent European Parliament resolutions (Abdel Kader Mohamed Ali and Arie Oostlander) on

Islam—both urging the EU to do more to understand Islam and improve relations with the Islamic communities in the Union.[3] This increased interest in Islam at the European level is an attempt to counter the considerable ignorance about Islam and Muslim traditions in the EU. Islam is rarely studied, and most people associate the word Islam with "fundamentalism" and "terrorism." The media's first reaction whenever there is a terrorist incident is to blame "Islamic fundamentalists." Certainly, the conduct of some Islamic states, such as Iran, Sudan and Afghanistan, does little to allay the fears of Western publics and governments. But this fear of fundamentalism also leads to a less than objective assessment of foreign policy issues and especially the relative role of Islam in determining the behavior of Muslim states toward the outside world. Yet, as Shireen Hunter has noted:

> The international relations of Muslim states have been determined historically not by Islam but mostly by other dynamics and determinants of state behaviour—security, economic needs, ruling-elite interests, and the search for prestige and influence. Commitment to Islam has not been a bond sufficiently strong to allow Muslims to form a united front against the outside world; thus Islam has not prevented conflicts that pit Muslim states against each other. Nor has Islam proved to be an insurmountable barrier to co-operation between Muslims and non-Muslims. Quite the contrary; the history of the Muslims has been one of internecine conflict, inability to unite even in the face of common enemies, and co-operation with non-Muslims against fellow Muslims.[4]

This situation has both advantages and disadvantages. On the plus side, the fact that Muslim states behave largely out of motives similar to those of non-Muslim states means that a process of mutual accommodation can produce constructive and mutually beneficial relations. On the minus side, the absence of a single interlocutor makes developing and executing a coherent strategy toward the Islamic world more difficult.

THE ROLE OF MUSLIM COMMUNITIES

For their part, the Muslim communities in Europe also lack a coherent and coordinated approach toward foreign policy. In fact, they are interested primarily in local and daily issues such as ensuring freedom of religion, retaining social and cultural life styles, and securing employment. They show little interest in foreign affairs. The main cause of friction between Muslims and indigenous European populations in recent times has been questions related to schooling (headscarves), the law (turbans/crash helmets), social customs (slaughtering of animals—

for *halal* food—in public), and not foreign policy-related issues. This is due partly to the fact that, while Muslims have some representation at the national level in the EU member states, they have little or no representation at the EU level. There are hardly any Muslim Members of Parliament, members of European Parliament, or effective Muslim organizations at the European or international level. This may reflect competing priorities, lack of understanding of the EU's importance, or the Muslims' inability to coordinate their actions—or a combination of all these factors.

Therefore, regarding major EU external policies likely to be of interest to Muslim communities, there is little evidence that they lobby actively. There has been no obvious Muslim pressure on EU authorities to influence Russia's attitude on the Chechen conflict, despite the massacre of many Muslim civilians. Between 1992 and 1995, there was some lobbying on the Bosnian conflict, but the Kosovo war was undertaken primarily for humanitarian reasons—not to support an independent Muslim state. With regard to Algeria, there were mixed attitudes in the Muslim communities over the ambivalent reaction of the EU following the annulment of the 1992 parliamentary elections that FIS (*Front Islamique de Salut* [Islamic Salvation Front]) had won but had stolen by the Algerian military. As to East Timor, there were hardly any statements or comments by Muslims in the EU when the largest Muslim country in the world—Indonesia—faced a major internal crisis and ultimately had to accept the demands of the Timorese separatists.

PROSPECTS FOR CHANGE: A GREATER MUSLIM INVOLVEMENT IN FOREIGN POLICY?

There are signs that Muslims are beginning to operate as a more cohesive force in Europe, a development that could increase their engagement in trying to shape aspects of EU foreign policy. The level and character of Muslims' actions vary from state to state and are often determined by underlying political and social conditions or tensions within each country or region. In the Balkans, the violent collapse of Yugoslavia has determined the way in which Muslim communities are perceived by others and see themselves, and hence also the social, economic, and organizational priorities adopted both by the Muslims and by wider society. Such extremes of ethnoreligious tensions have not occurred in countries like Bulgaria, Rumania, and Poland, where Muslims are a much smaller part of the population, although in Bulgaria they are a substantial minority.

The organizational and behavioral pattern of Muslim communities is also influenced by the cultures of their countries of origin. No doubt, the fact that most British Muslims are from the Indian subcontinent marks the character of the UK's Muslim community and its foreign policy concerns. Thus, there were demonstrations by Indian and Pakistani communities in Britain following the EU's condemnation of the nuclear tests by India and Pakistan. Similarly, the existence of large numbers of Turks and Maghrebiens in Germany and France, respectively, determines the range of foreign policy issues in which they are interested.

THE EXTREMIST FRINGE AND ITS IMPACT

The overwhelming majority of Europe's Muslim populations, whatever their religious proclivities—reformist, traditionalist, or secular—are peaceful citizens and harbor no subversive goals. Nevertheless, there is an extremist fringe connected to militant groups in the Muslim world, especially the Middle East and South Asia. Some of these elements engage in activities aimed at undermining their home governments; others are political refugees who, although not often actually engaged in active subversion, do write and speak against the policies of their home governments. These activities often create tensions in bilateral relations of some EU members and certain Muslim countries. The latter, at times, demand that these political dissidents be extradited to their home countries, thus posing serious dilemmas for European countries in terms of human rights. Some EU member states also complain that some others are too permissive regarding the activities of these dissident elements. However, not all political dissidents originating from countries where Islam is the majority religion are Islamists or even practicing Muslims. Many are secular and espouse a variety of leftist or nationalist ideas.

The activities of this extremist fringe sometimes create tensions in the EU's relations with the United States. However, despite being an irritant, these groups have no influence in determining EU policies, beyond overall efforts to eliminate the root causes of extremism in the Muslim world, especially the Mediterranean region.

NEW DYNAMICS

In the future, several new dynamics will determine the pattern of interaction between Europe's Muslim communities and broader society, including the level of their engagement in political life and thus in foreign policy issues. Among these new dynamics are the evolution of the relative balance between "inclusive" and "exclusive" political movements, including the impact of racist and xenophobic trends. Depending on how these trends develop, they will influence the expectations of Europe's Muslims and hence their attitudes toward society, political participation, and political power. Another factor that will have a long-term impact on relations between Muslims and others in European society is the debate about religion's proper role. How this debate evolves and the way in which church-state relations in European countries try to adapt and make space for new Muslim communities will influence the way Muslims view the public space. Perhaps the most influential factors will be a major demographic shift and a growing linkage between Europe and the "other (Muslim) side" of the Mediterranean.

Another major development is the "Europeanization" of the Muslim communities, with direct consequences for the character of their relations with state and society. First, the younger generation is taking over leadership of the community's organizations and representative structures from the older generations. Just as local and national governments and their civil servants had begun to get used to working with the representatives of the immigrant generation, they are now faced with their children, who often have different perceptions and priorities. In particular, the younger leaderships have a much better understanding of how their countries' political and administrative processes function, and they are clearly prepared to use them. On the whole, they appear to want a much more constructive engagement with local and national institutions. They want to take part in society at all levels, to be recognized and respected as native citizens—but as *Muslim* native citizens. Yet, it would be naive to interpret this new attitude as willingness to assimilate completely into existing structures and to accept all inherited European perceptions of the place of religion in society. Rather, the younger Muslims are looking for an active Muslim presence—including religious—in society. This desire coincides with a renewed debate concerning the place of religion in society within wider circles in European countries.

Second, there is a widespread intellectual movement among European Muslims, especially within the growing numbers of well-educated professionals, directed toward rethinking traditional Islamic concepts and their expression in a specific cultural form. The Islamic expression of the immigrant generations was closely integrated with the cultural frameworks and practices of the regions of origin, which usually were rural rather than urban. The new generation actively separates the culturally specific from the "universally" Islamic in a process that reclothes the latter in a new cultural "dress" that is oriented to the European environment. In this way, they are replacing, or at least significantly reinterpreting, the cultural dress that their parents brought from their home countries.

This development is making the traditional categorization of Islamic movements unsatisfactory. The political and social priorities both of the Muslim communities and of their European interlocutors are producing new types of Muslim organizations. These new institutions are trying to become more independent from institutions, ideologies, and objectives rooted in ancestral homelands. They are also becoming more open to cooperation with other religio-political movements. New organizations and alliances are emerging with reference to agendas and priorities associated with the European environment. There are now more Muslim umbrella organizations that can interact more effectively with local and national authorities. As shown by different authors in this volume, this process has been due partly to pressures from European governments, which have felt the need for viable interlocutors in the Muslim communities in order to address various issues. Meanwhile, political issues related to home countries, such as Kashmir in the case of British Muslims and Algeria in the case of France's Muslims, also play an important role in mobilizing the Muslim community's political interests. Should these trends continue, they may affect the formation of EU policy toward certain regions, if these institutions become activist.

Third, there is growing identification of sectors of the younger Muslim population with issues related to the broader Muslim world rather than solely countries of origin. These younger Muslims increasingly identify with Islam in general rather than with their parents' (or grandparents') countries of origin. For example, younger Turkish Muslims are becoming concerned about Muslim issues in places like Palestine, the northern Caucasus, or the southern Philippines, and not just with issues related to Turkey. The same trend has been observed among Muslims of South Asian and North African origin. This has already been reflected in the growth of Islamic emergency and relief agencies that are working with some success in crisis situations like those of Bosnia, Kosovo, and Sudan and the ability of such agencies to mobilize young people who have previously had little active mosque involvement. In the case of support for Bosnian Muslims, this effort was associated with a widespread perception that their fate was somehow vital for that of Muslims in Europe in general. Such broader identification should not be regarded as sinister: Essentially, it is no different from the tendencies of European Christians to identify with the fate of fellow believers in areas of conflict, such as southern Sudan, India, and Pakistan, where at times Christians suffer active discrimination or mob-generated aggression.

Moreover, these developments are also part of a wider European tendency that unites East and West. Following the collapse of the Soviet system a decade ago, questions related to the relationships between national, ethnic, and religious identities have become a priority. In the former Yugoslavia, they were a major factor in the disintegration of the multinational federation. While the extremes of Yugoslavia have so far been avoided elsewhere, such risks still exist, as illustrated by Kosovo and Macedonia. Moreover, the main issue remains alive, and its negotiation is contributing to changes in public discourse, political perceptions, and self-awareness of national identity. In Europe, with very different histories, the presence of large, relatively new ethnic and religious minorities has raised anew precisely the same issues. How do countries that have inherited a self-understanding of a *folk*, sharing a common history, culture, and collective self-awareness, part of which is often a shared religious tradition and national church, integrate people who do not share that common heritage? There are profound issues of local, regional, national, and continental identities and self-awareness converging across Europe, East and West. This situation has wide-ranging implications for the debate over a common European identity.

ASSESSING FUTURE TRENDS AND IMPLICATIONS FOR FOREIGN POLICY

A few other new factors need to be taken into account before assessing the implications of future trends. The first is leadership. What will be the profile of future leaders of Islam in Europe? Until now, "natural" leaders coming from the first generation, along with leaders imported from Muslim spaces or Europeans converted to Islam, have dominated Muslim communities. But as the new generation emerges, what models of Islam will it adopt? How will it position itself in the European body politic? How will it react to various challenges at the European level, including foreign policy?

The second factor is organizational. The local and federative organizational capacity of European Muslims has been considerable. But there has been little sign that they are willing to engage at the European level. Will the new generation change this pattern of behavior?

A third factor is cultural. What does it mean to be a Muslim in modern Europe? How much of traditional identity can be maintained in a Europe that itself is changing at break-neck speed, in an attempt to keep pace with globalization? How will European Muslims steer a path between secularization and ethnic identification (e.g., Arab, Turk, Pakistani, African)?

A fourth factor relates to Muslim countries. It is impossible accurately to predict the worldwide evolution of Islam. But certain "centers of Islam" will clearly continue to focus attention. How will European Muslims react to these centers in terms of symbols, ideas, behavior, and organization?

Thus, only tentative and speculative predictions can be made regarding the way Muslim communities in Europe might seek to influence and shape EU foreign policy. Their behavior will depend on the interplay between domestic politics and foreign policy. Some Muslims worry about an institutional integration of Islam and are developing a European Islamic discourse while maintaining cultural and symbolic ties with worldwide Islam. Some reject any European paradigm and prefer the Islam of Malcolm X. Another factor is that many Muslims consider themselves, and are considered by others, to be appendices, an expression of geopolitical strategies developed on the basis of centers of Islam. The various diaspora are often active in this context, leading to conflicts of loyalty.

Interestingly, in periods of major crisis in European-Muslim relations, such as during the Persian Gulf War of 1991, until now European Muslims have remained quiescent even if they do not approve of their governments' policies. Beneath such specific factors and responses lies a blunt choice for European society with regard to the presence of ethnic and religious minorities and in particular the presence of Muslim communities: Integrate or expel. There is no "third way," least of all denial of the realities of immigration and its consequences. The economic and political choice in favor of integration has essentially been made, even if to some extent by default rather than by deliberate choice. If the option of integration is to succeed, the fundamental assumptions of European democratic traditions should be observed—namely, that good government and sociopolitical stability rest on a foundation of the consent of the governed, a "contract" where loyalty and consent are granted in exchange for participation and access to social and political "goods."

CONCLUSION

Muslim countries are becoming increasingly important to member states of the EU. Apart from energy supplies, European trade with neighboring Muslim states and with other Muslim countries located beyond the immediate borders of the EU is increasing rapidly. Europe is generally viewed positively by most Arab and Muslim states, and the successful process of European integration in the postwar period is seen as a possible paradigm for peaceful settlement of ongoing regional disputes. The growth in the Muslim population of EU member states challenges European citizenry and leadership to forge new paths of cultural and religious inclusion. Though Europe's record in this area is mixed, the issue of an increasingly multicultural Europe is present in the minds of all Europeans—from officials in Brussels to inhabitants of provincial France and the suburbs of Berlin.

Muslims are not yet sufficiently and effectively organized at either the national or the EU level, but fundamental changes are underway within Europe's Muslim communities. So far, Europe's Muslims have had little direct impact on EU's external relations. Nevertheless, their presence has influenced policymakers' calculations regarding the merits of different options and strategies. This Muslim passivity in the foreign policy area could change in the future, and Europe's Muslims could exert more influence in shaping EU foreign policy.

NOTES

The author writes in a personal capacity.

1. On the Euro-Med Partnership, among others. "Euro-Mediterranean Partnership" (Brussels: European Commission, 1997).

2. For details of the Accession Partnership, consult EUROPA Web site http://europa.eu.int/.

3. See DOC. EN/RR/338/338209, *Explanatory Statement Fundamentalism: A Challenge to the European Legal Order Rapporteur Arie Oostlander*. Also *Report on Islam and European Averroes Day Committee on Culture, Youth, Education and the Media* (European Parliament report).

4. Shireen T. Hunter, *The Future of Islam and the West: Clash of Civilizations or Peaceful Coexistence?* (Westport, CT: Praeger/CSIS, 1998).

Conclusions and Outlook for European Islam

Shireen T. Hunter

This book has surveyed the history and dynamics of the arrival, implantation, and gradual domestication of Muslim immigrants and their culture in a dozen European countries and examined a number of important thematic issues such as the dynamics of identity formation among Muslim youth; the dual processes of Islamization of Europe and Europeanization of Islam; and the relationship among processes of European unification, growing multiculturalism, and the place and role of Islam in this context. By doing so, it has sought to identify and delineate the multiple cross-cutting and often contradictory contexts and discourses within which the process of mutual adaptation and adjustment of Islam and Europe is taking place. The country-specific studies, and those dealing with issues that transcend national frontiers, have revealed certain patterns of diversity and unity across geographical and intellectual boundaries. They have also pointed to the emergence of contradictory trends in various socioeconomic, political, and cultural contexts.

These analyses have also demonstrated that the process of Islam's and Muslims interaction with European societies and peoples is taking place within a historical—both old and more recent—context of inherited and deep-rooted cultural and religious prejudices and political and other grievances. They have shown that the simultaneous processes of Europe's unification and globalization are creating a much more complex environment within which Islam's and Europe's encounter is taking place. In the foreseeable future, these dynamics are unlikely to change. Rather, most probably, they will grow in complexity. What is certain is that the dynamics of Europe's Muslim communities, plus the gradual development of a European Islam—notwithstanding local varieties—will affect developments in the Muslim world and will increase the interpenetration of the European and Islamic spaces. In Europe, this phenomenon will contribute to the reopening of old debates about the place of religion and spirituality in public life. In the Islamic world, it will intensify the debate about the relations between Islam and modernity and how they can be reconciled and will lead to new interpretations and synthesis.

PATTERNS OF DIVERSITY AND UNITY

Europe's Muslim communities are very diverse; they are divided along ethnic, sectarian, and socioeconomic lines, although in a number of key European countries such as France, Germany, and the United Kingdom, one or two ethnic groups have such a numerical superiority that their specific religious and cultural traditions and traits mark the characteristics of that country's Islam. They are also different in regard to their level of integration into the societies in which they have settled, their ideological orientations, and the nature of their relations both with the host societies and with their countries of origin.

The European societies in which Muslims have settled also have diverse cultural, religious, and political traditions, which affect their attitudes toward Muslims and their mode of interaction with them. Thus, different patterns of Muslim and European accommodation can be observed in different countries.

Beneath this diversity, Europe's Muslim communities have much in common in terms of their experiences of alienation and integration, their struggles for social and economic advancement and religious and cultural recognition and legitimacy, challenges and barriers that they face in trying to achieve these goals, and the opportunities that European societies offer them.

ISLAM NO LONGER A TRANSITORY PHENOMENON

When Muslim immigrant workers arrived in Europe in the 1960s, they were viewed as a temporary and transient phenomenon. Certainly, there was no expectation that Islam could become part of Europe's religious and cultural landscape or that Muslims would demand a legitimate place within the European space. By the early 1980s, however, the changing composition of the Muslim populations and the development of Muslim organizations, especially cathedral mosques—the most obvious outward sign of Islam—caused a sudden awareness among European publics that Islam was to stay in Europe. The emergence of a new generation of

Muslims born and raised in Europe has eliminated any remnants of the myth of "returning home," although periodically right-wing groups and parties call for the forced expulsion of immigrants including, and perhaps especially, Muslims.

PATTERNS OF MUSLIM-EUROPEAN INTERACTION: ASSIMILATION, COMMUNITARIANISM, OR NEW MODES OF INTEGRATION

The question of the nature of the relationship between the Muslim communities and the European countries has generally been posed in terms of either complete assimilation or the development of communitarian structures that, in their extreme form, could be a type of de facto segregation. This simplistic division is appealing to some Europeans and Muslims alike.

The assimilationists tend to believe that Muslims should accept the totality of the cultural and political ethos of their country of residence or citizenship. They can, of course, remain Muslim, but their religion must be a private matter and publicly invisible. The one-time French Minister of the Interior Charles Pasqua expressed well the assimilationist philosophy when he said that it was not "enough simply to have Islam in France. . . . There must be a French Islam." German politicians have talked about a high German culture (*Leitkultur*) that all residents and citizens of Germany must follow. Assimilationist tendencies are also present among Muslims, especially those who arrived late in the 1980s and 1990s, following revolutions and civil wars in Iran, Algeria, and Yugoslavia, and a considerable portion of the second or third generations of Muslims who want to become French, British, or German to the extent that their respective societies will permit.

Communitarians—both European and Muslim—prefer Muslims to form cohesive communities, which can then enter into systematic dialogue with state and society. Some Muslims prefer to live in complete isolation according to strict Islamic rules.

In reality, however, Muslim communities have evolved along different lines, ranging from assimilationist to communitarian. But the most important movement, especially among the youth, is integration without complete assimilation. The policies of various European countries, too, in practice, have had elements of both assimilationist and communalist tendencies. Presently, all these different patterns coexist in most countries with substantial Muslim populations. But in the future, the philosophy of integration without assimilation is most likely to shape the pattern of Muslim–European relations and the intellectual evolution of Islam in Europe. This philosophy accepts the basic legal and political principles of the country of residence or citizenship, reinterprets Islamic concepts, such as *Dar ul-Islam* and *Dar ul-Harb,* in a way to make Europe an acceptable place for Muslims to live—*Dar ul-Ahd.* Its promoters are eager to become engaged in social and political life of the country but are unwilling to compromise on the essentials of the Muslim faith, or as Tariq Ramadan has put it, to relinquish its claim to universality.

These processes are taking place in different forms in different countries, thus giving rise to national varieties of Islam. Yet, because of interconnections that exist among various Muslim communities and the similarities of their problems and concerns in different countries, coupled with the process of European integration, what could be called a European Islam is also slowly emerging. This process is similar to that of Islam's implantation over centuries in Asia and Africa and reflects its ability to adapt to local and preexisting cultures and traditions while retaining its spiritual and universal essence.

PERSISTING DISPARITIES AND LIMITS OF MULTICULTURALISM

Despite some progress and some bright spots, most of Europe's Muslim communities constitute an underprivileged class, clustered in ghetto-like neighborhoods imbued with a culture of deprivation and alienation and with antisocial propensities. Yet, despite these conditions, only a very small percentage of them are attracted to extremist ideas. This situation has complex causes, as demonstrated in various chapters. But persisting prejudice and discrimination against Muslims at various levels are among its primary causes.

The number of Muslims with European citizenship has increased, but there is still resistance in some countries to easing the process of naturalization, thus limiting the level of Muslim political participation and representation.

In the cultural domain, because of the process of European unification and the development of a European identity, which, for many of Europe's citizens, is a difficult and anxiety-producing experience, and the fear of the corrosive effects of globalization, many Europeans have difficulty in accepting Islam as a legitimate component of their cultural landscape and their emerging European identity. Rather, at this early stage, the formation of a European identity, as Sami Zemni and Christopher Parker point out, tends to perpetuate and even intensify the perception of Islam as the hostile "other." The individual Muslim becomes conflated with global Islam. Despite the secular nature of their societies, many Europeans find disquieting the intrusion of Islam in their predominantly Christian religious landscape. In short, multiculturalism in Europe, as it applies to the Muslims, still has serious limits at national and local levels, although in principle it has been adopted by the European Union.

RELATIONS WITH THE MUSLIM WORLD: EUROPE AS THE NEW INTELLECTUAL FRONTIER

Europe's Muslim communities interact at several levels with the Islamic world. The most extensive relations are still those with the immigrants' countries of origin. However, as European Muslims are increasingly becoming rooted in the countries of settlement and are trying to become full participants in their social and political life, the nature of the relationship with the countries of origin is growing increasingly complex.

For example, conflict of interest in many regards is emerging between the immigrant communities and their home countries. Especially, many European Muslims resent the tendency of the authorities of their home countries to exert control over them or to discourage them from participating in the political life of their adopted countries. The governments of immigrants' home countries, for their part, are concerned about the contagious effect of the more liberal and modernist interpretations of Islam that are developing in Europe. They fear that immigrant Muslims' experience of living in democratic societies could increase demands for political liberalization among their own populations.

Europe's Muslim communities also interact closely with transnational Muslim organizations and movements. The influence of some of these institutions is less than positive, especially in terms of the integrative processes. Some have a decidedly negative impact because they propagate unrealistic and, at times, extremist ideologies, which strain relations between Muslim communities and the host societies and solidify Islam's negative image.

The existence of Muslim communities has also affected Europe's geopolitical priorities and aspects of its foreign policy. Their presence has intensified and expanded the ties that exist between Europe and the Muslim world, notably the Mediterranean region.

Europe's Muslims, so far, have not been very active in trying to influence Europe's foreign policy in regard to the Islamic world and issues of concern to the Muslims. Nevertheless, their mere presence has affected the attitudes and approaches of Europe's policymakers toward a number of key issues, notably the Arab–Israeli conflict.

Europe has become a major and vital center of Islamic intellectual activity. The more open atmosphere of Europe and new challenges that Muslims have had to face have led to new, creative, and diverse thinking. The ramifications of this development for the cultural and political development of the Islamic world cannot be fully measured. What is certain is that it will set in motion new dynamics. Equally, the Muslim presence and the Muslims' demands have opened a new debate on the role of religion and spirituality in Europe.

In the coming decades, the Muslim presence in Europe is likely to grow, both quantitatively and qualitatively. Eventually, Islam is bound to find its place in the sociocultural and political landscape of Europe. But the road to mutual acceptance and accommodation will not be free of tension or strife. Nor will it be uniform and linear. Rather, in the foreseeable future, many processes, at times contradictory, will characterize the pattern of interaction between Muslim communities and European societies.

Afterword

The terrorist attacks on the World Trade Center in New York and the Pentagon in Washington, DC on September 11, 2001, along with the events that followed—notably US retaliation against Osama bin Laden's terrorist organization, Al Qaeda, and the Afghan Taliban regime that supported it—have had significant and multi-dimensional consequences at both regional and international levels.

What happened on September 11 and afterward has also had significant and mostly negative consequences for the Muslim communities in Europe, and has set back the process of mutual accommodation between Muslim and European populations and the integration of both Islam and Muslims into Europe's social, cultural, and political landscape.

In addition to the general and justified anger generated by the terrorist attacks on the World Trade Center, during which many European citizens also died, the events of September 11 intensified Europeans' fears about their own vulnerability to such acts. The fact that a key figure in those heinous acts, Muhammad Atta, had spent several years in Germany and did not fit the stereotype of a Muslim terrorist, cast a shadow over Europe's Muslims in the minds of many of its citizens. Although, as demonstrated in various chapters of this book, hard-core extremists potentially capable of carrying out violent acts are a small minority among Europe's Muslims, the discovery that Osama bin Laden and his terrorist network had sympathizers and collaborators among European Muslims has put the entire community under a shadow of suspicion. Moreover, the events of September 11 have strengthened already existing anti-Muslim prejudices and have made it legitimate for those political groups espousing anti-immigrant and xenophobic views to express them openly and, in many instances, to translate them into acts of violence against Muslims and Muslim institutions.

Yet the reactions of European governments and Europe's Muslim communities to the tragic events of September 11 have shown that neither side is willing to allow the extremists to gain the upper hand in deciding how relations between Muslim communities and their adopted countries will evolve. Several European leaders have made clear that the overwhelming majority of peaceful and law-abiding Muslims should not be blamed for the inhuman and unacceptable acts of the extremists.

For their part, most European Muslims have shown that they value their positions as citizens and residents of Europe too much to jeopardize them out of misplaced sympathy for a group of misguided co-religionists, who have been deluded into engaging in violence and terror in the name of Islam. Indeed, despite some early concerns, there was no rush of Muslims, including those of Pakistani descent, to Afghanistan to fight on the side of the Taliban, although a small number of British subjects of Pakistani descent did do so. Nor were there massive protests against military operations against the Taliban and Osama bin Laden and his terror network. In fact, the post-September 11 reaction of Europe's Muslims has validated one of the principal conclusions of this volume: that the overwhelming majority of Europe's Muslims want to become full-fledged and loyal citizens of Europe.

The events of September 11, especially the European connections of some of the perpetrators, have highlighted the necessity and importance of better understanding the characteristics of Europe's Muslim communities and the dynamics that are operating within them, notably the more progressive and integrational tendencies. These events have further emphasized the need for European societies and their Muslim communities to do a better job of mutual acceptance and accommodation. European societies must realize the importance of preventing the marginalization and alienation of their growing youthful Muslim populations. Muslim communities, for their part, must work harder at protecting themselves against the dangerous and disruptive influences of extremists and try to isolate them.

As explained in various chapters of this volume, even before September 11, these were extremely complex and difficult tasks, as was the process of incorporating Islam and Muslims into the European landscape. This has become more daunting since then. What remains unchanged is the reality of the Muslim presence in Europe, Europe's proximity to the Islamic world, the complex web of interconnections between the two, and hence the need for the gradual integration of Islam and Muslims in Europe.

The insights provided by the contributors to this volume into the psychology and workings of Europe's Muslim communities and the forces that affect relations between them and the majority societies can offer useful guidelines for advancing the process of mutual accommodation and acceptance, and thus they remain highly relevant.

Shireen T. Hunter
April 2002

Selected Bibliography

Abul Ala Mawdudi, Sayyid. *Towards Understanding Islam.* Leicester: Islamic Foundation, 1981.

Ahmed, Akbar. *Post-Modernism and Islam: Predicament and Promise.* London: Routledge & Kegan Paul, 1992.

Ahmed, Ishtiaq. *The Concept of an Islamic State.* London: Pinter, 1987.

Allievi, Stefano; Bidussa, David; and Naso, Paolo. *Il libro e la spada. La sfida dei fondamentalismi* [The book and the sword. The challenge of fundamentalisms]. Turin: Claudiana, 2000.

Anwar, Muhammad. *Ethnic Minorities and the British Political System.* University of Warwick, Coventry: Centre for Research in Ethnic Relations, 1998.

Anwar, Zainah. *Islamic Revivalism in Malaysia: Dawah among the Students.* Selangor Darul Ehsan, Malaysia: Pelanduk Publications, 1987.

Bartels, Dieter. *Moluccans in Exile: A Struggle for Ethnic Survival.* Leiden: COMT, 1989.

Bell, David S. *Democratic Politics in Spain: Spain's Politics after Franco.* Londres: Frances Printer, 1983.

Bistolfi, Robert, and Zabbal, François. *Islams d'Europe, intégration ou insertion communautaire?* [Islams in Europe, integration or communitarian insertion?] Paris: Editions de l'Aube, 1995.

Blommaert, J., and Verschueren, J. *Het Belgische migrantendebat: De pragmatiek van de abnormalisering.* [The Belgian immigration debate: From pragmatism to normalization]. Antwerpen: IprA Research Center, 1992.

———. *Debating Diversity. Analyzing the Discourse of Tolerance.* London: Routledge, 1998.

Christinakis, Panagiotis. *Elliniko ekklisiatiko dikaio* [Hellenic ecclesiastical law]. Athens: Simmetria Editions, 1995.

Commission for Racial Equality. *British Bureaucracy and the Multi-Ethnic Society.* New Brunswick, NJ: Transaction Publishers, 1998.

Dassetto, Felice. *La construction de l'islam Européen. Approche socio-anthropologique* [The construction of European Islam. A socio-anthropological approach]. Paris: L'Harmattan, 1996.

———, ed. *Islam en Belgique et en Europe; facettes et questions. Facettes de l'islam belge* [Islam in Belgium and in Europe: dimensions and questions. Dimensions of Belgian Islam]. Louvain-la-Neuve: Academia Bruylant, 1997.

Dodos, Dimosthenis X. *Eklogiki geografia ton meionotiton* [Electoral geography of the minorities]. Athens: Eksadas Editions, 1994.

Driessen, Henk. *On the Spanish–Moroccan Frontier. A Study in Ritual, Power and Ethnicity.* Oxford: Berg Publishers, 1992.

El Fadl, Khaled Abou. *Authoritative and Authoritarian in Islamic Discourses: A Contemporary Case Study.* Austin, TX: Dar Taiba, 1997.

Esposito, John L. *Islam and Politics*, 3rd ed. Syracuse: Syracuse University Press, 1998.

Esposito, John L., and Voll, John O. *Islam and Democracy.* New York: Oxford University Press, 1996.

Evers Rosander, Eva. *Women in a Borderland. Managing Muslim Identity Where Morocco Meets Spain.* Estocolmo: Stockholm Studies in Social Anthropology, 1991.

Ferrari, Silvio, ed. *L'islam in Europa. Lo statuto giuridico delle comunità musulmane* [Islam in Europe. The juridical status of Muslim communities in Europe]. (Bologna: Il Mulino, 1996).

Ferrari, Silvio, and Bradney, A., eds. *Islam and European Legal Systems.* Aldershot: Ashgate, 2000.

Finkielkraut, Alain. *La défaite de la pensée* [The defeat of thought]. Paris: Folio Essais/Gallimard, 1987.

Gabrieli, Francesco. *Storici arabi delle crociate* [Arab historians of the Crusades]. Turin: Einaudi, 1987.

Hidiroglou, Paul. *The Greek Pomaks and Their Relation with Turkey.* Athens: Proskinio Editions, 1991.

Hoodbhoy, Pervez. *Islam and Science. Religious Orthodoxy and the Battle for Rationality.* London: Zed Books, 1991.

Hunter, Shireen T., ed. *The Politics of Islamic Revivalism: Diversity and Unity.* Bloomington: Indiana University Press, 1988.

Hunter, Shireen T. *The Future of Islam and the West: Clash of Civilizations or Peaceful Coexistence?* Westport, CT: Praeger/CSIS, 1998.

Jacobson, J. *Islam in Transition: Religion and Identity among British Pakistani Youth.* London: Routledge, 1998.

Joly, Daniele. *Britain's Crescent: Making a Place for Islam in British Society.* Aldershot: Avebury, 1995.

Kepel, Gilles. *Les banlieues de l'islam* [The suburbs of Islam]. Paris: Seuil, 1987.

Khosrokhavar, F. *L'islam des jeunes* [Islam of the youth]. Paris: Flammarion, 1997.

Kitromilides, Paschalis, and Veremis, Thanos, eds. *The Orthodox Church in a Changing World.* Athens: Hellenic Foundation for European and Foreign Policy, Center for Asia Minor Studies, 1998.

Landman, Nico. *Imamopleiding in Nederland, kansen en knelpunten* [Training imams in the Netherlands, chances and problems]. Den Haag: SDU, 1996.

Lebor, Adam. *A Heart Turned East.* London: Little, Brown, 1997.

Lewis, Phillip. *Islamic Britain: Religion, Politics and Identity among British Muslims.* London: I.B. Tauris, 1994.

López Barrios, Fernando, and Hagherty, Miguel José. *Murieron para vivir. El resurgimiento del Islam y el Sufismo en España* [To die or to live. The resurgence of Islam and Sufism in Spain]. Barcelona: Argos Vergara, 1983.

Metcalf, Barbara Daly, ed. *Making Muslim Space in North America and Europe.* Berkeley: University of California Press, 1996.

Modood, Tariq; Berthoug, Richard; Lakey, Jane; Nazroo, James; Smith, Patten; Veidee, Satnam; and Beiskon, Sharon. *Ethnic Minorities in Britain.* London: Policy Studies Institute, 1997.

Nielsen, Jørgen S. *Muslims in Western Europe*, 2nd ed. Edinburgh: Edinburgh University Press, 1995.

Nonneman, Gerd; Niblock, Tim; and Szajkowski, Bogdan. *Muslim Communities in the New Europe.* Reading: Ithaca Press, 1996.

Ramadan, Tariq. *To Be a European Muslim.* Leicester: Islamic Foundation, 1999.

Rex, John, and Moore, Robert. *Race, Community and Conflict.* Oxford: Oxford University Press, 1967.

Rex, John, and Tomlinson, Sally. *Colonial Immigrants in a British City—A Class Analysis.* London: Routledge & Kegan Paul, 1979.

Robinson, Vaughan. *Transients, Settlers or Refugees: Asians in Britain.* Oxford: Clarendon Press, 1986.

Roy, Olivier. *The Failure of Political Islam.* London: I.B. Tauris, 1994.

Sachedina, Abdulaziz. *The Islamic Roots of Democratic Pluralism.* New York: Oxford University Press/CSIS, 2000.

Schmidt di Friedberg, O Havia. *Islam, solidarietà e lavoro. I muridi senegalesi in Italia* [Islam, solidarity and work. The Senegalese Mourids in Italy]. Turin: Fondazione Agnelli, 1994.

Shadid, W.A.R., and van Koningsveld, P.S., eds., *Religious Freedom and the Position of Islam in Western Europe.* Kampen: Kok Pharos, 1995.

———. *Muslims in the Margin. Political Responses to the Presence of Islam in Western Europe.* Kampen: Kok Pharos, 1996.

Solomos, John, and Back, Les. *Race, Politics and Social Change.* London: Routledge, 1995.

Stenberg, Leif. *The Islamization of Science. Four Muslim Positions Developing an Islamic Modernity.* Stockholm: Almquist & Wiksell, 1996.

Steward, Charles, and Shaw, Rosalind, eds. *Syncretism/Anti-Syncretism: The Politics of Religious Synthesis.* London: Routledge, 1994.

Vertovec, Steven, and Peach, Ceri, eds. *Islam in Europe. The Politics of Religion and Community.* London/New York: Macmillan/St. Martin's Press, 1997.

Voll, John O. *Islam: Continuity and Change in the Modern World*, 2nd ed. Syracuse: Syracuse University Press, 1994.

Waardenburg, J.D. *L'islam en Europe. Aspects religieux* [Islam in Europe. Religious Aspects]. Lausanne: Université de Lausanne, 1994.

Wahlbeck, Osten. *Kurdish Diasporas: A Comparative Study of Kurdish Refugee Communities.* Basingstoke: Macmillan, 1999.

Westerlund, David, and Svanberg, Ingvar, eds. *Islam outside the Arab World*. Richmond: Curzon Press, 1999.

Zeginis, Efstratios. *Oi Mousoulmanoi Athiganoi tis Thrakis* [The Muslim Athiganoi of Western Thrace]. Thessaloniki: Institute for Balkan Studies, 1994.

———. *O Bektasismos sti Ditiki Thraki* [Bektashiism in Western Thrace]. Thessaloniki: Institute for Balkan Studies, 1996.

Index

In the index ''n'' indicates a note; ''t'' indicates a table.

About the Editor and Contributors

STEFANO ALLIEVI is a researcher at the University of Padua, Italy, where he also teaches sociology in the faculty of sciences of communication.

DIMITRIS A. ANTONIOU is a researcher at the Hellenic Foundation for European and Foreign Policy (ELIAMEP) in Athens, Greece.

FRASER CAMERON is a former academic and British diplomat and head of political and academic affairs at the European Commission Delegation in Washington, DC, USA.

ANA I. PLANET CONTRERAS teaches Arabic and Islamic studies at the University of Alicante in Spain.

THANOS P. DOKOS is director of studies at the Hellenic Foundation for European and Foreign Policy (ELIAMEP) in Athens, Greece.

JOHN L. ESPOSITO is a professor at Georgetown University and founding director of the Center for Muslim-Christian Understanding in Washington, DC, USA.

BERNABÉ LÓPEZ GARCÍA is professor of history of the Middle East at the University Autonoma in Madrid, Spain.

ANDREAS GOLDBERG is managing director and head of the migration department at the Centre for Studies on Turkey (CST) at the University of Essen in Germany.

SHIREEN T. HUNTER is director of the Islam Program at the Center for Strategic and International Studies (CSIS) in Washington, DC, USA.

SABINE KROISSENBRUNNER works at the Austrian Ministry of Foreign Affairs.

NICO LANDMAN is assistant professor of Islamic history and culture at the Department of Oriental Studies at Utrecht University in the Netherlands.

REMY LEVEAU is professor of political science at the Institut d'Etudes Politiques de Paris (Institute of Political Studies of Paris) in France.

FERNANDO SOARES LOJA is an attorney-at-law in Lisbon, Portugal.

PETER P. MANDAVILLE is assistant professor of government and politics at George Mason University, Fairfax, Virginia, USA.

CHRISTOPHER PARKER is a research fellow and Ph.D. candidate at the Center for Third World Studies at Ghent University in Belgium.

TARIQ RAMADAN is professor of philosophy at the College of Geneva and of Islamic studies at the University of Fribourg in Switzerland.

JOHN REX is emeritus professor at the University of Warwick in England.

SIMON SERFATY is director of the Europe Program at the Center for Strategic and International Studies (CSIS) in Washington, DC, and professor of US foreign policy at Old Dominion University in Norfolk, Virginia, USA.

LIEF STENBERG is assistant professor at Lund University in Sweden.

SAMI ZEMNI is a Ph.D. candidate at Ghent University in Belgium.

About CSIS

For four decades, the Center for Strategic and International Studies (CSIS) has been dedicated to providing world leaders with strategic insights on—and policy solutions to—current and emerging global issues.

The CSIS staff of 190 researchers and support staff focus primarily on three subject areas. First, CSIS addresses the full spectrum of new challenges to national and international security. Second, it maintains resident experts on all of the world's major geographical regions. Third, it is committed to helping develop new methods of governance for the global age; to this end, CSIS has programs on technology and public policy, international trade and finance, and energy.

Headquartered in Washington, DC, USA, CSIS is private, bipartisan, and tax exempt. CSIS does not take specific policy positions; accordingly, all views expressed herein should be understood to be solely those of the authors.

Center for Strategic and International Studies
1800 K St. N.W.
Washington, DC 20006, USA
Tel: (202) 887–3119
Fax: (202) 775–3199
Web: http://www.csis.org/